Essay On The Golden Verses of Pythagoras

By

Fabre d'Olivet

First published in 1813

Published by Left of Brain Books

Copyright © 2023 Left of Brain Books

ISBN 978-1-397-66769-4

First Edition

All rights reserved. No part of this publication may be reproduced, distributed, or transmitted in any form or by any means, including photocopying, recording, or other electronic or mechanical methods, without the prior written permission of the publisher, except in the case of brief quotations permitted by copyright law. Left of Brain Books is a division of Left Of Brain Onboarding Pty Ltd.

PUBLISHER'S PREFACE

About the Book

"Fabre d'Olivet (b. 1768, d. 1825), a French esoteric writer, originally published this book in 1813. The first section, an essay on esoteric Poetics, was dedicated to the Section of Literature of the Imperial Institute of France. The second portion contains the Greek text of the Golden Verses, along with French and English translations. The final part of the book is an extended essay on the Golden Verses."

(Quote from sacred-texts.com)

About the Author

Fabre d'Olivet (1768 - 1825)

"Antoine Fabre d'Olivet (December 8, 1767-March 25, 1825) was a French author, poet and composer whose Biblical and philosophical hermeneutics influenced many occultists, such as Eliphas Lévi and Gerard Encausse. His best known work today is his research on the Hebrew language, Pythagoras's thirty-six Golden Verses and the sacred art of music. His interest in Pythagoras and the resulting works started a revival of Neo-Pythagoreanism that would later influence many occultists and new age spiritualists. He attempted an alternate interpretation of Genesis, based on what he considered to be connections between the Hebrew alphabet and Hieroglyphs. The discovery of the rosetta stone and the subsuquent understanding of Egyptian Hieroglyphs that followed would prove much of this particular work technically mistaken. He was declared a non-person by Napoleon I and condemned by the Pope. An interesting story involves his healing a deaf boy of his hear impairment, and then having Napoleon officially declare that he is never again to heal another person of deafness. He indicates that he kept the letter of notice out of amusement. Outside of esotericism, he also invented the poetic measure of eumolpique."

(Quote from wikipedia.org)

CONTENTS

PUBLISHER'S PREFACE
TRANSLATOR'S FOREWORD 1
DISCOURSE UPON THE ESSENCE AND FORM OF POETRY 3
    INTRODUCTION 4
        I. 6
        II. 14
        III. 23
        IV. 28
        V. 38
        VI. 50
        VII. 59
    THE GOLDEN VERSES OF PYTHAGORAS 77
EXAMINATIONS OF THE GOLDEN VERSES 82
    THE GOLDEN VERSES OF THE PYTHAGOREANS 83
    RENDER TO THE IMMORTAL GODS THE CONSECRATED CULT; GUARD THEN THY FAITH 85
    REVERE THE MEMORY OF THE ILLUSTRIOUS HEROES, OF SPIRITS DEMI-GODS 88
    BE A GOOD SON, JUST BROTHER, SPOUSE TENDER, AND GOOD FATHER 92
    CHOOSE FOR THY FRIEND, THE FRIEND OF VIRTUE; YIELD TO HIS GENTLE COUNSELS, PROFIT BY HIS LIFE, AND FOR A TRIFLING GRIEVANCE NEVER LEAVE HIM 95
    IF THOU CANST AT LEAST: FOR A MOST RIGID LAW BINDS POWER TO NECESSITY 98
    STILL IT IS GIVEN THEE TO FIGHT AND OVERCOME THY FOOLISH PASSIONS: LEARN THOU TO SUBDUE THEM 102
    BE SOBER, DILIGENT, AND CHASTE; AVOID ALL WRATH. IN PUBLIC OR IN SECRET NE'ER PERMIT THOU ANY EVIL; AND ABOVE ALL ELSE RESPECT THYSELF 109
    SPEAK NOT NOR ACT BEFORE THOU HAST REFLECTED; BE JUST 111
    REMEMBER THAT A POWER INVINCIBLE ORDAINS TO DIE 112
    THAT RICHES AND THE HONOURS EASILY ACQUIRED, ARE EASY THUS TO LOSE 113
    AS TO THE EVILS WHICH DESTINY INVOLVES 116
    EVEN AS TRUTH, DOES ERROR HAVE ITS LOVERS 121
    LISTEN, AND IN THINE HEART ENGRAVE MY WORDS 124
    CONSULT, DELIBERATE, AND FREELY CHOOSE 128

LET FOOLS ACT AIMLESSLY AND WITHOUT CAUSE, THOU SHOULDST, IN THE PRESENT, CONTEMPLATE THE FUTURE 129

THAT WHICH THOU DOST NOT KNOW, PRETEND NOT THAT THOU DOST. INSTRUCT THYSELF: FOR TIME AND PATIENCE FAVOUR ALL............. 134

NEGLECT NOT THY HEALTH 138

DISPENSE WITH MODERATION, FOOD TO THE BODY, AND TO THE MIND REPOSE 139

TOO MUCH ATTENTION OR TOO LITTLE SHUN; FOR ENVY THUS, TO EITHER EXCESS IS ALIKE ATTACHED 140

LUXURY AND AVARICE HAVE SIMILAR RESULTS. ONE MUST CHOOSE IN ALL THINGS A MEAN JUST AND GOOD 141

LET NOT SLEEP E'ER CLOSE THY TIRED EYES, WITHOUT THOU ASK THYSELF; WHAT HAVE I OMITTED, AND WHAT DONE? 143

ABSTAIN THOU IF 'TIS EVIL; PERSEVERE IF GOOD 149

MEDITATE UPON MY COUNSELS, LOVE THEM; FOLLOW THEM: TO THE DIVINE VIRTUES WILL THEY KNOW HOW TO LEAD THEE 156

I SWEAR IT BY THE ONE WHO IN OUR HEARTS ENGRAVED THE SACRED TETRAD, SYMBOL IMMENSE AND PURE, SOURCE OF NATURE AND MODEL OF THE GODS 164

BUT BEFORE ALL, THY SOUL TO ITS FAITHFUL DUTY, INVOKE THESE GODS WITH FERVOUR, THEY WHOSE AID, THY WORK BEGUN, ALONE CAN TERMINATE... 169

INSTRUCTED BY THEM, NAUGHT SHALL THEN DECEIVE THEE; OF DIVERSE BEINGS THOU SHALT SOUND THE ESSENCE; AND THOU SHALT KNOW THE PRINCIPLE AND END OF ALL 176

IF HEAVEN WILLS IT, THOU SHALT KNOW THAT NATURE, ALIKE IN EVERYTHING, IS THE SAME IN EVERY PLACE 182

SO THAT, AS TO THY TRUE RIGHTS ENLIGHTENED, THINE HEART SHALL NO MORE FEED ON VAIN DESIRES 184

THOU SHALT SEE THAT THE EVILS WHICH DEVOUR MEN ARE OF THEIR CHOICE THE FRUIT 185

THAT THESE UNFORTUNATES SEEK AFAR THE GOODNESS WHOSE SOURCE WITHIN THEY BEAR... 190

FOR FEW KNOW HAPPINESS: PLAYTHINGS OF THE PASSIONS.................... 191

GOD! THOU COULDST SAVE THEM BY OPENING THEIR EYES 193

BUT NO: 'TIS FOR THE HUMANS OF A RACE DIVINE, TO DISCERN ERROR, AND TO SEE THE TRUTH 199

NATURE SERVES THEM... 200

THOU WHO FATHOMED IT. O WISE AND HAPPY MAN, REST IN ITS HAVEN. BUT OBSERVE MY LAWS, ABSTAINING FROM THE THINGS WHICH THY SOUL MUST FEAR, DISTINGUISHING THEM WELL; LETTING INTELLIGENCE O'ER THY BODY REIGN 204

SO THAT, ASCENDING INTO RADIANT ETHER, MIDST THE IMMORTALS, THOU SHALT BE THYSELF A GOD 206

ENDNOTES.. 208

TRANSLATOR'S FOREWORD

IN this twentieth century, the sacred books of the ancients are undoubtedly better understood than they were even by their contemporaries, for their authors, by the greatness of their genius, are as much nearer to us, as they were distant from them. At the close of the eigh-teenth century, the light which came from the illimitable mind of Fabre d'Olivet shone with solitary splendour and was destined to be seen by only a few devoted followers. But history shows that a great inspirer always appears at the beginning of every great epoch, and however small the number of his disciples, these disciples with their pupils form the magnetic chain which, according to Plato, carries his thought out into the world.

Fabre d'Olivet, born at Ganges, Bas-Languedoc, Dec. 8, 1768, was distinguished even in his own day not only for the extent of his learning but for the rectitude of his judgment and the sublimity of his conceptions. If one can infer from the all too scarce records available since the calamitous fire which destroyed so many of his valued manuscripts, he evidently suffered keenly from the fetters of mortality, and sought with unfailing fervour what Porphyry so aptly called the "Olympia of the Soul."

Saint Yves d'Alveydre, writing of him in La France vraie, says, that it was in 1790, while in Germany, he received his Pythagorean initiation, the profound imprint of which marked all his later productions. After returning to Paris he applied himself to philological and philosophical studies undisturbed by the terrible revolutionary storm. In obscure seclusion he amassed, to quote Sédir, "a disconcerting erudition." He became familiar with all the Semitic tongues and directs, the Aryan languages, and even penetrated the secrets of the Chinese hieroglyphics.

It was during these ten years of retirement that he wrote his Examinations of the Golden Verses which were not published until 1813, with its dedication to the Section of Literature of the Imperial Institute of France. It is known that the Golden Verses of Pythagoras were originally transcribed by Lysis and that it is to Hierocles we owe the version which has come down to us. Fabre d'Olivet has translated them into French verse, the style of which he calls eumolpique, that is, subject to measure and harmonious cadence but free from rhyme, with alternate masculine and feminine terminations. In the Essence and Form of Poetry which precedes the Golden Verses, he illustrates this melodious style, in applying it to the opening lines of some of the well-known classics, and to others not so well-known.

These Golden Verses, so remarkable for their moral elevation, present the most beautiful monument of antiquity raised in honour of Wisdom. They formed the credo of the adepts and initiates. In his recondite Examinations, Fabre d'Olivet has drawn the metaphysical correlation of Providence, Destiny, and the Will of Man, in which combined action Destiny reigns over the past, the Will of Man over the future, and Providence over the present, which, always existing, may be called Eternal. One will find this given at greater length in his Hermeneutic Interpretation of the Origin of the Social State of Man and the Destiny of the Adamic Race: admirable work of this little known theosophist, "to give him the name he loved best to hold," says Pierre Leroux in De l'Humanité.

The inequality of human conditions, upon which depend the social and political questions, forms one of the vital subjects of these esoteric teachings. He has also endeavoured to explain the true opinion of Pythagoras concerning metempsychosis which was his sacred dogma, and said that the dogma of transmigration of souls, received by all peoples and revealed in the ancient mysteries, has been absolutely disfigured in what the moderns have called metempsychosis.

His strange death, which occurred March 25, 1825, is mentioned by des Essarts in Les Hiérophantes, and other authorities including Pierre Leroux, have asserted that he died at the foot of his altar.

NAYÁN LOUISE REDFIELD.

HARTFORD, CONN., October, 1916.

DISCOURSE UPON THE ESSENCE AND FORM OF POETRY

INTRODUCTION [1]

Messieurs:

BEFORE publishing the translation of the Golden Verses of Pythagoras, such as I have made it, in French verse which I have designated by the expression eumolpique,[2] I would have liked to be able to submit it to you and thus be enlightened by your counsels or sustained by your approbation; but academic laws and usages, whose justice I have felt, have prevented my enjoying this advantage. The innovation, however, which I have endeavoured to make in French poetry and the new explanation which I have tried to give of one of the most celebrated pieces of Greek poetry, have seemed to me to hold too closely to your labours and to enter too deeply into your literary provinces, for me to believe myself able to dispense with calling your attention to them. I crave your indulgence, if in the demonstration of a just deference to your judgment I involuntarily neglect certain formalities; and I beg you to judge the purity of my intentions.

I claim not to be a poet; I had even long ago renounced the art of verse, but notwithstanding that, I am now presenting myself in the poetic career to solicit the hazardous success of an innovation! Is it the love of glory which inspires in me this temerity, which dazzles me today as my autumn advances, whereas it was unable to move me when the effervescence of my springtime ought to have doubled its strength? No: however flattering the wreaths that you award to talent, they would not concern me; and if an interest, as new as powerful, had not induced me to address you, I would keep silent. This interest, Messieurs, is that which science itself inspires in me, and the desire, perhaps inconsiderate but commendable, of co-operating with my limited ability for the development of a language whose literary and moral influence, emerging from the bourns of Europe and the present century, ought to invade the world and become universal like the renown of the hero who extends his conquests with those of the empire whose foundations he has laid.

I feel, Messieurs, that I should explain my thought. My assertion, well founded as it may be, appears none the less extraordinary, and I am bound to admit this. The disfavour which is attached to all new ideas, to all innovations, the just defiance that they inspire, the element of ridicule that springs from their downfall, would have arrested my audacity, if I had had audacity alone, and if the worthy ambition of effecting a general good had not raised me above a particular evil which might have resulted for me. Besides I have counted upon the judicious good-will of the two illustrious Academies to which I am addressing myself: I have thought that they would distinguish in the verse which I am presenting for their examination, both as a means of execution in French poetry and as a means of translation in ancient and foreign poetry, the real utility that they can offer, of the fortuitous beauty which they lack, and which a more capable hand would have been able to give them; I flatter myself, at length, that they would grant to the end, without prejudice, the attention which is necessary, and that if they refused an entire approbation to my efforts, they would at least render justice to my zeal and commend the motives which have made me attempt them.

I.

WHEN, after the revival of letters in Europe, Chancellor Bacon, legislator of thought, sketched with bold strokes the tree of human knowledge, and brought back each branch of science to that of the moral faculties upon which it depends, he did not fail to observe sagaciously that it was necessary to distinguish in poetry two things, its essence and its form [3]: its essence as pertaining wholly to the imagination, and composing by itself alone one of the principal branches of science [4]; its form, as making part of the grammar, and entering thus into the domain of philosophy and into the rational faculty of the understanding. [5] This celebrated man had borrowed this idea from a man much older and more celebrated than himself, Plato. According to this admirable philosopher, poetry is either a simple talent, an art which one uses to give to his own ideas a particular form, or it is a divine inspiration by means of which one clothes in the human language and transmits to men the ideas of the gods. [6] It is because, never having felt sufficiently this important distinction and having confused two ideas that ought to be separated, the essence and the form of poetry, which are as the soul and body of this science, that so many men among the modern nations proclaimed themselves poets, whereas they were, in strict truth, only clever versifiers. For it does not suffice, as Plato again said, to have poetic talent, it does not suffice to make verse and even good verse, to be called a poet [7]; it is necessary to possess that divine enthusiasm, that inspiration which elevates the soul, enlightens it, transports it, as it were, to intellectual regions and causes it to draw from its source the very essence of this science.

How they delude themselves, those who, habitually deceived, foolishly imagine that the lofty fame of Orpheus, Homer, Pindar, Æschylus, or Sophocles and the immortality which they enjoy, belongs only to the plan of their works, to the harmony of their verse, and to the happy use of their talent! These flattering appearances which constitute the form of their poetry would have disappeared long ago, they would have become broken, like fragile vases, upon the torrent of centuries, if the intelligence which animated them had not eternalized their duration. But this secret intelligence does not reside, as certain other superficial readers persuade themselves, being still deceived, in the simple interest that the characters mise en scène inspire; this interest, which results from their contrast and from the shock of the passions, is another sort of form, more hidden, and less frail, than the former, it is true, but as variable generally and subject to the great revolution of customs, laws, and usages. True poetry does not depend upon that; it depends upon the primordial ideas which the genius of the poet in his exaltation has seized in the intellectual nature, and which his talent has shown afterwards in the elementary nature, thus adapting the simulacra of physical things to the movement inspired by the soul, instead of adapting this movement to those same simulacra, as those who write history. This is what Bacon, the modern philosopher whom I have already cited, has felt so perfectly. [8] He says:

As the sentient world is inferior to the human soul, it is for poetry to give to this nature what reality has refused it, lending to it the faculties of the intellectual world; and as the acts and events which make the subject of true history have not that grandeur and that sublimity for which the human soul seeks, it is necessary that poetry create acts and events greater and more heroic. All must be increased and embellished by its voice and receive from it a new existence; it is necessary even that virtue shine with an éclat [acclaim—JBH] more pure; that the veil which covers truth be lifted from its eyes and that the course of Providence, better discerned, be allowed to penetrate into the most secret causes of events.

The philosopher who expressed thus his thought regarding the essence of poetry, was far from believing, as the vulgar have always believed, and as certain modern writers have wished to convince the savants, [9] that, of the two parts of poetry, the positive form might be the only genuine; that is to say, that they do not by any means consider that the human characters put upon the stage by the poets whom I have just named, were historic characters. Bacon understood well that Achilles, Agamemnon, Ulysses, Castor and Pollux, Helen, Iphigenia, Œdipus, Phædra, etc., are somewhat more than they appear to be, and that their virtues or their vices, their heroic actions, even their crimes, celebrated by poetry, contain a profound meaning wherein lie buried the mysteries of religion and the secrets of philosophy. [10]

It belongs only to the men to whom poetry is known by its exterior forms alone and who have never penetrated as far as its essence, to imagine that a small city of Asia, unknown to all Asia, around which the King of kings of Greece waited in vain for ten years to avenge the honour of his brother betrayed by his wife, should be able during three thousand years to occupy the greatest minds of Europe, on account of a quarrel which was raised in the tenth year of the siege, between this King of kings and a petty prince of his army, angry and sulky, named Achilles. It is only permitted to the phlegmatic chronologists, whom the muses have never visited in their studies, to seek seriously to fix the year and the day when this quarrel took place. A man, strongly imbued with the spirit of Homer or of Sophocles, would never see in Ulysses a real man, a king who, returning to his isle after long wanderings, kills in cold blood a crowd of lovers of his wife and rests confident of the conjugal fidelity of that spouse abandoned for twenty years, and whom he had won in the course, [11] although, according to the most common reports, she was delivered of a son in his absence [12]; nor in Œdipus, another king, who, without knowing it, without wishing it, always innocent, kills his father, espouses his mother and, driven to parricide and incest by an irresistible destiny, tears out his eyes and condemns himself to wander over the earth, to be a frightful example of celestial wrath. The platitudes and ridicule of the deed related by Homer, and the horror which resulted from that presented on the stage by Sophocles, are sufficient evidence against their reality. If the poem of the one and the tragedy of the other do not conceal, under the coarse exterior which covers them, a secret fire which acts unknown to the reader, never would a sane man tolerate a presentation, on the one side, of vice changed into virtue, and on the other, virtue changed into vice, and the gods operating this strange metamorphosis against all the laws of natural justice. He would throw aside the book with disgust, or, agreeing with the judicious reflection of an ancient Greek writer, exclaim with him [13]:

If Homer had merely thought with respect to the gods what he said, he would have been an impious, sacrilegious man, a veritable Salmoneus, a second Tantalus; but let us guard against doing him this wrong, or taking for guides those who, misunderstanding the allegorical genius of this great poet, and hesitating before the outer court of his mysterious poetry, have never succeeded in understanding the sublime philosophy which is enclosed therein.

You are not, Messieurs, of those designated by Heraclides in the words I have just quoted. Members of these celebrated Academies where Homer and Sophocles have found so many admirers, defenders, and illustrious disciples, you can easily admit that I see in these great men more than ordinary poets, that I place their glory elsewhere than in their talent, and that I say, particularly of Homer, that his most just claims to immortality are less in the form than in the essence of his poetry, because a form, however admirable it may be, passes and yields to time which destroys it, whereas the essence or the spirit which animates it, immutable as the Divinity from which it emanates by inspiration, resists all vicissitudes and seems to increase in vigour and éclat, in proportion as the centuries passing away reveal its force and serve as evidence of its celestial origin. I flatter myself that my sentiments in this regard are not foreign to yours and that the successors of Corneille, Racine, and Boileau hear with pleasure these eulogies given to the creator of epopœia, to the founders of dramatic art, and agree with me in regarding them as particular organs of the Divinity, the instruments chosen for the instruction and civilization of men.

If you deign, Messieurs, to follow the development of my ideas with as much attention as indulgence, you already know that what I call the essence or spirit of poetry, and which, following upon the steps of the founder of the Academy and of the regenerator of the sciences of Europe, I distinguish from its form, is no other thing than the allegorical genius, immediate production of the inspiration; you also understand that I mean by inspiration, the infusion of this same genius into the soul which, having power only in the intellectual nature, is manifested in action by passing into the elementary nature by means of the inner labour of the poet who invests it with a sentient form according to his talent; you perceive finally, how, following this simple theory, I explain the words of Plato, and how I conceive that the inspired poet transmits to men the ideas of the gods.

I have no need I think of telling you that I make an enormous difference between this divine inspiration which exalts the soul and fills it with a real enthusiasm, and that sort of inner movement or disorder which the vulgar also call inspiration, which in its greatest perfection is only passion excited by the love of glory, united with a habit of verse making, which constitutes the talent, and in its imperfection is only a disordered passion called by Boileau, an ardour for rhyming. These two kinds of inspiration in no wise resemble each other; their effects are as different as their causes, their productions as different as their sources. The one, issuing from the intellectual nature, has its immutability: it is the same in all time, among all peoples, and in the heart of all men who receive it; it alone produces genius: its first manifestation is very rare, but its second manifestation is less so, as I will show later on. The other inspiration, inherent in sentient nature, born of passion, varies with the whim of men and things, and takes on the hue of the customs and the times; it can bring forth talent or at least modify it, and when it is seconded by a great facility, can go to the extent of feigning genius but never farther: its real domain is the mind. Its possession is not very rare even in its perfection. One can sometimes find it united with the true inspiration, first as in Homer, or second as in Vergil; and then the form which it unceasingly works over, joining its sentient beauties to the intellectual beauties of genius, creates the monuments of science.

It may be that the development which I have just given of my ideas on the essence of poetry will appear new, although I must acknowledge that in reality they are not I am addressing men who are too enlightened to ignore what the ancients have said in this respect. Heraclides, whom I have already cited, is not the only one who has given this impression. Strabo assures positively that ancient poetry was only the language of allegory [14], and he refutes Eratosthenes who pretended that the aim of Homer was only to amuse and please. In this he is in accord with Denys of Halicarnassus who avows that the mysteries of nature and the most sublime conceptions of morals have been covered with the veil of allegory. [15] Phurnutus goes farther: he declares that the allegories used by Hesiod and by Homer do not differ from those which other foreign poets have used before them. [16] Damascius said as much of the poems of Orpheus, [17] and Plutarch confirms it in a passage which has been preserved to us by Eusebius. [18]

In the first ages of Greece, poetry, consecrated to the service of the altars, left the enclosures of the temples only for the instruction of the people: it was as a sacred language in which the priests, entrusted with presiding at the mysteries of religion, interpreted the will of the gods. The oracles, dogmas, moral precepts, religious and civil laws, teachings of all sorts concerning the labours of the body, the operations of the mind, in fact all that which was regarded as an emanation, an order, or a favour from the Divinity, all was written in verse. To this sacred language was given the name Poetry, that is to say, the Language of the Gods: a symbolic name which accords with it perfectly, since it expressed at the same time its origin and its usage. [19] It was said to have come from Thrace, [20] and the one who had invented it and caused its first accents to be heard was called Olen. [21] Now these are again two symbolic names perfectly adapted to the idea that one had of this divine science: it was descended from Thrace, that is to say, from the Ethereal Space; it was Olen who had invented it, that, is to say, the Universal Being. [22] To understand these three etymologies which can be regarded as the fundamental points of the history of poetry, it is necessary to remember, first, that the Phœnicians, at the epoch when they covered not only Greece but the coasts of the rest of Europe with their colonies, brought there their language, and gave their names to the countries of which they had taken possession; secondly, that these names drawn almost always from objects symbolic of their cult, constituted for these countries a sort of sacred geography, which Greece above all others, was faithful in preserving. [23] It was thus (for there is nothing under the sun which cannot find either its model of its copy) when the Europeans took possession of America and colonized it, and carried to those regions their diverse dialects and covered it with names drawn from the mysteries of Christianity. One ought therefore, when one wishes to understand the ancient names of the countries of Greece, those of their heroic personages, those of the mysterious subjects of their cult, to have recourse to the Phœnician dialect which although lost to us can easily be restored with the aid of Hebrew, Aramaic, Chaldean, Syriac, Arabic, and Coptic.

I do not intend, Messieurs, to fatigue you with proofs of these etymologies which are not in reality the subject of my discourse. I am content to place them on the margin for the satisfaction of the curious. Thus I shall make use of them later, when occasion demands. But to return to Thrace, this country was always considered by the Greeks as the place peculiar to their gods and the centre of their cult; the divine country, par excellence. All the names that it has borne in different dialects and which in the course of time have become concentrated in particular regions, have been synonyms of theirs. Thus, Getæ, Mœsia, Dacia, all signify the country of the gods. [24] Strabo, in speaking of the Getæ, said that these peoples recognized a sovereign pontiff to whom they gave the title of God, the dignity of which existed still in his time. [25] This sovereign pontiff resided upon a mountain that d'Anville believes he has recognized, between Moldavia and Transylvania. The Thracians had also a sovereign pontiff instituted in the same manner as that of the Getæ, and residing likewise upon a sacred mountain. [26] It was, no doubt, from the heights of these mountains that the divine oracles, the laws and teachings which the great pontiffs had composed in verse, were at first spread throughout Greece; so that it might be said, literally as well as figuratively, that poetry, revered as the language of the gods, production of an Eternal Being, descended from the ethereal abode and was propagated upon earth for the instruction and delight of mortals. It appears to me very certain that the temple of Delphi, erected upon the famous mountain of Parnassus, differed not essentially at first from those of Thrace; and what confirms me in this idea is that, according to an ancient tradition, it was Olen who, coming out from Lycia, that is to say from the light, caused all Greece to recognize the cult of Apollo and Diana; composed the hymns which were chanted at Delos in honour of these two divinities and established the temple of Delphi of which he was the first pontiff. [27] Thus the temple of Delphi rivalled those of Thrace. Its foundation, doubtless due to some innovator priest, was attributed by a poetic metaphor to the divinity which had inspired it. At that time a schism arose and two cults were formed, that of the Thracians consecrated to Bacchus and Ceres, or Dionysus the divine spirit, and Demeter the earth-mother [28]; and that of the Greeks, properly speaking, consecrated to the sun and the moon, adored under the names of Apollo and Diana. It is to this schism that one should ascribe the famous dispute which was raised, it is said, between Bacchus and Apollo concerning the possession of the tripod of Delphi. [29] The poetic fable woven from this subject was made to preserve the remembrance of the moral incident and not of the physical event; for at this remote epoch, when verse only was written, history, ever allegorical, treated only of moral and providential matters, disdaining all physical details deemed little worthy of occupying the memory of men.

However that may be, it appears certain, notwithstanding this schism, that the cult of the Thracians dominated Greece for a long time. The new source of poetry opened at Delphi and on Mount Parnassus, destined in time to become so celebrated, remained at first somewhat unknown. It is worthy of observation that Hesiod, born in the village of Ascra, a short distance from Delphi, makes no mention either of the oracle or of the temple of Apollo. All that he said of this city, which he named Pytho, has reference to the stone which Saturn had swallowed, believing to devour his son. [30] Homer does not mention this Pytho in the Iliad; he mentions in the Odyssey an oracle delivered by Apollo upon Parnassus. For a long time, the peoples of Greece, accustomed to receive from the ancient mountains of Thrace both their oracles and their instructions, turned toward that country and neglected the new sacred mount. This is why the most ancient traditions place in Thrace, with the supremacy of cult and sacerdotalism, the cradle of the most famous poets and that of the Muses who had inspired them: Orpheus, Musæus, Thamyris, and Eumolpus were Thracians. Pieria, where the Muses were born, was a mountain of Thrace; and when, at length, it was a question of rendering to the gods a severe and orthodox cult, it was said that it was necessary to imitate the Thracians, or, as one would say in French, thraciser. [31]

Besides it must be observed, that at the epoch when the temple of Delphi was founded,, the new cult, presented to the Greeks under the name of the universal Olen, tended to unite Apollo and Diana, or the sun and the moon, under the same symbolic figure, and to make of it only one and the same object of adoration, under the name of Œtolinos, that is to say, Sun-moon. [32] It was proclaimed that the middle of the earth, its paternal and maternal umbilicus, was found placed exactly on the spot where the new sacred city was built, which was called for this mystical reason Delphi. [33] But it seems that the universality of this Œtolinos was never well understood by the Greeks, who, in their minds, united only with difficulty that which custom and their senses had taught them to separate. Moreover one can well conjecture that, as in all religious schisms, a host of difficulties and contradictory opinions were raised. If I can believe the sacerdotal traditions of India, that I encounter, the greatest difficulty was, not knowing which sex dominated in this mysterious being whose essence was composed of the sun and moon and whose hermaphroditic umbilicus was possessed in Delphi. This insoluble question had more than once divided mankind and stained the earth with blood. But here is not the place to touch upon one of the most important and most singular facts of the history of man. I have already deviated too much from my subject, and I return to it asking pardon of my judges for this necessary digression.

II.

POETRY, transported with the seat of religion from the mountains of Thrace to those of Phocis, lost there, as did religion, its primitive unity. Not only did each sovereign pontiff use it to spread his dogmas, but the opposed sects born of the rending of the cult, vying with each other, took possession of it. These sects, quite numerous, personified by the allegorical genius which presided over poetry, and which, as I have said, constituted its essence, were confused with the mind which animated them and were considered as a particular being. Thence, so many of the demi-gods, and the celebrated heroes, from whom the Greek tribes pretended to have descended; thence, so many of the famous poets to whom were attributed a mass of works that emanated from the same sanctuary, or were composed for the support of the same doctrine. For it is well to remember that the allegorical history of these remote times, written in a different spirit from the positive history which has succeeded it, resembled it in no way, and that it is in having confused them that so many grave errors have arisen. It is a very important observation that I again make here. This history, confided to the memory of men or preserved among the sacerdotal archives of the temples in detached fragments of poetry, considered things only from the moral side, was never occupied with individuals, but saw only the masses; that is to say, peoples, corporations, sects, doctrines, even arts and sciences, as so many particular beings that it designated by a generic name. It is not that these masses were unable to have a chief to direct their movements, but this chief, regarded as the instrument of a certain mind, was neglected by history which attached itself to the mind only. One chief succeeded another without allegorical history making the least mention of it. The adventures of all were accumulated upon the head of one alone. It was the moral thing whose course was examined, whose birth, progress, or downfall was described. The succession of things replaced that of individuals. Positive history, which ours has become, follows a method entirely different. The individuals are everything for it: it notes with scrupulous exactitude dates and facts which the other scorns.

I do not pronounce upon their common merit. The moderns would mock that allegorical manner of the ancients, if they could believe it possible, as I am persuaded the ancients would have mocked the method of the moderns, had they been able to foresee its possibility in the future. How approve of what is unknown? Man approves of only what he likes; he always believes he knows all that he ought to like.

I can say, after having repeated this observation, that the poet Linus, who is regarded as the author of all the melancholy chants of the ancient world, represents nothing less than lunar poetry detached from the doctrine of Œtolinos, of which I have spoken, and considered as schismatic by the Thracians; I can also say, that the poet Amphion, whose chants were, on the contrary, so powerful and so virile, typifies the orthodox solar poetry, opposed by these same Thracians; whereas the prophet Thamyris, who, it is said, celebrated in such stately verse the creation of the world and the war of the Titans, [34] I represents quite plainly the universal doctrine of Olen, re-established by his followers. The name of Amphion signifies the orthodox or national voice of Greece; that of Thamyris, the twin lights of the gods. [35] One feels, accordingly, that the evils which came to Linus and to Thamyris, one of whom was killed by Hercules, [36] and the other deprived of sight by the Muses, [37] are, in reality, only some sort of criticism or unfortunate incident sustained by the doctrines which they represented, on account of the opposition of the Thracians. What I have said concerning Linus, Amphion, and Thamyris, can be applied to the greater part of the poets who preceded Homer, and Fabricius names seventy of these [38]; one could also extend it to Orpheus, but only on a certain side; for although it may be very true, that no positive detail is possessed regarding the character of the celebrated man, founder or propagator of the doctrine which has borne this name; although it may be very true, that all that concerns his birth, his life, and his death is completely unknown, it is none the less certain that this man has existed, that he has been actually the head of a very extended sect, and that the allegorical fables which remain to us on this subject depict, more particularly than they have done with any other, the course of his thoughts and the success of his institutions.

Orpheus belongs, on the one side, to anterior times, and on the other, to times merely ancient. The epoch when he appeared is the line of demarcation between pure allegory and mixed allegory, the intelligible and the sentient. He taught how to ally the rational faculty with the imaginative faculty. The science which was a long time after called philosophy, originated with him. He laid its first basis.

One should guard against believing, following in the footsteps of certain historians deceived by the meaning of allegorical fables, that when Orpheus appeared, Greece, still barbarous, offered only the traces of a civilization hardly outlined, or that the ferocious animals, tamed by the charm of his poetry, should represent, in effect, the inhabitants of this beautiful country. Men capable of receiving a cult so brilliant as that of Orpheus, a doctrine so pure, and mysteries so profound; men who possessed a language so formed, so noble, so harmonious as that which served that inspired man to compose his hymns, were far from being ignorant and savage to this degree. It is not true, as has been said and repeated without examination, that poetry had its birth in the forests, in regions rough and wild, nor above all, that it may be the concomitant of the infancy of the nations and the first stammerings of the human mind. Poetry, on the contrary, having attained its perfection, indicates always a long existence among the peoples, a civilization very advanced and all the splendour of a virile age. The sanctuary of the temple is its true cradle. Glance over the savage world and see if the Iroquois or the Samoyeds have a poetry. Have the peoples who were found in their infancy in the isles of the Pacific shown you hymns like those of Orpheus, epic monuments like the poems of Homer? Is it not known that the Tartars who have subjugated Asia, those proud Manchus who today reign over China, have never been able to derive from their language, rebellious to all kinds of melody and rhythm, a single verse,[39] although since their conquests they have felt and appreciated the charms of this art?[40]

Bears and lions, tamed and brought nearer together by Orphic poetry, have no reference to men, but to things: they are the symbols of rival sects which, imbibing their hatred at the very foot of the altars, diffused it over all that surrounded them and filled Greece with troubles.

For a long time this country was a prey to the double scourge of religious and political anarchy. In detaching herself from the cult of the metropolis, she also detached herself from its government. Once a colony of the Phœnicians, she had thrown off their yoke, not however spontaneously and en masse, but gradually, over and over again; so that there were twenty rival temples, twenty rival cities, twenty petty peoples divided by rite, by civil interest, and by the ambition of the priests and princes who governed them. The Thracians, remaining faithful to the ancient laws, were styled superstitious or enslaved, whereas the innovators and the insurgents were considered, by the Thracians and often by themselves, schismatics and rebels. Phoenicia had vainly wished to oppose this general desertion. Asia came to experience the most terrible shocks. India, which had long held the sceptre there, was buried for fifteen hundred years in her Kaliyoug, or her age of darkness, and offered only the shadow of her ancient splendour. [41] For fifteen centuries she had lost her unity by the extinction of her imperial dynasties. Many rival kingdoms were formed, [42] whose constant quarrels had left them neither the leisure nor the possibility of watching over and supporting their colonies from afar. The gradual lowering of the Mediterranean, and the alluvial deposit of the shores of Egypt raising the Isthmus of Suez, [43] had cut off all communication between this sea and the Red Sea, and, by barriers difficult to surmount, separated the primitive Phœnicians, established upon the shores of the Indian Ocean, from those of Palestine. [44] The meridional Arabs were separated from the septentrional, and both had broken with the Indians to whom they had formerly belonged. [45] Tibet had adopted a particular cult and form of government. [46] Persia had been subject to the empire of the Assyrians. [47] At last the political ties which united all these states, and which once formed only a vast group under the domination of the Indian monarchs, had become relaxed or broken on all sides. Egypt, long subject to the Philistines, known under the name of Shepherds, came at length to drive them out, and emerging from her lethargy prepared herself to seize the influence which Asia had allowed to escape. [48] Already the most warlike of her kings, Sethos, had extended his empire over both Libya and Arabia; Phoenicia and Assyria had been subjugated; he had entered triumphant into Babylon and was seated upon the throne of Belus. [49] He would not have hesitated to attempt the conquest of Greece, if he had been able as easily to lead his army there; but it was difficult for him to create a marine force, and above all to overcome the invincible repugnance that the Egyptians had for the sea. [50] Obliged to employ the Phœnicians, his ancient enemies, he was able to draw from them only mediocre service. In spite of these obstacles and the stubborn resistance of the Greeks, he succeeded nevertheless in making some conquests and forming some partial settlements. Athens, so celebrated later, was one of the principal ones. [51] These events, these revolutions, calamitous in appearance, were in reality to produce great benefits. Greece, already impregnated with the learning of the Phœnicians, which she had obtained and elaborated, afterward received that of the Egyptians and elaborated it still further. A man born in the heart of Thrace, but carried in his childhood into Egypt through the desire for knowledge, [52] returned to his country with one of the Egyptian colonies, to kindle there the new light. He was initiated into all the mysteries of religion and science:

he surpassed, said Pausanias, all those who had preceded him, by the beauty of his verse, the sublimity of his chants, and the profoundness of his knowledge in the art of healing and of appeasing the gods.[53] This was Orpheus: he took this name from that of his doctrine[54] which aimed to cure and to save by knowledge.

I should greatly overstep the limits that I have prescribed for this discourse if I should recall in detail all that Greece owed to this celebrated man. The mythological tradition has consecrated in a brilliant allegory the efforts which he made to restore to men the truth which they had lost. His love for Eurydice, so much sung by the poets, is but the symbol of the divine science for which he longed.[55] The name of this mysterious spouse, whom he vainly wished to return to the light, signified only the doctrine of the true science, the teaching of what is beautiful and veritable, by which he tried to enrich the earth. But man cannot look upon the face of truth before attaining the intellectual light, without losing it; if he dare to contemplate it in the darkness of his reason, it vanishes. This is what the fable, which everyone knows, of Eurydice, found and lost, signifies.

Orpheus, who felt by his own experience, perhaps, the great disadvantage that he had here, of presenting the truth to men before they might be in condition to receive it, instituted the divine mysteries; an admirable school where the initiate, conducted from one degree to another, slowly prepared and tried, received the share of light in proportion to the strength of his intelligence, and gently enlightened, without risk of being dazzled, attained to virtue, wisdom, and truth. There has been but one opinion in antiquity concerning the utility of the mysteries, before dissolution had stained its precincts and corrupted its aim. All the sages, even Socrates, have praised this institution,[56] the honour of which has been constantly attributed to Orpheus.[57] It is not improbable that this sage had found the model in Egypt and that he himself had been initiated, as Moses[58] and Pythagoras[59] had been before and after him; but in this case an imitation was equivalent to a creation.

I have said that after the appearance of Orpheus, poetry had lost its unity: as divided as the cult, it had sustained its vicissitudes. Entirely theosophical in its principle, and calm as the Divinity which inspired it, it had taken in the midst of the opposed sects a passionate character which it had not had previously. The priests, who used it to uphold their opinions, had found, instead of the real inspiration, that sort of physical exaltation which results from the fire of passions, whose movement and fleeting splendour entrance the vulgar. Vying with each other they had brought forth a mass of theological systems, had multiplied the allegorical fables concerning the universe, and had drowned, as it were, the unity of the Divinity in the vain and minute distinction of its infinite faculties; and as each composed in his own dialect and in pursuance of his own caprice, each devised unceasingly new names for the same beings, according as they believed they caught a glimpse of a certain new virtue in these beings that another had not expressed, it came to pass that not only were the gods multiplied by the distinction of their faculties, but still more by the diversity of names employed in expressing them. Very soon there was not a city nor a town in Greece, that did not have, or at least believed that it had, its own particular god. If one had carefully examined this prodigious number of divinities, one would have clearly seen that they could be reduced, by elimination, to a small number and would finally end by being mingled in a sole Universal Being; but that was very difficult for people, flattered, moreover, by a system which compared the condition of the gods with theirs, and offered them thus, protectors and patrons so much the more accessible as they were less occupied and less powerful. [60] Vainly, therefore, the Egyptian colony established at Athens presented to the adoration of this people imbued with the prejudice of polytheism, the sovereign of the gods under the title of the Most-High [61]; the veneration of this people was turned wholly towards Minerva, who became its patron under the name of Athena, [62] as Juno was that of Argos, [63] Ceres, that of Eleusis, Phigalia, Methydrium, [64] etc.

Orpheus, instructed as was Moses, in the sanctuaries of Egypt, had the same ideas as the legislator of the Hebrews upon the unity of God, but the different circumstances in which he found himself placed did not permit him to divulge this dogma; he reserved this for making it the basis of his mysteries, and continued, in the meantime, to personify in his poetry the attributes of the Divinity. His institutions, drawn from the same source, founded upon the same truths, received the imprint of his character and that of the people to whom he had destined them. As those of Moses were severe and, if one must admit, harsh in form, enemies of the sciences and arts, so those of Orpheus were brilliant, fitted to seduce the minds, favourable to all the developments of the imagination. It was beneath the allurements of pleasure, of joy, and of fêtes, that he concealed the utility of his lessons and the depth of his doctrine. Nothing was more full of pomp than the celebration of its mysteries. Whatever majesty, force, and grace, poetry, music, and painting had, was used to excite the enthusiasm of the initiate. [65] He found no pretext advantageous enough, no form beautiful enough, no charm powerful enough to interest the hearts and attract them toward the sublime truths which he proclaimed. These truths, whose force the early Christians have recognized, [66] went much further than those of which Moses had been the interpreter; they seemed to anticipate the times. Not only did he teach of the unity of God, [67] and give the most sublime ideas of this unfathomable Being [68]; not only did he explain the birth of the Universe and the origin of things [69]; but he represented this unique God under the emblem of a mysterious Trinity endowed with three names [70]; he spoke of the dogma which Plato announced a long time after concerning the Logos, or the Divine Word; and, according to Macrobius, taught even its incarnation or its union with matter, its death or its division in the world of sense, its resurrection or its transfiguration, and finally its return to the original Unity. [71]

This inspired man, by exalting in Man the imagination, that admirable faculty which makes the charm of life, fettered the passions which trouble its serenity. Through him his disciples enjoyed the enthusiasm of the fine arts and he insisted that their customs should be pure and simple. [72] The régime that he prescribed for them was that which Pythagoras introduced later [73]. One of the most pleasing rewards which he offered to their endeavours, the very aim of their initiation into his mysteries, was, putting themselves in communion with the gods [74]; freeing themselves from the cycle of generations, purifying their soul, and rendering it worthy of projecting itself, after the downfall of its corporal covering toward its primal abode, to the realms of light and happiness. [75]

Despite my resolution to be brief, I cannot resist the pleasure of speaking at greater length of Orpheus, and of recalling, as is my custom, things which, appearing today wholly foreign to my subject, nevertheless, when examined from my viewpoint, belong to it. Poetry was not at all in its origin what it became later, a simple accomplishment, regarded by those who profess to be savants as even rather frivolous [76]; it was the language of the gods, par excellence, that of the prophets, the ministers of the altars, the preceptors and the legislators of the world. I rejoice to repeat this truth, after rendering homage to Orpheus, to this admirable man, to whom Europe owes the éclat with which she has shone and with which she will shine a long time. Orpheus has been the real creator of poetry and of music, [77] the father of mythology, of morals, and of philosophy: it is he who has served as model for Hesiod and Homer, who has illumined the footsteps of Pythagoras and Plato.

After having wisely accommodated the outward ceremonies to the minds of the people whom he wished to instruct, Orpheus divided his doctrine into two parts, the one vulgar, and the other mysterious and secret, following in this the method of the Egyptians, whose disciple he had been [78]; then, turning his attention to poetry, and seeing into what chaos this science had fallen and the confusion that had been made of divine and profane things, he judiciously separated it into two principal branches, which he assigned, the one to theology, the other to natural philosophy. It can be said that he gave in each the precept and the example. As sublime a theosophist as he was profound as a philosopher, he composed an immense quantity of theosophical and philosophical verses upon all sorts of subjects. Time has destroyed nearly all of them; but their memory has been perpetuated. Among the works of Orpheus that were cited by the ancients and whose loss must be deplored, were found, on the subject of theosophy, The Holy Word or The Sacred Logos, [79] by which Pythagoras and Plato profited much; the Theogony, which preceded that of Hesiod more than five centuries; The Initiations to the Mysteries of the Mother of the Gods, [80] and The Ritual of the Sacrifices, wherein he had recorded, undoubtedly, the divers parts of his doctrine [81]: on the subject of philosophy, a celebrated cosmogony was found, in which an astronomical system was developed that would be an honour to our century, touching the plurality of the worlds, the station of the sun at the centre of the universe, and the habitation of the stars. These extraordinary works emanated from the same genius who had written in verse upon grammar, music, natural history, upon the antiquities of the many isles of Greece, upon the interpretation of signs and prodigies, and a mass of other subjects, the details of which one can see in the commencement of the Argonautica of Onomacritus, which is attributed to him.

But at the same time that Orpheus opened thus to his successor two very distinct careers, theosophical and philosophical, he did not entirely neglect the other parts of this science: his hymns and his odes assigned him to a distinguished rank among the lyric poets; his Démétréide presaged the beauties of Epopœia, and the representations full of pomp, that he introduced into his mysteries, gave birth to Greek Melopœia whence sprang dramatic art. He can therefore be regarded, not only as the precursor of Hesiod and Epimenides, but even as that of Homer, Æschylus, and Pindar. I do not pretend, in saying this, to take away anything from the glory of these celebrated men: the one who indicates a course, yields to the one who executes it: now this, especially, is what Homer did.

III.

HOMER was not the first epic poet in the order of time, but in the order of things. Before him many poets were skilled in Epopœia; but no one had known the nature of this kind of poetry [82]; no one had united the opposed qualities which were necessary. There existed at this epoch a multitude of allegorical fables which had emanated at divers times from different sanctuaries. These fables, committed at first to memory, had been collected in several sets of works which were called cycles. [83] There were allegorical, mythological, and epic cycles. [84] We know from certain precious texts of the ancients, that these sorts of collections opened generally with the description of Chaos, with the marriage of Heaven and Earth; contained the genealogy of the Gods and the combats of the Giants; included the expedition of the Argonauts, the famous wars of Thebes and of Troy; extended as far as the arrival of Ulysses at Ithaca, and terminated with the death of this hero, caused by his son Telegonus. [85] The poets who, before Homer, had drawn from these cycles the subject of their works, not having penetrated as far as the allegorical sense, lacking inspiration, or being found incapable of rendering it, lacking talent, had produced only cold inanimate copies, deprived of movement and grace. They had not, however, omitted any of the exploits of Hercules or of Theseus, nor any of the incidents of the sieges of Thebes or Troy; and their muse, quite lifeless, fatigued the readers without interesting or instructing them. [86] Homer came. He, in his turn, glanced over this pile of sacerdotal traditions, and raising himself by the force of his genius alone to the intellectual principle which had conceived them, he grasped the ensemble, and felt all its possibilities. The faculties of his soul and the precious gifts which he had received from nature had made him one of those rare men who present themselves, at long intervals, upon the scene of the world to enlighten it, shining in the depths of centuries and serving as torches for mankind. In whatever clime, in whatever career destiny had placed him, he would have been the foremost. Ever the same, whether under the thatched roof or upon the throne, as great in Egypt as in Greece, in the Occident as in the Orient of Asia, everywhere he had commanded admiration. Some centuries earlier this same attribute might have been seen in Krishna or in Orpheus, some centuries later, in Pythagoras or in

Cyrus. Great men are always great by their own greatness. Incidents which depend upon chance can only modify. Homer was destined to poetry by favourable circumstances. Born upon the borders of the river Meles, of an indigent mother, without shelter and without kindred, he owed, to a schoolmaster of Smyrna who adopted him, his early existence and his early instructions. He was at first called Melesigenes, from the place of his birth. [87] Pupil of Phemius, he received from his benevolent preceptor, simple but pure ideas, which the activity of his soul developed, which his genius increased, universalized, and brought to their perfection. His education, begun with an assiduous and sedentary study, was perfected through observation. He undertook long journeys for the sole purpose of instructing himself. The political conditions, contrary to every other project, favoured him.

Greece, after having shaken off the yoke of the Phœnicians and having become the friend of Egypt rather than her subject, commenced to reap the fruits of the beautiful institutions that she had received from Orpheus. Powerful metropolises arose in the heart of this country, long regarded as a simple colony of Asia, and her native strength being progressively augmented by the habit of liberty, she had need of extending herself abroad. [88] Rich with the increase of population, she had reacted upon her ancient metropolis, had taken possession of a great number of cities on the opposite shores of Asia, and had colonized them. [89] Phoenicia humiliated, torn by internal dissensions, [90] tossed between the power of the Assyrians and that of the Egyptians, [91] saw this same Greece that she had civilized and to whom she had given her gods, her laws, and even the letters of her alphabet, ignore, deny her benefits, [92] take up arms against her, carry away her colonies from the shores of Italy and of Sicily, and becoming mistress of the islands of the Archipelago, tear from her her sole remaining hope, the empire of the sea. [93] The people of Rhodes were overpowered.

Homer, of Greek nationality although born in Asia, profited by these advantages. He set sail in a vessel, whose patron, Mentes of Leucas, was his friend, wandered over all the possessions of Greece, visited Egypt, [94] and came to settle at Tyre. This was the ancient metropolis of Greece, the source and sacred repository of her mythological traditions. It was there, in this same temple of the Master of the Universe, [95] where twelve centuries before Sanchoniathon had come to study the antiquities of the world, [96] that Homer was able to go back to the origin of Greek cult and fathom the most hidden meanings of its mysteries [97]; it was there that he chose the first and noblest subject of his chants, that which constitutes the fable of the Iliad. [98] If one must believe in the very singular accounts which time has preserved to us, thanks to the blind zeal of certain Christians who have treated them as heresies, this Helen, whose name applied to the moon signifies the resplendent, this woman whom Paris carried away from her spouse Menelaus, is nothing else than the symbol of the human soul, [99] torn by the principle of generation from that of thought, on account of which the moral and physical passions declare war. But it would be taking me too far away from my subject, examining in detail what might be the meaning of the allegories of Homer. My plan has not been to investigate this meaning in particular, but to show that it exists in general. Upon this point I have not only the rational proof which results from the concatenation of my ideas, but also proof of the fact, which is furnished to me by the testimonials of the ancients. These testimonials are recognized at every step, in the works of the philosophers and chiefly in those of the Stoics. Only a very superficial erudition is necessary to be convinced of this. [100] But I ought to make an observation, and this observation will be somewhat novel: it is that, the poetic inspiration being once received by the poet and his soul finding itself transported into the intelligible world, all the ideas which then come to him are universal and in consequence allegorical. So that nothing true may exist outside of unity, and as everything that is true is one and homogeneous, it is found that, although the poet gives to his ideas a form determined in the sentient world, this form agrees with a multitude of things which, being distinct in their species, are not so in their genus. This is why Homer has been the man of all men, the type of all types, the faithful mirror, [101] wherein all ideas becoming reflected have appeared to be created. Lycurgus read his works, and saw there a model of his legislation. [102] Pericles and Alcibiades had need of his counsels; they had recourse to him as a model of statesmen. [103] He was for Plato the first of the philosophers, and for Alexander the greatest of kings; and what is more extraordinary still, even the sectarians, divided among themselves, were united in him. The Stoics spoke only of this great poet as a rigid follower of the Porch [104]; at the Academy he was considered as the creator of dialectics; at the Lyceum, the disciples of Aristotle cited him as a zealous dogmatist [105]; finally, the Epicureans saw in him only a man calm and pure, who, satisfied with that tranquil life where one is wholly possessed by it, seeks nothing more. [106] The temples, which devout enthusiasm consecrated to him, were the rendezvous for mankind. [107] Such is the appanage of universal ideas: they are as the Divinity which inspires them, all in all, and all in the least parts.

If, at the distance where I am placed, I should dare, traversing the torrent of ages and opinions, draw near to Homer and read the soul of this immortal man, I would say, after having grasped in its entirety the allegorical genius which makes the essence of poetry, in seeking to give to his universal ideas a particular form, that his intention was to personify and paint the passions, and that it was from this that epopœia had birth. I have not sufficient documents to attest positively that the word by which one characterizes this kind of poetry after Homer, did not exist before him; but I have sufficient to repeat that no one had as yet recognized its real nature. [108] The poems of Corinna, of Dares, or of Dictys, were only simple extracts from the mythological cycles, rude copies from certain theosophical fragments denuded of life; Homer was the first who caused the Voice of Impulse, that is to say Epopœia, to be understood [109]: that kind of poetry which results from intellectual inspiration united to the enthusiasm of the passions.

In order to attain to the perfection of this kind of poetry, it is necessary to unite to the imaginative faculty which feeds the genius, the reason which regulates the impulse, and the enthusiasm which inflames the mind and supplies the talent. Homer united them in the most eminent degree. Thus he possessed the first inspiration and the complete science, as much in its essence as in its form; for the poetic form is always dependent upon talent.

This form was then highly favourable to genius. The Greek verse, measured by musical rhythm and filled with a happy blending of long and short syllables, had long since shaken off the servile yoke of rhyme. Now, by rhythm was understood the number and respective duration of the time of which a verse was composed. [110] A long syllable was equal to a time divided in two instants, and equivalent to two short syllables. A foot was what we name today a measure. The foot contained two times, made up of two long, or of one long and two short syllables. The verse most commonly used was the hexameter, that is, that in which the extent was measured by six rhythmic feet and of which the whole duration was twelve times. Thus poetry received only the laws of rhythm; it was a kind of music whose particular harmony, free in its course, was subject only to measure.

I have never found any authentic evidence that the Greeks had ever used the rhyme in their verse. It is stated, however, that they have not differed from other nations in this respect. Voltaire said so but without proof. [111]

What is most certain is that, taking the word epos, [112] a verse, in its most restricted acceptance, expressing a turn, a turning around again, the early poets constructed their verse in form of furrows, going from right to left and returning from left to right. [113] Happily this bizarrerie did not last long. If the Greek verses had thus turned one upon another, or if the rhyme had forced them to proceed in couplets bent beneath a servile yoke, Homer would not have created the Epopœia, or these frivolous obstacles would have vanished before him. His genius, incapable of enduring chains, would have refused to clothe itself in a form capable of stifling it. But this celebrated man would no doubt have changed it; one can judge by the energetic manner with which he attacked that which he found in use. The Greek language, which preserved still in his time something of the Phœnician stiffness and the Celtic roughness, obliged to adapt itself to all the movements of his imagination, became the most flexible and the most harmonious dialect of the earth. One is astonished, in reading his works, at the boldness of his composition. [114] One sees him without the least effort, bending words at his pleasure, lengthening them, shortening them to produce something new, reviving those no longer in use, uniting them, separating them, disposing of them in an unaccustomed order, forcing them to adapt themselves everywhere to the harmony that he wishes to depict, to sentiments of elevation, of pleasure or terror, that he wishes to inspire.

Thus genius, dominating form, creates master-pieces; form, on the contrary, commanding genius, produces only works of the mind. I must say finally and no longer veil from the attention of my judges, the aim of this discourse: whenever rhyme exists in the poetic form, it renders the form inflexible, it brings upon it only the effort of talent and renders that of intellectual inspiration useless. Never will the people who rhyme their verses attain to the height of poetic perfection; never will real epopœia flourish in their breasts. They will hear neither the accents inspired by Orpheus, nor the stirring and impassioned harmonies of Homer. Far from drawing the allegorical genius at its source and receiving the first inspiration, it will not even recognize the second one. Its poets will polish painfully certain impassioned or descriptive verses, and will call beautiful the works which will only be well done. A rapid glance over the poetic condition of the earth will prove what I have advanced. But I ought to explain beforehand what I understand by first and second inspiration; the moment has arrived for holding to the promise that I made at the beginning of this discourse.

IV.

YOU recall, Messieurs, that wishing, with Chancellor Bacon, to distinguish the essence and the form of Poetry, I have taken my text from the works of Plato. It is again from this man, justly called divine even by his rivals, from the founder of the Academy, that I have borrowed the germ of my idea. This philosopher compares the effect which the real poets have upon those who hear them, with the magnetic stone which not only attracts rings of iron, but communicates to them also the virtue of attracting other rings. [115]

In order to appreciate well the force of this thought, and to follow all the inferences, it is necessary to state a truth de facto: namely, that the men destined by Providence to regenerate the world, in whatever manner it may be, to open any sort of a career, are extremely rare. Nature, docile to the impulse which she has received of bringing all to perfection by means of time, elaborates slowly the elements of their genius, places them at great distances upon the earth, and makes them appear at epochs very far removed one from the other. It is necessary that these events, which determine these men toward an end, should be brought about in advance; that the physical conditions in which they are born coincide with the inspiration which attends them; and therefore everything prepares, everything protects, everything serves the providential design. These men, thus scattered over the earth, come among nations to form them, to give them laws, to enlighten and to instruct them. They are the beacon-lights of mankind; these are those to whom I attribute the first inspiration. This inspiration is immediate; it emanates from the first principle of all intelligence, in the same manner, to use the comparison of Plato, that the magnetic force which animates the loadstone, emanates from its cause. It is profoundly hidden from our eyes: it is this which fires the genius of a theosophist such as Thoth, Orpheus, and Zoroaster; the genius of a theocrat, such as Krishna, Moses, or Mohammed; the genius of a philosopher, such as Kong-Tse, Pythagoras, or Socrates; the genius of a poet, such as Homer or Valmiki; and of a triumphant hero, such as Cyrus, Alexander, or Napoleon.

Those who follow in the footprints of these primordial men, who allow themselves to be impressed by their genius, receive what I call the second inspiration. They can still be great men; for those who assist them are very great; they can also communicate the inspiration, for it acts in them with an exuberant force. Let us confine ourselves to the poetic inspiration and listen to the voice of Plato:

The Muse inspires the poets directly, and these, communicating to others their enthusiasm, form a chain of inspired men. It is by means of this chain that the Divinity attracts the souls of men, and moves them at his pleasure, causing his virtue to pass from link to link, from the first inspired poet to the last of his readers or his rhapsodists. [116]

It is by means of this magnetic chain that one can, in another sphere of movement, explain this truth so well known, that great kings make great men; it is also in this manner that one can understand how a monarch, called to found a vast empire, makes his will penetrate all hearts, take possession of all souls, and propagating his valour more and more, electrify his army and fill it with a multitude of heroes.

Homer received therefore a first inspiration; he was created to become the poetic motive of Europe, the principle of a magnetized chain which, appropriating unceasingly new links, was to cover Europe with its numberless extensions. His first conquests were in Greece. His verses, carried from city to city by actors known under the name of rhapsodists, [117] excited the keenest enthusiasm; they passed soon from mouth to mouth, fixed the attention of legislators, were the ornament of the most brilliant fêtes, [118] and became everywhere the basis of public instruction. [119] The secret flame which they concealed, becoming developed in young souls, warmed there the particular germ which they possessed, and according to their divers specie and the fertility of the soil, brought forth many talents. [120] The poets who were found endowed with a genius vast enough to receive the second inspiration in its entirety, imitated their model and raised themselves to epopœia. Antimachus and Dicæogenes are noticeable, the one for his Thebaïs, and the other for his cyprien verses. [121] Those to whom nature had given passions more gentle than violent, more touching than vehement, inclinations more rustic than bellicose, whose souls contained more sensitiveness than elevation, were led to copy certain isolated groups of this vast tableau, and placing them, following their tastes, in the palace or in the thatched cottage, caused accents of joy or of sorrow, the plaints of heroes or the sports of shepherds to be heard, and thus created elegy, eclogue, or idyl. [122] Others, on the contrary, whose too vehement enthusiasm shortened the duration of it, whose keen fiery passions had left little empire for reason, who allowed themselves to be drawn easily toward the object of which they were momentarily captive, created the ode, dithyramb, or song, according to the nature of their genius and the object of their passion. These were more numerous than all the others together, and the women who were here distinguished, rivalled and even surpassed the men; Corinna and Myrtis did not yield either to Stesi`chorus, [123] or to Pindar; Sappho and Telesilla effaced Alcæus and Anacreon. [124]

It is said that the art with which Homer had put into action gods and men, had opposed heaven and earth, and depicted the combats of the passions; this art, being joined to the manner in which the rhapsodists declaimed his poems [125] by alternately relieving one another, and covering themselves with garments of different colours adapted to the situation, had insensibly given rise to dramatic style and to theatrical representation. [126] This, true in a sense. has need of a distinction: it will serve at the same time to throw light upon what I am about to say.

One should remember that the intellectual and rational poetry, or theosophical and philosophical, illustrated by Orpheus and which Homer had united with the enthusiasm of the passions in order to constitute epopœia, although separated from the latter, existed none the less. Whereas the disciples of Homer, or the Homeridæ, [127] spread themselves abroad and took possession of the laic or profane world, the religious and learned world was always occupied by the disciples of Orpheus, called Eumolpidæ. [128] The hierophants and philosophers continued to write as formerly upon theology and natural philosophy. There appeared from time to time theogonies and cosmological systems, [129] dionysiacs, heraclides, [130] oracles, treatises on nature and moral apologues, which bore no relation to epopœia. The hymns or pæans which had emanated from the sanctuaries in honour of the Divinity, had in no wise resembled either the odes or the dithyrambs of the lyric poets [131]: as much as the former were vehement and passionate, so much the latter affected to be calm and majestic. There existed therefore, at this epoch, two kinds of poetry, equally beautiful when they had attained their respective perfection: Eumolpique Poetry and Epic Poetry: the first, intellectual and rational; the other, intellectual and passionate.

However, the divine mysteries, hidden from the profane, manifested to the initiates in the ceremonies and symbolic fables, had not as yet issued from the sanctuaries: it had been nearly a thousand years since they had been instituted by Orpheus [132] when suddenly one saw for the first time certain of these fables and these ceremonies ridiculously travestied, transpiring among the people and serving them for amusement. The fêtes of Dionysus, celebrated in the times of vintage, gave place to this sort of profanation. The grape-gatherers, besmeared with lees, giving way in the intoxication of wine to an indiscreet enthusiasm, began to utter aloud from their wagons the allegories that they had learned in their rural initiations. These allegories, which neither the actors nor the spectators had comprehended in reality, appeared, nevertheless, piquant to both through the malicious interpretations which they gave them. [133] Such were the feeble beginnings of dramatic art in Greece [134]; there was born the profanation of the Orphic mysteries, in the same manner that one sees it reborn among us, by the profanation of the Christian mysteries. [135] But this art was already old in Asia when it sprang up in Europe. I have already said that there was in the secret celebration of the mysteries, veritable dramatic representations. These mystic ceremonies, copied from those which had taken place in the celebration of the Egyptian mysteries, had been brought into Egypt by the Indian priests at a very remote epoch when the empire of Hindustan had extended over this country. This communication, which was made from one people to another, has been demonstrated to the point of evidence by the learned researches of the academicians of Calcutta, Jones, Wilford, and Wilkin, [136] who have proved what Bacon had previously said in speaking of the Greek traditions, "that it was only a very light air which, passing by means of an ancient people into the flutes of Greece, had been modulated by them into sounds more sweet, more harmonious, and more conformable to the climate and to their brilliant imagination."

A singular coincidence, Messieurs, which will not escape your sagacity, is that dramatic art, whose origin is lost in India in the night of time, has likewise had its birth in the mysteries of religion. It is during the Ram-Jatra, a fête celebrated annually in honour of Rama, the same as Dionysus of the Greeks, or Bacchus of the Latins, that one still sees theatrical representations which have served as models for the more regular works that have been made in the course of time. [137] These representations, which run through nearly all the exploits of Rama and through the victory that this beneficent god gained over Rawhan, the principle of evil, are mingled with chants and recitations exactly as were those of the ancient Greeks. You understand, Messieurs, that the first efforts of tragedy were to celebrate the conquests of Bacchus and his triumph, of which that of Apollo over the serpent Python, celebrated by the Pythian games, was the emblem. [138] Those of the Indians who appear to have preserved the most ancient traditions, since the sacred books were written in the Pali language, considered as anterior to the Sanskrit by some savants, the Burmans, have from time immemorial recorded the mysteries of Rama in scenic dramas which are still performed in public on the fête day of this god. [139] I do not consider it amiss to mention here that the name of Rama, which in Sanskrit signifies that which is dazzling and beautiful, that which is sublime and protective, has had the same signification in Phœnician, [140] and that it is from this same name to which is joined a demonstrative article common to Aramaic, Chaldean, and Syriac, that the word drama [141] is formed, and which being adopted by the Greek tongue, has passed afterwards into the Latin tongue and into ours. This word has expressed an action, because, in truth, it depicts one in the mysteries and besides its primitive root refers to regular movement in general.

But as my purpose is not to follow at present dramatic art in all its ramifications and as it suffices me to have indicated clearly the origin, I return to Greece.

The spectacle of which I have spoken, effect of a Bacchic enthusiasm, and at first abandoned to the caprice of certain rustic grape-gatherers whose indiscretions did not appear formidable, struck so forcibly by its novelty and produced such a marvellous effect upon the people, that it was not long before certain men of most cultivated minds were seen desirous of taking part either from liking or from interest. Thespis and Susarion appeared at the same time and each seized, according to his character, one the noble and serious side and the other the ridiculous and amusing side of the mythological fables; dividing thus from its birth, dramatic art and distinguishing it by two kinds, tragedy and comedy: that is, the lofty and austere chant, and the joyous and lascivious chant. [142] [143]

In the meantime, the governments, until then quite indifferent to these rustic amusements, warned that certain liberties permitted by Thespis were becoming too flagrant, began to see the profanations which had resulted, and of which the Eumolpidæ had no doubt pointed out the consequences. [144] They tried to prevent them, and Solon even made a law regarding this subject [145]; but it was too late: the people attracted in crowds to these representations, all informal as they were, rendered useless the foresight of the legislator. It was necessary to yield to the torrent and, being unable to arrest it, to strive at least to restrain it within just limits. A clear field was left open for the good that it was able to do, in fertilizing the new ideas, and severe rules were opposed to check whatever dangers its invasions might have for religion and for customs. The dramatic writers were permitted to draw the subject of their pieces from the source of the mysteries, but it was forbidden them, under penalty of death, to divulge the sense. Æschylus, first of the dramatic poets, having involuntarily violated this law, ran the risk of losing his life. [146] Discriminating judges were established to pronounce upon the excellency of the works offered in the competition, and one was very careful not to abandon oneself at first to the passionate acclamations of the people, and the approbations or disapprobations of the maxims which were therein contained. [147] These judges, proficient in the knowledge of music and of poetry, had to listen in silence until the end, and maintain all in order and decency. Plato attributes to the desuetude into which this law fell, and to the absolute dominion which the people assumed over the theatre, the first decadence of the art and its entire corruption.

Æschylus, whom I have just named, was the true creator of dramatic art. Strong with the inspiration which he had received from Homer, [148] he transported into tragedy the style of epopœia, and animated it with a music grave and simple. [149] Not content with the moral beauties with which his genius embellished it, he wished that music, painting, and dancing might lend their aid and contribute to the illusion of the senses. He caused a theatre to be built where the most ingenious devices, the most magnificent decorations displayed their magic effects. [150] One saw in the tragedy of Prometheus, the earth trembling, clouds of dust rising in the air; one heard the whistling of wind, the crash of thunder; one was dazzled by the lightnings. [151] Old Ocean appeared upon the waves, and Mercury came from the heights of heaven to announce the commands of Jupiter. In the tragedy of the Eumenides, these infernal divinities appeared upon the scene to the number of fifty, clothed in black robes; blood-stained, the head bristling with serpents, holding in one hand a torch and in the other a lash. [152] They replied to the shade of Clytemnestra, who invoked them, by a choir of music so frightful, that a general terror having struck the assembly, certain of the women experienced premature pains of confinement. [153]
One feels, after this, that Greek tragedy had in its theatrical forms, much in common with our modern operas; but what eminently distinguishes it is

that, having come forth complete from the depths of the sanctuaries, it possessed a moral sense which the initiates understood. This is what put it above anything that we might be able to conceive today; what gave it an inestimable price. Whereas the vulgar, dazzled only by the pomp of the spectacle, allured by the beauty of the verse and the music, enjoyed merely a fleeting gratification, the wise tasted a pleasure more pure and more durable, by receiving the truth in their hearts even from the deceitful delusions of the senses. This pleasure was as much greater as the inspiration of the poet had been more perfect, and as he had succeeded better in making the allegorical spirit felt, without betraying the veil which covered it.

Æschylus went further in comprehension of the subject than any of his successors. His plans were of an extreme simplicity. He deviated little from the mythological tradition. [154] All his efforts tended only to give light to their teachings, to penetrate into their hidden beauties. The characters of his heroes, strongly drawn, sustained them at heights where Homer had placed them. He caused terror to pass before them that they might be frightened. [155] His aim was to lead them to virtue by terror, and to inspire the soul with a force capable of resisting alike the intoxications of prosperity and the discouragements of poverty.

Sophocles and Euripides followed closely Æschylus and surpassed him in certain portions of the art; the first, even triumphed over him in the eyes of the multitude [156]; but the small number of sages, faithful to the true principles, regarded him always as the father of tragedy. [157] One can admit that Sophocles was more perfect in the conduct of his plans, in the regularity of his style [158]; that Euripides was more natural and more tender, more skilful in arousing interest, in stirring the passions [159]; but these perfections, resulting from the form, had not been acquired without the very essence of drama being altered; that is to say, without the allegorical genius which had presided at the composition of the fables that the poets had always drawn from the religious mysteries, suffering many deviations, which rendered it often unrecognizable through the foreign adornments with which it was burdened. Sophocles and above all Euripides, by devoting themselves to perfecting the form, really harmed therefore the principle of the art and hastened its corruption. If the laws which had at first been promulgated against those who in treating of the tragic subjects vilified the mysterious sense had been executed, Euripides would not have been allowed to depict so many heroes degraded by adversity, so many princesses led astray by love, so many scenes of shame, of scandal, and of crime [160]; but the people, already degraded and bordering upon corruption, allowed themselves to be drawn along by these dangerous tableaux and hastened half-way to meet the poisoned cup which was offered to them.

It must candidly be admitted, that it is to the very charm of these tableaux, to the talent with which Euripides understood how to colour them, that the decadence of Athenian manners and the first harm done to the purity of religion must be attributed. The theatre, having become the school of the passions, and offering to the soul no spiritual nourishment, opened a door through which doubt, contempt, and derision for the mysteries, the most sacrilegious audacity, and utter forgetfulness of the Divinity, insinuated themselves even unto the sanctuaries. Æschylus had represented in his heroes, supernatural personages [161]; Sophocles painted simple heroes, and Euripides, characters often less than men. [162] Now these personages were, in the eyes of the people, either children of the gods, or the gods themselves. What idea could be formed then of their weaknesses, of their crimes, of their odious or ridiculous conduct, particularly when these weaknesses or these crimes were no longer represented as allegories from which it was necessary to seek the meaning, but as historical events or frivolous plays of the imagination? The people, according to the degree of their intelligence, became either impious or superstitious; the savants professed to doubt all, and the influential men, by feigning to believe all, regarded all parties with an equal indifference. This is exactly what happened. The mysteries became corrupt because one was accustomed to regard them as corrupt; and the people became intolerant and fanatical, each one cringing with fear, lest he be judged what he really was, namely, impious.

Such was the effect of dramatic art in Greece. This effect, at first imperceptible, became manifest to the eyes of the sages, when the people became the dictators of the theatre and ignored the judges named to pronounce upon the works of the poets; when the poets, jealous of obtaining the approval of the multitude, consulted its taste rather than truth, its versatile passions rather than reason, and sacrificed to its caprices the laws of honesty and excellence. [163]

As soon as tragedy, disparaging the mysteries of the fables had transformed them into historical facts, it needed only a step to raise historical facts to the rank of subjects of tragedy. Phrynichus was, it is said, the first who had this audacity. He produced in the theatre, the Conquest of Miletus. [164] The people of Athens, with a whimsicality which is characteristic of them, condemned the poet to a very heavy fine, for having disobeyed the law and crowned him because of the tears which they shed at the representation of his work. But this was not enough, confounding thus reality and allegory; soon, sacred and profane things were mingled by forging without any kind of moral aim, subjects wholly false and fantastic. The poet Agathon, who was the author of this new profanation had been the friend of Euripides. [165] He proved thus that he knew nothing of the essence of dramatic poetry and makes it doubtful whether Euripides knew it any better.

Thus, in the space of less than two centuries, tragedy, borne upon the car of Thespis, elevated by Æschylus to a nobler theatre, carried to the highest degree of splendour by Sophocles, had already become weakened in the hands of Euripides, had lost the memory of its celestial origin with Agathon, and abandoned to the caprices of a populace as imperious as ignorant, inclined toward a rapid degeneration. [166] Comedy less reserved did not have a happier destiny. After having hurled its first darts upon the heroes and demigods of Greece, having taken possession of certain very unguarded allegories, to turn even the gods to ridicule [167]; after having derided Prometheus and Triptolemus, Bacchus and the Bacchantes, after having made sport of heaven and earth, of the golden age and the seasons [168]; it attacked men in general and in particular, ridiculed their absurdities, pursued their vices, real or imaginary, and delivered them both unsparingly, without pity, to derision and contempt. [169] Epicharmus, who gave certain rules to the indecent farces of Susarion, was followed by Magnes, Cratinus, Eupolis, and a crowd of other comic poets, until Aristophanes whose bitter satires no longer finding sufficient influence in certain obscure ridicules, applied themselves to disparaging science and virtue, and twenty years beforehand, prepared and envenomed the hemlock by which Socrates was poisoned. It is true that some time after, Menander tried to reform this terrible abuse and gave to comedy a form less revolting; but he was only able to do so by detaching it completely from its origin, that is to say, by severing it from all that it had preserved, intellectually and allegorically, and reducing it to the representation of certain tableaux and certain events of the social life.

In going back, as I have just done, to the origin of poetic science in order to distinguish first, its essence from its form and afterwards, to follow its diverse developments, in genus and in kind, I have related many things and cited a great number of subjects with which you are familiar; but you will no doubt excuse, Messieurs, these numerous reminiscences and citations, in reflecting that although but little necessary for you, they were infinitely so for me, since presenting myself in the lists and wishing to give an added form to this science which belongs to you, I must prove to you that I have at least studied it profoundly.

V.

NOW, summing up what I have said, it will be found that poetry, entirely intellectual in its origin and destined only to be the language of the gods, owed its first developments in Greece to Orpheus, its second to Homer, and its last to Æschylus. These three creative men, seizing the different germs of this science still shrouded in their formless rudiments, warmed them with the fire of their genius and according to the particular inspiration of each, led them to the perfection of which they were susceptible. All three of them were the object of a first inspiration, although influenced one by the other, and were able to communicate the magnetic power to new disciples. Orpheus possessor of intellectual and rational poetry, constituted that which I call Eumolpœia, which, being divided into theosophy and philosophy, produces all the works which treat of the Divinity, of the Universe, of Nature, and of Man in general. [170] Homer, in joining to this spiritual poetry the enthusiasm of the passions, created Epopœia, whose magnificent genus envelops a multitude of specie, where the intellectual faculty and passion dominate with more or less energy under the influence of imagination. Homer rendered sentient that which was intelligible and particularized that which Orpheus had left universal: Æschylus, trying to bring into action what these two divine men had left with potentiality, formed the idea of dramatic or active poetry, in which he claimed to include whatever Eumolpœia and Epopœia had in common, that was moral, allegorical, and passionate. He would have succeeded, perhaps, and then would have produced the most perfect work of thought, passion, and action possible for men, conceived by genius and executed by talent; but Greece, exhausted by the abundant harvest obtained by Orpheus and Homer, lacked the sap to give nourishment to this new plant. Corrupted in its germ, this plant degenerated rapidly, deteriorated, and put forth only a vain show of branches without elevation and without virtue. The heroes of Thermopylæ succumbed under the burden of their laurels. Given over to a foolish arrogance, they covered with an unjust contempt their preceptors and their fathers; they persecuted, they assassinated their defenders and their sages and, base tyrants of the theatre, they prepared themselves to bow the head beneath the yoke of the king of Macedonia.

This king, victor at Chæronea, became arbiter of Greece, and his son, providential instrument of the ascendancy which Europe was to have over Asia, crossing the Hellespont at the head of an army that his genius alone rendered formidable, overthrew the empire of Cyrus and stood for a moment upon its débris: I say for a moment, because it was not here that the new empire was to be established: Europe had still obeyed; she was one day to command. Rome was already, in the thought of the future, the culminating point of the earth. A few centuries sufficed for this city, then unknown, [171] to attain to the height of glory. Emerging from her obscurity, conquering Pyrrhus, dominating Italy, combating and overthrowing Carthage, conquering Greece, and trampling under foot twenty diadems borne by the successors of Alexander, was for this ambitious Republic the work of a few centuries. But it is not true, although certain men whose virtue was not enlightened by the torch of experience may have been able to say it; it is not true that a republic, already perplexed in governing itself, can govern the world. It requires an empire, and this empire is created.

Cæsar laid its foundation, Augustus strengthened it. The sciences and arts, brought to Rome from the heart of Greece, came out then from their lethargy and flourished with a new éclat. Poetry, especially, found numberless admirers. Vergil, strongly attracted by the magnetic flame of Homer, dared to tread in his light, overthrew all the obstacles that time had raised, and drawing near to this divine model, received from him the second inspiration without intermediary and without rival. Ovid, less determined, hovering between Orpheus and Homer, succeeded, however, in uniting the second inspiration of the one to the third inspiration of the other, and left in his book of Metamorphoses a monument not less brilliant and more inimitable than the Æneid. Horace, little satisfied with succeeding Pindar, sought and found the means of uniting to the enthusiasm of the passions the calm of rational poetry, and, establishing himself a legislator of Parnassus, dictated laws to the poets, or jeered at the absurdities of men.

This poetry of reason had long since fallen into desuetude. The false movement that dramatic poetry had taken in Greece, the contempt that it had come to inspire for gods and men, had reacted upon it. The philosophers, disdaining a science which, by its own admission, was founded upon falsehood, had driven it from their writings. As much as they searched for it, when they believed it an emanation of the Divinity, so much had they fled from it since they had come to see in it only the vain production of an insensate delirium. Here is an observation, Messieurs, somewhat new, with which I may engage your attention: the first comedies appeared five hundred and eighty years before our era, which was about twenty years after Pherecydes wrote the first work in prose. [172] This philosopher doubtless, did not believe that a language prostituted to the burlesque parodies of Susarion should be useful further to the meditations of the sages. It is not, however, that at long intervals certain philosophers such as Empedocles, Parmenides, and many others of their disciples, have not written in verse [173]; but the remains of the ancient usage soon gave way, especially when Plato had embellished prose with the charm of his captivating eloquence. Before this philosopher, Herodotus had read in the assembly of the Olympic games an history of Greece connected with that of the greater part of the neighbouring nations. [174] This work, written in a fluent style, clear and persuasive, had so enchanted the Greeks, that they had given to the nine books which he composed, the names of the nine Muses. Nevertheless, an observation which will not be wholly foreign here, is, that the admission of prose in philosophy, instead of rational poetry, produced a style of work hitherto unknown, and of which the moderns made much; I am speaking of positive history. Before this epoch, history written in verse was, as I have said, allegorical and figurative, and was occupied only with the masses without respect to individuals. Thus the evil which resulted on the one side, from the degradation experienced by poetry in one of its branches, was balanced by the good which was promised on the other, from the purification of prose for the advancement of exact knowledge.

But returning to what I said just now on the subject of rational poetry, joined by the Romans to the passionate part of that science, I will say that this union created a new style, of which Horace was the originator: this was the didactic style. This style ought not to be confused with rational poetry, of which Hesiod has made use in his poem of Works and Days, and which pertains to Eumolpœia; nor with pure rational poetry, such as one finds in the writings of Parmenides and Empedocles: it is a sort of poetry which, attaching itself to form alone, depends much upon dramatic art. The didactic, satirical, or simply descriptive poet is similar to an actor on the stage declaiming a long monologue. Rational poetry was welcomed at Rome, and drawn from the long oblivion into which it had fallen, by [paragraph continues] Lucretius who, being inspired by the works of Leucippus and of Epicurus [175] wrote a book upon the nature of things, which has never been as yet well comprehended or well translated, the language not being understood.

Comedy, reformed by Menander, was again improved by Plautus and by Terence who acquired much reputation in this style; as to dramatic art in itself, it remained in its inertia. The Romans having the same gods and nearly the same mythology as the Greeks, were neither sufficiently elevated in intelligence to reinstate this art and make of it the masterpiece of the human mind; nor sufficiently advanced in exact knowledge to change wholly its forms and make of it, as we have, a new art, whence allegory and the moral part of Eumolpœia have been completely banished. But what the Romans were unable to do for dramatic art, they unfortunately were able to do for Epopœia. Certain writers, able versifiers, but absolutely deprived of intellectual inspiration, incapable of distinguishing in poetry the essence from the form, following what the degenerated theatre and the inspired declamations of Euhemerus [176] had taught them, imagined foolishly that the gods and heroes of antiquity having been only men stronger and more powerful than the others, mythology was only a crude collection of historic facts disfigured, and Epopœia only an emphatic discourse upon these same facts. [177] Thereupon they believed that it was only a question of taking any historic subject whatever, and relating it in verse with certain embellishments, to create an epic poem. Lucan and Silius Italicus, in choosing, the one the misfortunes of Pompey, and the other the victories of Hannibal, considered themselves superior to Homer or Vergil, as much as they supposed Rome or Carthage superior to Ilium. But a just posterity, notwithstanding the prejudices of their panegyrists, has put them in their place. It has considered them merely the inventors of a kind of bastard poetry, which might be called historic poetry. This poetry, entirely separated from Eumolpœia, whose moral essence it is unable to realize, preserves only the material and physical forms of true Epopœia. It is a body without soul, which is moved by a mechanical mainspring applied by a skilful workman.

As to the poetic form in itself, its only point of variance with the Greeks and Romans was that of elegance. The verses written in the same manner, depended likewise upon a fixed number of time or of feet regulated by musical rhythm. If rhyme had been admitted there in the first ages, it had been excluded early enough so that there remained no longer the least trace of it. The Latin tongue, very far from the Greek in flexibility, variety, and harmony, for a long time treated with contempt by the Greeks who, regarding it as a barbarous dialect, only learned it with repugnance [178]; the Latin tongue, I say, unpleasing, obscure, not even supporting the mediocrity of ordinary elocution, became, through the laborious efforts of its writers, a tongue which in the works of Vergil, for example, attained such a perfection, that it came to be doubted, owing to the grace, the justice, and the force of its expression, whether the author of the Æneid did not surpass the author of the Iliad. Such is the empire of forms. They alone make problematical that which, in its essence, should not be subject to the least discussion.

But at last the Roman Eagle, after having soared some time in the universe and covered with his extended wings the most beautiful countries of Europe, Asia, and Africa, fatigued by its own triumphs, sank down again, allowed its power to be divided, and from the summit of this same Capitol, whence it had for such a long time hurled its thunderbolts, saw the vultures of the North divide among them its spoils. The mythological religion, misunderstood in its principles, attacked in its forms, given over to the corruption of things and men, had disappeared to give place to a new religion, which born in obscurity, was raised imperceptibly from the ranks of the humblest citizens to the imperial throne. Constantine, who in embracing the Christian cult had consolidated that religious revolution, believed himself able to bring about another in politics, by transferring the seat of his empire to the Bosphorus. Historians have often blamed this last movement; but they have not seen that Providence, in inspiring this division of the empire, foresaw that the darkness of ignorance rolling with the waves of the barbarians was about to extend as far as Rome, and that it would be necessary to concentrate at one point a part of the learning, in order to save it from the general ruin. Whereas the Empire of the Occident, assailed on all sides by the hordes from the North, was overthrown, torn, divided into numberless small sovereignties whose extent was often limited to the donjon where the sovereign resided; the Empire of the Orient sustained the weight of the hordes from the South, nourished continually in its midst certain men, guardians of the sacred fire of science, and did not fall until more than nine centuries later; and learning, commencing its revival in the Occident, put minds in condition there, to appreciate the models which were about to be presented to them and rendered them capable of receiving their inspiration.

It was a very remarkable epoch, Messieurs, which saw grouped about it in the space of less than a half century and coincident with the downfall of the Empire of the Orient, the use of gunpowder, of the compass, of the telescope in the Occident; the invention of engraving upon copper, that of movable characters for printing, the extension of commerce and navigation by the passage around the cape of Storms, and finally the discovery of America. It was a very extraordinary century, in which were born Mohammed II. and Lorenzo de' Medici, Vasco da Gama and Christopher Columbus, Theodoros Gaza and Pico della Mirandola, Leonardo da Vinci and Bojardo, Leo X. and Luther. After the invasion of the barbarians, Christian Europe had lost its political unity: it was as a great republic whose divided members, struggling continuously one against the other, tearing by turn a shadow of supremacy, were the realms, the pontifical or laic principalities, the republics, the free and commercial cities. The two chiefs of this gigantic and badly organized body, the German Emperor and the Pope, bishop of Rome, were vested only with a grandeur of opinion; their real power was void: they were nothing more, in fact, than that which they appeared in form. Since Charlemagne, who, in a century of darkness enlightened with his own genius, had had the force to grasp the débris of the empire, uniting them in his hand and giving them a momentary existence, it had not had an emperor. The vain efforts of Hildebrand and of Charles V. had served only at different times and under different conditions to demonstrate their impotence. It was reserved for a much greater man to dominate Europe regenerated by violent shocks, and to show to the universe the legitimate successor of Augustus wreathed with the imperial crown.

But without in any way anticipating time, without even leaving our subject which is poetry, let us continue to follow the developments of this science.

The original poets of Greece and Rome, brought into Italy by the savants whom the taking of Constantinople forced to go back towards the Occident of Europe, brought there an unexpected brilliancy, which, with the ancient germs deeply buried in its midst, soon awakened certain new germs that the peculiar circumstances had also brought there. In explaining what these germs were, I am giving occasion for thinkers to make certain reflections, and critics to form certain singular conjectures upon works hitherto badly judged.

It is necessary at first, that I repeat a truth which I have already said: that intellectual nature is always one and the same, whereas physical nature varies, changes unceasingly with time and place, and is modified in a thousand ways according to circumstances. Now, it is this latter nature which gives the form, that is to say, which renders sentient and particular that which the former gives to it as universal and intelligible; so that its aptitude more or less great, in receiving and in working upon the intelligence, can make the things which are more homogeneous in their principle appear more dissimilar in their effect. I will give a proof. Whilst the most profound obscurity covered Europe, whilst ignorance spread on all sides its baleful veils, there were found, however, at long intervals, certain privileged men, who, raising themselves above these thick vapours, came to grasp certain faint glimmerings of the light shining always above them. These men possessors of such rare gifts, would have indeed wished to communicate them to their contemporaries, but if they imprudently opened their mouths, the blind and fanatic horde which surrounded them cried out forthwith against the heretic, the magician, the sorcerer, and conducted them to torture as the price of their lessons. [179] After several sorry examples, these men, having become prudent, assumed the part of silence by retiring into monasteries or hermitages, studying Nature there in quietude, and profiting alone by their discoveries. If certain ones still dared to speak, it was by borrowing the style of religion, or history, diverting from the ordinary sense certain ideas received, explaining themselves by enigmas, or by figures, which, when necessary, they were able to explain as they wished.

Among this number was a man of strong imagination and of a genius really poetic, who, having grasped certain truths of nature, and judging it proper not to divulge them, took the expedient of enclosing them in a book which he entitled: Les Faits et Gestes de Charles-Magne. This extraordinary man who has, in these modern times, obtained an ascendancy greater than one could ever have imagined, since he is the vital source whence have come all the orders, all the institutions of chivalry with which Europe has been inundated; this man, I say, was a monk of Saint-André de Vienne, living from the tenth to the eleventh century and perhaps a little before. [180] The book that he composed had a success as much the more prodigious as it was misunderstood, and such was the ignorance not only of the people, but even of the clergy, that the most palpable fictions were taken for realities. There are historians even who pretend that the council of Rheims, celebrated in 1119, declared this work authentic [181]; and thence came the habit of attributing it to Archbishop Turpin. However that may be, it is to the allegorical history of Charlemagne, to that of his twelve paladins, called peers of France, to that of the four sons of Aymon and of Chevalier Bayard, to that of Renaud, Roland, Richard, and the other heroes of the bibliothèque bleue, for a long time our only bibliotheca, that we owe a new style of poetry, called Romanesque, on account of the Romance tongue in which it had birth. [182] This style is to the eumolpique style, as a wild offshoot, growing laboriously in an arid and bramble-covered land, is to a cultivated tree which rises majestically in the heart of a fertile country.

It was with the chivalrous ideas, inspired by the book of the monk of Saint André, that the first poetic ideas were brought forth in France. The Oscan troubadours seizing these first glimmerings of genius, threw themselves with enthusiasm into a career which offered at the same time pleasures, glory, and the gifts of fortune. [183] They sang of the fair, of gallants and of kings; but their verses, monotonous enough when a real passion did not animate them, hardly reached above eulogy or satire. But little capable of feeling the moral beauties of poetry, they stopped at form. The rhyme for them was everything. For them the supreme talent was only rhyming much and with difficulty. One could not imagine to what lengths they went in this style. Not content with restricting themselves to follow the same rhyme throughout the entire course of the poem, they sometimes doubled it at the end of each verse, rhyming by echo, or else they made an initial rhyme. [184] These obstacles becoming multiplied stifled their muse in its cradle. All that art owed to these first modern poets was limited to a sort of song, gay and sprightly, ordinarily a parody upon a more serious subject, and which, because it was quite frequently sung with an air of the dance accompanied by the vielle or hurdy-gurdy, their favourite instrument, was called vau-de-vielle, or as is pronounced today, vaudeville. [185]

The Italians and Spaniards, who received from the Oscan troubadours their first impulse toward poetry, would have been perhaps as limited as they, to composing amorous sonnets, madrigals or, at the most, certain vehement sylves, [186] if the Greeks, driven from their country by the conquests of Mohammed II., had not brought them the works of the ancients as I have already said. These works, explained in the chaire publique, due to the munificence of the Medicis, struck particularly the Italians: not however by exciting their poets to take them as models; the turn of their mind and the form of their poetry, similar in everything to that of the troubadours, were opposed too obviously here; but by giving them that sort of emulation which, without copying the others, makes one strive to equal them. At this epoch the book of the monk of St. André, attributed as I have said to Archbishop Turpin, already more than four centuries old, was known by all

Europe, whether by itself, or whether by the numberless imitations of which it had been the subject. Not only France, Spain, Italy, but also England and Germany were inundated with a mass of romances and ballads, wherein were pictured the knights of the court of Charlemagne and those of the Round Table. [187] All these works were written in verse, and the greater part, particularly those composed by the troubadours or their disciples, intended to be sung, were cut into strophes. Those of the imitator poets, who had had the force to go back to the allegorical sense of their model, had only developed and enriched it with their own knowledge; the others, following their various methods of considering it, had chosen subjects real and historical, or indeed had followed ingenuously without aim or plan, the impulse of their vagabond imagination. In France could be seen represented by the side of the stories of Tristan, of Lancelot, of the Grail, and of Ogier-le-Danois, that of Alexander the Great and of the Bible, that of the Seven Sages and of Judas Maccabeus, that of the History of the Normands and the Bretons, and finally that of the Rose, the most famous of all. A certain Guilhaume had published a philosophical romance upon the nature of beasts. [188]

Already the Italian poets, after having received from the troubadours the form of their verses and that of their works, had surpassed their masters and had caused them to be forgotten. Petrarch in the sonnet and Dante in the sirvente assumed all the glory of their models, and left not any for the successors [189]; already even Bojardo and some others had attempted, with the example of Homer, to bring back to the unity of epopœia, the incongruous and fantastic scenes of the romance, when Ariosto appeared. This man, gifted with a keen and brilliant imagination, and possessor of a matchless talent, executed what no one else had been able to do before him; he was neither inspired by Homer, nor by Vergil; he copied no one. He learned from them only to raise himself to the poetic source, to see it where it was and to draw from it his genius. Then he received a first inspiration and became the creator of a particular style of poetry which may be called romantic. Undoubtedly this style is greatly inferior to epopœia; but after all it is original: its beauties as well as its faults belong to him.

Almost the same moment when Ariosto enriched Europe with his new poetry, Camoëns wished to naturalize it in Portugal; but the mélange of Vergil and Lucan that he essayed to make, betrayed his lack of understanding and he did not succeed. I mention it only that you may observe,

Messieurs, that the form adopted by the Portuguese poet is exactly the same as the one which Ariosto, his predecessors and his successors, have followed in Italy: it is that of the troubadours. The poems of each are long ballads, intersected by strophes of eight lines of alternate rhymes which, succeeding one another with the same measure, can be sung from one end to the other, with an appropriate air, and which in fact, as J. J. Rousseau has very well remarked, were sung frequently. In these poems, the essence is in accord with the form, and it is this that makes their regularity. It is not the epopœia of Homer drawn from the Orphic source, it is the romantic poetry of Ariosto, an issue of the fictions attributed to Archbishop Turpin, which is associated with the verses of the troubadours. These verses subjected to rhyme are incapable in any tongue of attaining the sublime heights of Eumolpœia or of Epopœia.

The French poets soon proved it, when coming to understand the works of Homer and Vergil, they thought themselves able to imitate them by making use of the same poetic forms by which the authors of Perceval or Berthe-au-grand-pied had profited. It was all to no purpose that they worked these forms, striking them upon the anvil, polishing them, they remained inflexible. Ronsard was the first who made the fatal experiment; and after him a crowd of careless persons came to run aground upon the same reef. These forms always called up the spirit with which they were born; the melancholy and unceasing sound, sonorous with their rhymes in couplets or alternate, had something soporific which caused the soul to dream and which allured it in spite of itself, not into the sublime regions of allegory where the genius of Eumolpœia was nourished, but into vague spaces of fictions, where, under a thousand whimsical forms the romantic mind evaporates. Doubtless one would have been able, in France, to limit the Italian poets, as had been done in Spain and Portugal; but besides, as it would have been necessary to confine itself to the second inspiration in a style already secondary, the spirit of the nation, sufficiently well represented by that of Ronsard, foreseeing from afar its high destinies, wished to command the summit of Parnassus, before having discovered the first paths.

The disasters of the first epic poets did not discourage their successors; vying with each other they sought to make amends; but instead of seeing the obstacle where it really was, that is to say, in the incompatible alliance of the essence of Epopœia with the form of romance, they imagined that lack of talent alone had been prejudicial to the success of their predecessors. Consequently they devoted themselves to work with an indefatigable ardour, polishing and repolishing the rhyme, tearing to pieces and revising twenty times their works, and finally bringing the form to the highest perfection that they were able to attain. The century of Louis XIV., so fertile in able versifiers, in profound rhymers, saw, however, the dawn of Epic poems only as a signal of their failure. Chapelain had, nevertheless, shown talent before his catastrophe; wishing to interest the French nation, he had chosen in its history the sole epic subject which he found there. Why had he not succeeded? This point was considered, and the truth still lacking, they went on to imagine that the fault was inherent in the French tongue, and that it was no longer capable of rising to the heights of Epopœia: deplorable error, which for a long time has been harmful to the development of a tongue destined to become universal and to carry to future centuries the discoveries of past ones.

Ronsard had felt the difficulty most. Accustomed as he was to read Greek and Latin works in the original, he had seen clearly that what prevented the French tongue from following their poetic movement was particularly the restraint of the rhyme; he had even sought to free it from this servitude, endeavouring to make the French verses scan according to the ancient rhythm; but, in another way he had not appreciated the genius of that tongue which refused to follow this rhythm. Jodelle, Baïf, Passerat, Desportes, Henri-Etienne, and certain other savants, have made at different times the same attempt, and always without results.[190] Each tongue has its own character which it is necessary to know; ours has not at all the musical prosody of the Greek and Latin; its syllables are not determined, long and short, by the simple duration of time, but by the different accentuation and inflection of the voice. Among our writers the one who has best understood the nature of this prosody is certainly the abbé d'Olivet: he declared firstly that he did not believe it possible to make French verses measured by rhythm; and secondly, that even in the case where this might be possible, he did not see how this rhythm could be conformable to that of the Greeks and Latins.[191]

I am absolutely of his opinion on these two points; I am furthermore, en partie, on what he says of the rhyme. I know as he, that it is not an invention of the barbarous ages; I know even more, that it is the luxurious production of a very enlightened age; I must say that it has brought forth thousands of beautiful verses, that it is often to the poet like a strange genius which comes to the assistance of his own.[192] God forbid that I pretend to separate it from French verse of which it is a charm. Rhyme is necessary, even indispensable, to romantic poetry and to all that is derived from it; and songs, ballads, vaudevilles, sylves of whatever sort they may be, whatever form, whatever length they may have, cannot pass away. It adds an infinite grace to all that is sung or recited with the chivalrous sentiment. Even the lyric style receives from it a romantic harmony which accords with it. All the secondary styles admit of this. It can, up to a certain point, embellish descriptive verse, soften didactic verse, add to the melancholy of the elegy, to the grace of the idyl; it can at last become the ornament of dramatic art such as we possess—that is to say, chivalrous and impassioned; but as to real Eumolpœia and Epopœia—that is to say, as to what concerns intellectual and rational poetry, pure or mingled with the enthusiasm of the passions; prophetic verses or hymns, emanated from the Divinity or destined to be raised to it; philosophical verse adapted to the nature of things and developing the diverse moral and physical systems; epic verses uniting talent to allegorical genius and joining together the intelligible world to the sentient world; with all these, rhyme is incompatible. As much as it delights in works of the mind just so much is it rejected by genius. Fiction harmonizes with it, allegory is opposed to it. It is chivalrous and not heroic; agreeable, brilliant, clever, melancholy, sentimental, but it could never be either profound or sublime.

Let us clear this up with the light of experience, and now that we can do it to good purpose, let us make a rapid survey of the poetic condition of the principal nations of the earth.

VI.

THE Greeks and the Romans, as guilty of ingratitude as of injustice, have styled Asia barbarous, without thinking that they thus outraged their Mother, the one from whom both had their origin and their first instructions. Europe, more impartial today, begins to feel as she should toward this ancient and noble country, and rendering to her venerable scars a filial respect, does not judge her according to her present weakness, but according to the vigour that she possessed in the age of her strength, and of which her magnificent productions still bear the imprint. A philosophical observer, academician of Calcutta, turning an investigating eye upon that part of the terrestrial continent, has recognized there five principal nations, among which that of the Indians holds the first rank; the others are those of the Chinese, Tartars, Persians, and Arabs. [193] According to this able writer, primitive India should be considered as a sort of luminous focus which, concentrating at a very remote epoch the learning acquired by an earlier people, has reflected it, and has dispersed the rays upon the neighbouring nations. [194] She has been the source of Egyptian, Greek, and Latin theogony; she has furnished the philosophical dogmas with which the first poets of Thrace and Ionia have adorned the beauties of Eumolpœia and Epopœia; it is she who has polished the Persians, Chaldeans, Arabs, and Ethiopians; and who by her numerous colonies has entertained relations with the Chinese, Japanese, Scandinavians, Celts, Etruscans, and even with the Peruvians of the other hemisphere. [195]

If one listens to the discourse of those who have been much inclined to study the savant language of the Indians, Sanskrit, he will be persuaded that it is the most perfect language that man has ever spoken. Nothing, according to them, can surpass its riches, its fertility, its admirable structure; it is the source of the most poetic conceptions and the mother of all the dialects which are in use from the Persian Gulf to the waters of China. [196] It is certain that if anything can prove to the eyes of savants the maternal rights that this tongue claims over all the others, it is the astonishing variety of its poetry: what other peoples possess in detail, it possesses in toto. It is there that Eumolpœia, Epopœia, and Dramatic Art shine with native éclat: it is there that poetry divine and rational, poetry allegorical and passionate, poetry stirring and even romantic, find their cradle. There, all forms are admitted, all kinds of verse received. The Vedas, pre-eminently sacred books, are, like the Koran of Mohammed, written in cadenced prose [197] The Pouranas, which contain the theosophy and philosophy of the Brahmans, their system concerning Nature, their ideas upon morals and upon natural philosophy, are composed in philosophical verse not rhymed; they are attributed to Vyasa, the Orpheus of the Indians. Valmiki, who is their Homer, has displayed in the Ramayana an epopœia magnificent and sublime to the highest degree; the dramas, which they call Nataks, are, according to their style, rhymed and not rhymed: Bheret is considered as their inventor; Kalidasa as their perfecter. [198] The other kinds of poetry are all rhymed; their number is immense; their variety infinite. Nothing equals the industry and delicacy of the Indian rhymers in this style. The Arabs all skilful as they were, the Oscar troubadours whose rhyme was their sole merit, have never approached their models. [199] Thus, not only does one find among the Indians the measured verse of the Greeks and Romans, not only does one see there rhythms unknown to these two peoples, but one recognizes also there our rhyme with combinations of which we have no idea.

I ought to make an important observation here: it is, that whereas India, mistress of Asia, held the sceptre of the earth, she still recognized only the eumolpœia of the Vedas and the Pouranas, only the epopœia of Maha-Bharata and the Ramayana; her poetry was the language of the gods and she gave herself the name of Ponya-Rhoumi, Land of Virtues. It was only when a long prosperity had enervated her, that the love for novelty, the caprice of fashion and perhaps, as it happened in Greece, the deviation of the theatre, caused her to seek for beauties foreign to veritable poetry. It is not a rare thing to pass the point of perfection when one has attained it. The astonishing flexibility of Sanskrit, the abundance of its final consonants opens a double means for corruption. Poets multiplied words believing to multiply ideas; they doubled rhymes; they tripled them in the same verse believing to increase proportionably its harmony. Their imagination bending before an inspiring genius became vagabond; they thought to rise to the sublime, and fell into the bombastic. At last, knowing no longer how to give emphasis and importance to their extravagant thoughts, they created words of such length that, in order to contain them, it was necessary to forge verses of four cæsuras of nineteen syllables each. [200]

It was, therefore, at the epoch of the decadence of the Indian Empire, that rhyme usurped poetry. It would be difficult today to say whether it was an innovation or a simple renovation. However it may be, it is probable that it passed rapidly from the ruling nation to subject nations where it was diversely welcomed according to the language and particular mind of each people.

If one can believe the annals of the Indians, China was one of their colonies for a long time schismatic and rebellious. [201] If one can lend faith to the most ancient tradition of the Chinese, they form from time immemorial a body of autochthonous people. [202] The discussion of this historic difficulty would be out of place here. Suffice it to say, that the Chinese having commenced by having rhymed verses, and preserving by character and by religion, with an inviolable respect, the ancient usages, have never had but a mediocre poetry, absolutely foreign to epopœia. [203] Their principal sacred books, called Kings, are composed of symbolic or hieroglyphic characters, forming by groups sorts of tableaux, of profound and often sublime conception, but bereft of what we would call eloquence of language. These are mute images, incommunicable by means of the voice, and which the reader must consider with the eyes and meditate long upon in order to comprehend them.

The Tartars who reign today in China and who are distinguished from the others by the epithet of Manchus, although possessors of a formed tongue whose richness certain authors praise, [204] have not any kind of poetry as I have already remarked. [205] The other Tartars were hardly more advanced before being placed by their conquests within reach of the learning of the vanquished people. The Turks had no alphabetical characters. The Huns were ignorant even of its existence. The proud vanquisher of Asia, Genghis Khan did not find, according to the best historians, a single man among the Mongolians capable of writing his despatches. The alphabet of fourteen letters that the Uïgurian Tartars possess, appears to have been given them by the ancient Persians, [206] from whom they also received the little that they knew of poetry.

These Persians, today imitators of the Arabs, were in very remote times disciples of the Indians. Their sacred tongue then called Zend, in which are written the fragments that remain to us of Zoroaster, was a dialect of Sanskrit. [207] These fragments that we owe to the indefatigable zeal of Anquetil Duperron, appear to be written, as the Vedas, or as all the sacred books of India, in cadenced prose. After the Zend-Avesta, the most famous book among the Parsees is the Boun-Dehesh, written in Pehlevi, and containing the cosmogony of Zoroaster. Pehlevi, which is derived from Chaldaic Nabatæan, indicates a translation, [208] and testifies that Persia had already passed from under the dominion of India to that of Assyria. But when, thanks to the conquests of Cyrus, Persia had become free and mistress of Asia, Pehlevi, which recalled its ancient servitude, was banished from the court by Bahman-Espandiar, whom we call Artaxerxes Longimanus. [209] The Parsee replaced it; this last dialect, modified by Greek under the successors of Alexander, mixed with many Tartar words under the Parthian kings, polished by the Sassanidæ, usurped at last by the Arabs and subjected to the intolerant influence of Islamism, had no longer its own character: it has taken, in the modern Persian, all the movements of the Arabic, notwithstanding its slight analogy with it [210]; following its example, it has concentrated all the beauties of poetry in rhyme and since then it has had neither Eumolpœia nor Epopœia.

As to the Arab, no one is ignorant of the degree to which he is a slave to rhyme. Already, by a sufficiently happy conjecture, a French writer had made the first use of rhyme in France coincide with the irruption of the Moors into Europe at the beginning of the eighth century. [211] He has said that Provence had been the door by which this novelty was introduced into France. However difficult it may appear of proving rigorously this assertion, lacking monuments, it cannot, however, be denied that it may be very probable, above all considering what influence the Arabs exercised upon the sciences and arts in the south of France after they had penetrated through Spain. Now, there is no country on earth where the poetry that I have called romantic has been cultivated with more constancy and success than in Arabia; rhyme, if she has received it from India, was naturalized there by long usage, in such a way as to appear to have had birth there. If it must be said, the Arab tongue seems more apt at receiving it than the Sanskrit. Rhyme seems more requisite to poetry there, on account of the great quantity and inflexibility of the monosyllables, which joining together only with much difficulty to form the numerous and rhythmic combinations, had need of its assistance to soften their harshness and to supply the harmony which they lacked.

Nevertheless, whatever may be the pretension of Arabia to the invention of rhyme, and even to that of romantic poetry, one cannot be prevented, when one possesses without prejudice and to a certain extent the distinguishing character of the Asiatic languages, from seeing that there are proofs in the Arabic itself which give evidence in favour of India. Such is, for example, the word Diwan, [212] by which the Arabs designate the collection of their ancient poetries. [213] This word, which is attached to the Sanskrit expression Dewa or Diwa, designates all that is divine, celestial; all that emanates from the Universal Intelligence [214]: it is the poetry of the Greeks, the language of the gods, or the voice of the Universal Being of the Egyptians and the Phœnicians.

However, the Arabic Diwan—that is to say, the poetic collection of that nation, goes back to most ancient times. One finds in it verses attributed to the first Hebrew patriarchs and even to Adam [215]; for since the introduction of Islamism, the cosmogony of Moses has become that of the Mussulmans, as it has been ours since the establishment of Christianity. It is there, in this diwan, that the most authentic traditions are preserved: they are all in verse and resemble greatly, as to form and doubtless as to substance, that which the monk of St. André has transmitted to us through the court of Charlemagne. It is the same chivalrous spirit and the same romantic fictions. The Persian poet Firdausi appears to have followed similar traditions concerning the ancient kings of Iran, in his famous poem entitled Shah-Namah. [216] The wonders which reign in these traditions have been transmitted no doubt by the Arabs, with the artifice of rhyme: both have the same spirit. The protecting fairies of the knights, the giant persecutors of ladies, the enchanters, the magic, and all those illusions are the fruits of that brilliant and dreamy imagination which characterizes the modern Orientals. We have enthusiastically enjoyed them in the depths of the barbarity where we were plunged; we have allowed ourselves to be drawn by the charms of rhyme, like children in the cradle, whom their nurses put to sleep by the monotonous sound of a lullaby. Escaped from that state of languor, and struck at last with a gleam of real intelligence, we have compared Greece and Arabia, the songs of epopœia and those of the ballads; we have blushed at our choice; we have wished to change it; but owing to the captivating form always more or less the substance, we have only succeeded in making mixtures more or less happy, according to the secondary mode that we follow.

Rhyme, brought into Europe by the Arabs more than a thousand years ago, spread by degrees among all nations, in such a way that when one wishes to examine its origin with accuracy, one no longer knows whether it is indigenous there or exotic. One finds on all sides only rhymed verses. The Spanish, Portuguese, Italians, French, Germans of all dialects, Hollanders, Danes, Swedes and Norwegians, all rhyme. [217] The modern Greeks themselves have forgotten their ancient rhythm in order to assume our style. [218] If anything could, however, make one doubt that rhyme may be natural to Europe, it is that ancient Scandinavian, in which are written the precious fragments which have come down to us concerning the mythological cult of the Celts, our ancestors, does not rhyme; also it rises often to the sublimity of Eumolpœia. [219] This observation, which makes us reject Arabia, will take us back to India, if we consider that there is plausible presumption in believing that the Phœnicians and the Egyptians who had so much intercourse with the Arabs, did not rhyme, since the sacred book of the Hebrews, the Sepher, that we call the Bible, and which appears to have issued from the Egyptian sanctuaries, is written in cadenced rhyme, as the Zend-Avesta of the Parsees and the Vedas of the Indians. [220]

The outline that I have just sketched confirms, Messieurs, what I have wished to prove to you and which is the subject of this discourse, the distinction that should be made between the essence and the form of poetry, and the reciprocal influence that should be recognized between these two parts of the science. You have seen that wherever rhyme has dominated exclusively, as in Asia among the Chinese, Arabians, Persians; as in Europe among all the modern peoples, it has excluded epopœia and has replaced allegorical genius by the spirit of romantic fictions; you have seen that wherever eumolpique poetry has wished to appear, whether moral or rational, theosophical or philosophical, it has been obliged to have recourse to a particular prose, when the form of poetry has resisted it, as has happened in China for the Kings, in Persia for the Zend-Avesta, in Arabia for the Koran; you have seen that wherever poetry has been preserved purely rhythmical, as in Greece and with the Romans, it has admitted eumolpœia and epopœia without mixture; and finally, that wherever the two forms meet each other with all their modifications, as in India, it gives way in turn to all the different kinds, intellectual and rational, epic, dramatic, and romantic.

Now, what Hindustan was for Asia, France should be for Europe. The French tongue, as the Sanskrit, should tend towards universality; it should be enriched with all the learning acquired in the past centuries, so as to transmit it to future generations. Destined to float upon the débris of a hundred different dialects, it ought to be able to save from the shipwreck of time all their beauties and all their remarkable productions. Nevertheless, how will it be done, if its poetic forms are not open to the spirit of all the poetries, if its movement, arrested by obstacles cannot equal that of the tongues which have preceded it in the same career? By what means, I ask you, will it succeed to the universal dominion of Sanskrit, if, dragging always after it the frivolous jingling of Arabic sounds, it cannot even succeed to the partial domination of Greek or Latin? Must it be necessary then that it betray its high destinies, and that the providential decree which founds the European empire, exempt it from the glory which it promises to the French name?

I have told you, Messieurs, in beginning this discourse, that it was in the interest of science alone that I entered this career: it is assuredly not by my poor poetic talent that I have aspired to the honour of occupying your attention; but by a generous instinct, which, making me ignore many of the considerations which might have arrested me, has persuaded me that I could be useful. I have dared to conceive the possibility of composing, in French, eumolpique verse, which might neither be measured by musical rhythm foreign to our tongue, nor enchained by rhyme opposed to all intellectual and rational movement, and which however might have neither the harshness, nor the discord of that which has been called, up to this time, blank verse.

Many French writers have tried to make verse deprived of rhyme. Some have sought to imitate the measures of the ancients, others have satisfied themselves with copying certain moderns who do not rhyme. Each of them has misunderstood the essential character of his tongue. Vossius alone appears to have foreseen the principles without developing them, when he has said that French verse might be considered as having only one foot. [221] This is exactly true in examining rhythm only in itself, and giving to each hemistich the name of time: but if one considers this one foot, whether hexameter or pentameter, as formed of two times equal or unequal, it is perceived that it participates, through its final, in two natures: the one strong and forceful, that we name masculine; the other soft and languid, that we call feminine. Therefore, French verse having hut one rhythmic foot, differs, however, in the style of this foot and can be considered in two relations. Let us take for example the hexameter verse. The rhythmic foot which constitutes it is composed of two equal times distinguished by the cæsura, the last of which is masculine or feminine: Masculine, as in:

Rome, l'unique objet de mon ressentiment!
Rome, à qui vient ton bras d'immoler mon amant!
Feminine, as in:

Rome qui t'a vu naître et que ton cœur adore!
Rome enfin que je hais parce qu'elle t'honore!

In rhymed verses, such as these I have just cited, two feet of the same kind are obliged to follow one another on account of the rhyme which links them; they then form but one whole and, proceeding abreast without being separated, they injure by their forced mass the rapidity of expression and flight of thought. If a third foot of the same kind occur with the other two feet, rhyming together, it would have to rhyme with them to prevent an insupportable discordance, which is not tolerated; a fourth or a fifth foot would submit to the same law, so that, if the poet wished to fill his piece with masculine verses alone, it would be necessary that he should make them proceed upon a single rhyme, as the Arabs do today and as our early troubadours did, following their example. The French poet can vary his rhyme only by varying the style of his verses and by mingling alternately together the masculine and feminine finals.

As these two kinds of finals are dissimilar without being opposed, they may be brought together without the need of rhyming; their meeting, far from being disagreeable is, on the contrary, only pleasing; two finals of the same kind, whether masculine or feminine, can never clash without causing the same sound—chat is, without rhyming; but it is not thus with the finals of different kinds, since the rhyme is impossible in this case. So that, to make what I call eumolpique verses, it suffices to avoid the meeting of finals of the same kind, whose impact necessitates the rhyme, by making one kind succeed another continually, and opposing alternately the masculine and feminine, the mingling of which is irrelevant to eumolpœia. Here is all the mechanism of my verses: they are fluent as to form; as to the essence which is expedient for them—that is another thing: for it is rarely encountered.

Those who have made blank verse in French have spoken justly of it with the greatest contempt; these verses, miserable as to substance, without poetic fire, written as the flattest prose, lacking movement and grace, had, furthermore, the insupportable fault of not recognizing the genius of the French tongue, by making finals of the same kind clash constantly, and by not distinguishing that which is called rhyme from that which repels it.

Now that I have made as clear as possible my motives and my means, there remains only, Messieurs, for me to submit to your judgment the translation that I have made, in eumolpique verse, of the piece of Greek poetry which comprises the doctrine of Pythagoras in seventy-one lines called, par excellence, Golden Verses. This piece, venerable by its antiquity and by the celebrated philosopher whose name it bears, belonging to eumolpœia, without any mixture of passion, is sufficiently known to savants so that I need not speak about what concerns its particular merit. This would mean, moreover, a matter of some explanations At any rate, I believe it advisable before passing to this final subject, to give you certain examples of the use of my verses as applied to epopœia, so that you may judge, since they are in hands as incapable as mine, what they might become when used by men of superior genius and talent. I will choose, for this purpose, the exposition and invocation of the principal epic poems of Europe, in order to have a fixed subject for comparison. I will translate line by line, and will imitate, as well as is possible for me, the movement and harmony of the poet that I may have before me. This labour, which I hope will not be without some interest for the illustrious academicians whom I am addressing, will furnish me the occasion of showing by certain characteristic traits the genius of the language and poetry of the different modern peoples of Europe; and I will terminate thus the outline that I have sketched touching the poetic conditions of the principal nations of the earth.

VII.

I am beginning with the creator of epopœia, with Homer. It is easy to see by the manner in which this divine man blends, from the opening lines of the Iliad, the exposition and invocation, that, full of a celestial inspiration that he was the first to receive, he seeks to pour forth the superabundant fire which consumes him, and to throw into the soul of his hearer the impassioned enthusiasm which masters and controls his own. The following lines will suffice to make known the subject of a work which fills twenty-four cantos.

Déesse! viens chanter la colère d'Achille,
Fatale, et pour les Grecs si fertile en malheurs,
Qui, d'avance, aux enfers, précipitant en foule
Les âmes des héros, livra leurs corps sanglants
Aux dogues affamés: ainsi Jupiter même
Le voulut, quand la haine eut divisé les cœurs
Du roi des rois Atride et du divin Achille.
 Lequel des Immortels provoqua ce courroux?
Apollon irrité, qui, pour punir Atride,
Ravagea son armée: et les peuples mourraient!
O Goddess! sing the wrath of Peleus' son,
Achilles; sing the deadly wrath that brought
Woes numberless upon the Greeks, and swept
To Hades many a valiant soul, and gave
Their limbs a prey to dogs and birds of air,—
For so had Jove appointed,—from the time
When the two chiefs, Atrides, King of men,
And great Achilles, parted first as foes.
 Which of the gods put strife between the chiefs,
That they should thus contend? Latona's son
And Jove's. Incensed against the king, he bade
A deadly pestilence appear among
The army, and the men were perishing.
     BRYANT.

Μῆνιν ἄειδε, θεὰ Πηληϊάδεω Ἀχιλῆος,
οὐλομένην, ἣ μυρί' Ἀχαιοῖς ἄλγε' ἔθηκεν,
πολλὰς δ' ἰφθίμους ψυχὰς Ἄϊδι προϊαψεν
ἡρώων, αὐτοὺς δὲ ἑλώρια τεῦχε κύνεσσιν
οἰωνοῖσί τε πᾶσι (Διὸς δ'ἐτελείετο βουλή),
ἐξ οὗ δὴ τὰ πρῶτα διαστήτην ἐρίσαντε
Ἀτείδης τε, ἄναξ ἀνδρῶν, καὶ δῖος Ἀχιλλεύς.
 Τίς τ' ἄρ σφωε θεῶν ἔριδι ξυνέηχε μάχεσθαι;
Λητοῦς καὶ Διὸς υἱός. Ὁ γὰρ βασιλῆϊ χολωθεὶς
νοῦσον ἀνὰ στρατὸν ὦρσε κακὴν, ὀλέκοντο δὲ λαοί.

I dispense with making any reflection upon the charm of the original verses and upon the admirable sentiment which terminates them. It would be a very strange thing not to be impressed by the beauties of this poetry. Let us pass on to Vergil.

Even though I should not say it, it would suffice now to compare the Greek poet with the Latin poet, in order to perceive that the latter received only a second inspiration, transmitted by the inspiring power of the former. Vergil, less ardent, more tender, more correct, admits at once the luminous distinction; far from blending the exposition and invocation, he separates them, affects a tone more simple, promises little, exposes with timidity the subject of his poem, summons his Muse, and seems to persuade it, even less than the reader, to be favourable to him. He employs these lines:

Je chante les combats, et ce Héros troyen,
Qui, fuyant Ilion, aborda l'Italie
Le premier: sur la terre errant, et sur les mers,
En butte aux traits cruels de Junon irritée,
Il souffrit mille maux; avant qu'il établît
Ses Dieux chez les Latins, et fondât une ville,
Berceau d'Albe, de Rome et de ses hauts remparts.
 Muse! rappelle-moi quels motifs de vengeance
Excitaient la Déesse, et pourquoi son courroux
S'obstinait à poursuive un Héros magnanime?
Tant de haine entre-t-elle au cœur des Immortels!

Arms and the man I sing, who first,
By fate of Ilium realm amerced,
To fair Italia onward bore,

And landed on Lavinium's shore:—
Long tossing earth and ocean o'er,
By violence of heaven, to sate
Fell Juno's unforgetting hate:
Much laboured too in battle-field,
Striving his city's walls to build,
 And give his Gods a home:
Thence come the hardy Latin brood,
The ancient sires of Alba's blood,
 And lofty-rampired Rome.
Say, Muse, for godhead how disdained,
Or wherefore worth, Heaven's queen constrained
That soul of piety so long
'To turn the wheel, to cope with wrong.
Can heavenly natures nourish hate
So fierce, so blindly passionate?
                   CONINGTON.

Arma virumque cano, Trojæ qui primus ab oris
Italiam, fato profugus, Lavinaque venit
Litora, multum ille et terris jactatus et alto
Vi superûm, sævæ memorem Junonis ob iram,
Multa quoque et bello passus, dum conderet urbem
Inferretque deos Latio: genus unde Latinum,
Albanique patres atque altæ mœnia Romæ.
  Musa, mihi causas memora, quo numine læso,
Quidve dolens, regina deûm tot volvere casus
Insignem pietate virum, tot adire labores
Impulerit. Tantæne animis cœlestibus iræ?

It can be observed that Vergil, although he places himself foremost and although he says, I sing, begins nevertheless in a manner much less animated, much less sure than the Greek poet, who, transported beyond himself, seems to impose upon his Muse the subject of his songs, interrogates her, and then inspired by her, responds. The Latin poet finishes, like his model, with a sentence; but it is easy to feel that this apostrophe,

Can heavenly natures nourish hate
So fierce, so blindly passionate?

although very beautiful, contains less depth, less feeling, and holds less intimately to the subject than this sublime reflection:

... and the men were perishing!

Someone has said that Vergil had imitated in his exposition the commencement of the Odyssey of Homer; this is a mistake. One finds always in the exposition of the Odyssey the real character of a first inspiration blended with the invocation, although more calm and less alluring than in the Iliad. Here is the translation:

  Du plus sage Héros, Muse, dis les traverses
Sans nombre, après qu'il eut triomphé d'Ilion:
Rapelle les cités, les peuples, les usages,
Qu'il connut, et les mers où longtemps il erra:
A quels soins dévorants, à quels maux l'exposèrent
L'amour de la patrie et noble désir
D'y mener ses guerriers! Vain désir: ils osèrent,
Insensés! du Soleil dévorer les troupeaux;
Et ce Dieu, du retour leur ravit la journée.
Fais-nous part de ces faits, fille de Jupiter.
Tell me, O Muse, of that sagacious man
Who, having overthrown the sacred town
Of Ilium, wandered far and visited
The capitals of many nations, learned
The customs of their dwellers and endured
Great suffering on the deep; his life was oft
In peril, as he laboured to bring back
His comrades to their homes. He saved them not,
Though earnestly he strove; they perished all,
Through their own folly; for they banqueted,
Madmen! upon the oxen of the Sun,
The all-o'erlooking Sun, who cut them off
From their return. O Goddess, virgin-child
Of Jove, relate some part of this to me.
                    BRYANT.

Ἄνδρα μοι ἔννεπε, μοῦσα, πολύτροπον, ὃς μάλα πολλὰ
πλάγχθη, ἐπεὶ Τροίης ἱερὸν πτολίεθρον ἔπερσεν,
πολλῶν δ᾽ ἀνθρώπων ἴδεν ἄστεα καὶ νόον ἔγνω·

πολλὰ δ' ὅ γ' ἐν πόντῳ πάθεν ἄλγεα ὃν κατὰ θυμόν,
ἀρνύμενος ἥν τε ψυχὴν καὶ νόστον ἑταίρων.
ἀλλ' οὐδ' ὧς ἑτάρους ἐρρύσατο ἱέμενός περ·
αὐτῶν γὰρ σφετέρῃσιν ἀτασθαλίῃσιν ὄλοντο,
νήπιοι, οἳ κατὰ βοῦς Ὑπερίονος Ἠελίοιο
ἤσθιον· αὐτὰρ ὁ τοῖσιν ἀφείλετο νόστιμον ἦμαρ.
τῶν ἁμόθεν γε, θεὰ θύγατερ Διός, εἰπὲ καὶ ἡμῖν.

The talent of Homer shows itself completely in the Odyssey; it dominates the genius there, so to speak, as much as the genius had dominated it in the Iliad. The fire which animates the Iliad has been, with reason, compared to that of the sun arrived at the height of its course, and the splendour which shines in the Odyssey to that with which the occident is coloured on the evening of a fine day. Perhaps if we had his Thebaid, we would see those brilliant lights which accompany the aurora, developed there, and then we would possess in all its shades this immortal genius who depicted all nature.

There are people who, feeling by a sort of intuition that Homer had been created the poetic incentive of Europe, even as I have said, and judging on the other hand that Ariosto had made an epic poem, are convinced that the Italian poet had copied the Greek; but this is not so. Ariosto;, who has made only a romanesque poem, has not received the inspiration of Homer; he has simply followed the fictions attributed to Archbishop Turpin and clothing them with forms borrowed from the Arabs by the troubadours makes himself creator in this secondary style. The rhyme is as essential to it as it is harmful to veritable epopœia; this is why the eumolpique verses never conform to it in the slightest degree. To apply them to it, is to make serious what is by nature gay, it is to give a character of force and of truth to what is only light, airy, and fantastic. I am about, however, to translate the beginning of his poem, in order to furnish, by the shocking disparity which exists between the romantic essence of his poetry and the epic form that I here adapt, a new proof of what I have said.

   Je veux chanter les Dames, les Guerriers,
L'amour, l'honneur, et les jeux et les armes,
Durant ces temps où les fiers Sarrasins,
Des mers d'Afrique, abordèrent en France,
Pour seconder les fureurs d'Agramant,

Le jeune roi, dont l'orgueilleuse audace
Pensait venger la mort du vieux Trojan,
Sur l'empereur des Romains, Charlemagne.

  Je veux aussi raconter de Roland,
Chose inouïe, autant en vers qu'en prose;
Dire l'amour qui rendit furieux
Ce paladin, auparavant si sage;
Si toutefois celle qui m'a charmé,
Qui va minant ma raison d'heure en heure,
M'en laisse assez pour remplir dignement
Mon entreprise et tenir ma promesse.

  Of Loves and Ladies, Knights and Arms, I sing,
Of Courtesies, and many a Daring Feat;
And from those ancient days my story bring,
When Moors from Afric passed in hostile fleet,
And ravaged France, with Agramant their King,
Flushed with his youthful rage and furious heat;
Who on King Charles', the Roman emperor's head
Had vowed due vengeance for Troyano dead.

  In the same strain of Roland will I tell
Things unattempted yet in prose or rhyme,
On whom strange madness and rank fury fell,
A man esteemed so wise in former time;
If she, who to like cruel pass has well
Nigh brought my feeble wit which fain would climb
And hourly wastes my sense, concede me skill
And strength my daring promise to fulfil.
                W. R. ROSE.

  Le donne, i cavalier, l'arme, gl'amori
Le cortesíe, l'audaci imprese io canto,
Che furo al tempo the passaro i Mori
D'Africa il mare, e in Francia nocquer tanto,
Seguendo l'ire e i giovenil furori
D'Agramante lor re, che si diè vanto
Di vendicar la morte di Troiano
Sopra re Carlo imperator romano.

Dirò d'Orlando in un medesmo tratto
Cosa non detta in prosa mai, nè in rima;
Che per amor venne in furore e matto,
D'uom che sì saggio era stimato prima:
Se da colei che tal quasi m'ha fatto
Che'l poco ingegno ad or ad or mi lima,
Me ne sarà perd tanto concesso,
Che mi basti a finir quanto ho promesso.

It is very easy to see, in reading these two strophes, that there exists in the exposition no sort of resemblance either with that of Homer, or with that of Vergil. It is a third style, wholly foreign to the other two. Homer mingling the exposition and the invocation, commands his Muse to sing what she inspires in him; Vergil distinguishing one from the other, prays his Muse to acquaint him with what he is about to sing; whereas Ariosto, announcing simply the subject of his songs, makes no invocation. It is evident that he relies upon himself, and that in the style that he adopts he understands very well that he has no other Muse, no other guide than his imagination. His subject is in accord with his manner of treating it. If one wishes to reflect upon this decisive point, one will feel and realize, for the first time perhaps, why in the opinion of all the world concerning two works from the same hand, La Pucelle and La Henriade, the one is a poem, whereas the other, composed with a far greater pretension, is not. Voltaire, in imitating Ariosto in a subject that he has rendered romanesque and frivolous, has received the second inspiration; but in imitating Lucan in an historic subject he received nothing, for Lucan, creator of a mixed style, had no inspiration that he could communicate.

I have said what I thought of Camoens: it is useless to quote the exposition of his poem that has nothing remarkable, particularly since Tasso has so far surpassed him.

Tasso was worthy of receiving a veritable inspiration. His lofty genius, his pure and brilliant imagination brought him nearer to Vergil than to Ariosto; and if he had been inspired even through the Latin poet, he would have shown Europe what the magnetic power of Homer was, although acting only in its third degree. But the prejudices of education working in him even without his knowledge, and the influence that chivalresque poetry had attained in Italy, did not permit him either to forsake entirely the chronicles of Archbishop Turpin, or above all, to make any changes in the consecrated form. All that he could do in a most grave and serious historical subject was to mix a little allegorical genius with a great deal of romanesque fiction; so that, becoming inspired at the same time with Ariosto, Lucan, and Vergil, he made a mixed work, which, under the form of a lengthy song, contained the essence of epopœia, of history, and of romance. This work is one of the most entertaining poems that one can read; the only one perhaps which a translation in prose can harm but little. The inequality of its texture takes away nothing from the interest that it inspires. It pleases, but it does not instruct. If the eumolpique lines were applied to it throughout, it would not sustain them; for it is in substance only a very beautiful ballad; nevertheless, here and there are found parts which could become sublime. His exposition, imitating Vergil, reveals them very well. They are as follows:

Je chante les combats pieux, et le Guerrier
Qui délivra du Christ la tombe renommée.
Combien il déploya de génie et d'ardeur!
Combien il supporta de maux dans cette guerre!

Vainement les enfers s'armérent; vainement
Les peuples de l'Asie aux Africains s'unirent:
Favorisé du Ciel, sous ses drapeaux sacrés,
Vainqueur, il ramena ses compagnons fidèles.

Divine Muse! ô toi dont le front radieux
Ne ceint point sur le Pinde un laurier périssable,
Mais qui, parmi les chœurs des habitants du Ciel,
Chantes, le front orné d'étoiles immortelles,
Viens, inspire à mon sein tes célestes ardeurs;
Fais briller dans mes vers tes clartés, et pardonne
Si, parant quelquefois l'austère vérité,
Je mêle à tes attraits des grâces étrangères.

I sing the pious arms and Chief, who freed
The Sepulchre of Christ from thrall profane:
Much did he toil in thought, and much in deed;
Much in the glorious enterprise sustain;
And Hell in vain opposed him; and in vain
Afric and Asia to the rescue pour'd

Their mingled tribes;—Heaven recompensed his pain,
And from all fruitless sallies of the sword,
True to the Red-Cross flag his wandering friends restored.

  O thou, the Muse, that not with fading palms
Circlest thy brows on Pindus, but among
The Angels warbling their celestial psalms,
Hast for the coronal a golden throng
Of everlasting stars! make thou my song
Lucid and pure; breathe thou the flame divine
Into my bosom; and forgive the wrong,
If with grave truth light fiction I combine,
And sometimes grace my page with other flowers than thine!
                    WIFFEN.

  Canto l'armi pietose, e'l Capitano
Che'l gran sepolcro liberò di Christo:
Molto egli oprò col senno e con la mano;
Molto soffrì nel glorïoso acquisto:
E invano l'Inferno a lui s'oppose, e invano
S'arma d'Asia, e dì Libia il popol misto;
Chè il Ciel diè favore, e sotto ai santi
Segni ridusse i suoi compagni erranti.

  O Musa, tu, che di caduchi allori
Non circondi la fronte in Elicona
Ma su nel Ciel infra i beati cori,
Hai di stelle immortali aurea corona,
Tu spira al petto mio celesti ardori,
Tu rischiara il mio canto, e tu perdona,
S'intesso fregi al ver, s'adorno in parte
D'altri diletti, che de' tuoi, le carte.

The captivating enthusiasm of Homer, the majestic simplicity of Vergil are not there; there is a sweetness of expression, a purity of imagery which please. This might be greater, but then the melancholy of the romance would exclude it and the reader would demand the full force of epopœia.

Besides, the Italians have tried, over and over again, to vary the form of their verses; some have wished to measure them by musical rhythm;

others have contented themselves with making blank verse. They have neither succeeded completely nor failed completely. Their language sweet and musical lacks force whether in good or in evil. Its words might indeed, strictly speaking, be composed of long and short syllables; but as they terminate, nearly all, in the soft and languid style that we call feminine, it results, therefore, that in the measured verses the poets lack the long syllables to constitute the last foot and to form the spondee; and that in the blank verse they are obliged to terminate them all in the same style; so that with the measure they create only lame verses, and without the rhyme they make them all equally languid. [222]

I recall having sometimes read French writers who, not having investigated the character of their tongue, have reproached it for its feminine syllables and have believed that their concurrence was harmful to its force and its harmony. These writers have scarcely considered what this language would be, deprived of its feminine sounds. For with the little force that it would gain on one side, it would acquire such a harshness on the other, that it would be impossible to draw from it four consecutive lines that would be endurable. If all its finals were masculine, and if nothing could change it otherwise, it would be necessary to renounce poetry, or like the Arabs, be resolved to compose whole poems in the same rhyme.

We have just seen that the lack of masculine finals takes away all energy from the Italian tongue; a contrary defect would deprive the French of this mélange of sweetness and force which makes it the première langue of Europe. The English language is lacking in precisely what the writers of whom I have spoken desired eliminated from the French, without foreseeing the grave disadvantages of their desire: it has no feminine finals [223]; also it is in everything the opposite of the Italian. It is true that it possesses great energy, great boldness of expression, and a grammatical liberty which goes to the full extent; but deprived of sweetness and softness, it is, if I may say it, like those brittle metals whose strength is in stiffness, and which is broken when one would make them flexible. The poverty of its rhymes, denuded for the most part of accuracy of accent and of harmony in consonants, has for a long time engaged the English poets in making blank verse; and it must be admitted that, notwithstanding the defect inherent in their tongue and which consists, as I have just said, in the absolute lack of feminine finals, they have succeeded in this better than any of the poets of other nations. These lines, all imperfect in their harmony, are however, as to form, the only eumolpique verse that they could make. Shakespeare felt it and made use of it in his tragedies.

Shakespeare with the creative genius with which nature had endowed him, would have borne dramatic art to its perfection in these modern times, if circumstances had been as favourable to him as they were adverse. Emulator of Æschylus, he might have equalled and perhaps surpassed him, if he had had at his disposal a mine so rich, so brilliant as that of the mysteries of Orpheus; if he had made use of a language so harmonious, if his taste had been able to be refined at the school of Pindar or of Homer. At the epoch of his birth, Europe scarcely emerged from the gloom of barbarism; the theatre, given over to ridiculous mountebanks, profaned in indecent farces the incomprehensible mysteries of the Christian religion, and the English tongue, still crude and unformed, had not succeeded in amalgamating in one single body the opposed dialects of which it was successively formed. In spite of these obstacles, Shakespeare stamped upon England a movement of which Europe felt the influence. Raised by the sole force of his genius to the essence of dramatic poetry, he dared to seek for his subjects in the mythology of Odin, and put upon the stage, in Hamlet and in Macbeth, tableaux of the highest character. [224] Like Æschylus he conducted one to virtue by terror; but unfortunately the taste of the spectators, upon which he was forced to model his, led him to degrade his tableaux by grotesque figures: the English people were not sufficiently advanced to comprehend the moral end of the tragedy. They must be amused; and Shakespeare succeeded only at the expense of the beauties of the art. Historic facts and trivial scenes replaced the mysterious and sublime subjects.

In London, the dramatic muse was turbulent and licentious; as in Madrid it had been chivalrous and gallant. Everywhere the theatre had to accommodate itself to the taste of the people. The first regular tragedy which Pierre Corneille composed in France was derived from a Spanish ballad. Madrid at that time gave the tone to Europe. It needed much of the time and all the prosperity of Louis XIV. to throw off the unseasonable ascendancy that this proud nation had assumed over public opinion. [225] Notwithstanding the efforts of Corneille, of Racine, and of Molière, the Théâtre Français retained always the romanesque tone that it had originally received. All that these three men could do was, by lofty sentiments, by purity of forms, by regularity of the customs and characters, to pass over what was, in reality, defective. They came thus to give to modern dramatic art all the perfection of which it was susceptible. Shakespeare had been in London the successor of Æschylus; Corneille received in France the inspiration of Sophocles; Racine, that of Euripides; and Molière united as in a sheaf the spirit of Menander. of Terence, and of Plautus.

When I compare Shakespeare with Æschylus, I want to make it clearly understood that I regard him as the regenerator of the theatre in Europe, and superior to Corneille and Racine as to dramatic essence, although he may be assuredly much inferior to them as to form. Æschylus, in Greek, was inspired by Homer; while, on the contrary, it was Shakespeare who inspired Milton. It is known that Paradise Lost was at first conceived as the subject of a tragedy, and that it was only after reflection that the English poet saw therein the material for an epic poem. I will tell later on, in speaking of the Messiah of Klopstock, what has prevented these two subjects, which appear equally epics, from attaining wholly to the majesty of epopœia. As many of the motives that I have to offer apply to the two works, I will thus avoid useless repetition. I shall begin by translating the exposition and invocation of Milton, by imitating its movement and its harmony, as I have done with the other poets.

   De l'homme, viens chanter la disgrâce, et la fruit
De cet arbre fatal, dont le goût homicide
Livra le Monde au crime, à la mort, aux malheurs,
Et nous ravit Eden, jusqu'au moment qu'un Homme
Plus grand, par son trépas, racheta le séjour
Du bonheur: viens, ô Muse! ô toi qui, sur la cime
Se Sinaï, d'Oreb, en secret inspiras
La Berger d'Israël, quand d'une voix sacrée
Il enseignait comment et la terre et des cieux
Sortirent du Chaos! ou bien, si tu préfères
Les sommets de Sion, les bords du Siloë,
Qui, près du Temple saint, roule ses flots, ô Muse!
Viens protéger de là mes chants audacieux,
Mes chants qui, surpassant d'un essor non timide,
Les monts Aoniens, vont raconter des faits
Que n'ont point encor dits la prose ni la rime.

   Of Man's first disobedience, and the fruit
Of that forbidden tree, whose mortal taste
Brought death into the world, and all our woe,

> With loss of Eden, till one greater Man
> Restore us and regain the blissful seat,
> Sing, heavenly Muse, that, on the secret top
> Of Oreb or of Sinai, didst inspire
> That shepherd, who first taught the chosen seed,
> In the beginning how the heavens and earth
> Rose out of chaos; or if Sion hill
> Delight thee more, and Siloa's brook that flow'd
> Fast by the oracle of God; I thence
> Invoke thy aid to my adventurous song,
> That with no middle flight intends to soar
> Above the Aonian mount, while it pursues
> Things unattempted yet in prose or rhyme.

This invocation is manifestly in imitation of Homer, from whom Milton has received the second inspiration without the intermediary—Vergil. One can observe in the English poet the same movement and almost as much force as in the Greek poet, but much less clarity, precision, and particularly harmony. Nearly all of these defects pertain to his subject and his tongue. Circumstances were not favourable to Milton. His lines could not have been better with the elements that he was forced to employ. All imperfect as they are, they are worth much more than those of Klopstock; for at least they are in the character of his tongue, whereas those of the German poet are not. Milton is satisfied with throwing off the yoke of rhyme, and has made eumolpique lines of one foot only, measured by ten syllables. Their defect, inherent in the English idiom, consists, as I have said, in having all the lines bearing equally the masculine final, jarring continually one with the other. Klopstock has aspired to make, in German, verses measured by the musical rhythm of the Greeks; but he has not perceived that he took as long and short, in his tongue, syllables which were not such in musical rhythm, but by accent and prosody, which is quite different. The German tongue, composed of contracted words and consequently bristling with consonants, bears no resemblance to the Greek, whose words, abounding in vowels, were, on the contrary, made clear by their elongation. The rhythmic lines of Klopstock are materially a third longer than those of Homer, although the German poet has aspired to build them on an equal measure.[226] Their rhythmic harmony, if it exists there, is absolutely factitious; it is a pedantic imitation and nothing more. In order to make the movement of these lines understood in French, and to copy as closely as possible their harmony, it is necessary to compose lines of two cæsuras, or what amounts to the same, to employ constantly a line and a half to represent a single one. Here are the first fourteen lines which contain the exposition and invocation of the Messiah:

Des coupables humains, célèbre, Ame immortelle,
    l'heureuse délivrance,
Que sur terre envoyé le Messie accomplit
    dans son humanité:
Dis comment il rendit les fils du premier homme
    à leur Auteur céleste;
Souffrant et mis à mort, enfin glorifié.
    Ainsi s'exécuta
Le décret éternel. En vain Satan rebelle
    opposa son audace
A ce Fils du Très-Haut; et Judas vainement
    s'éleva contre lui:
Réconciliateur et Rédempteur suprême,
    il consomma son œuvre.
Mais quoi, noble action! que Dieu seul en son cœur
    miséricordieux,
Connaît, la Poésie, en son exil terrestre,
    pourra-t-elle te suivre?
Non, Esprit créateur, c'est à toi, devant qui
    je m'incline en tremblant,
A rapprocher de moi cette action divine,
    à toi-même semblable.
Viens donc, conduis-la-moi dans l'état immortel
    de toute sa beauté;
Remplis-la de ton feu, toi que, sondant l'abîme
    du Très-Haut, peux de l'homme
Issu de la poussière, et fragile et mortel,
    te faire un temple saint.

My Soul, degenerate man's redemption sing,
Which the Messiah in his human state
On earth accomplished, by which, suffering slain
And glorify'd, unto the Love of God
The progeny of Adam he restored.
Such was the everlasting Will divine,
Th' infernal Fiend opposed him, Judah stood

In opposition proud; but vain their rage:
He did the deed, he wrought out man's salvation.
 Yet, wondrous Deed, which th' all-compassionate
Jehovah alone completely comprehends,
May Poesy presume from her remote
Obscurity to venture on thy theme?
Creative Spirit, in whose presence here
I humbly' adore, her efforts consecrate,
Conduct her steps and lead her, me to meet,
Of transport full, with glorious charms endow'd
And power immortal, imitating Thee.
(EGESTORFF.)

Sing, unserterbliche Seele, der sündigen Menschen
    Erlösung,
Die der Messias auf Erden, in seiner Menscheit
    vollendet;
Und durch die er Adams Geschlecht zu der Liebe
    der Gottheit,
Leidend, getödtet und verherlichet, weider erhöhet
    hat.
Also geschah des Ewigen Wille. Vergebens erhub
    sich
Satan gegen der göttlichen Sohn; umsonst stand
    Juda
Gegen ihn auf; er that's, und wollbrachte die grosse
    Versöhnung.
Aber, o That, die allein der Albarmherzige
    kennet,
Darf aus dunckler Ferne sich auch dir nahen
    die Dichtkunst?
Weihe sie, Geist, Schöpfer, vor dem ich hier still
    anbete,
Führe sie mir, als deine Nachahmerin, voller
    Entzückung,
Voll unsterblicher Kraft, in verklärter Schönheit,
    entgegen.
Rüste mit deinem Feuer sie, du, der die Tiefen des
    Gottheit
Schaut und den Menschen, aus Staube gemacht, zum

Tempel sich heiligt!

It is evident that in this exposition the movement of Homer has been united by Klopstock to the ideas of Tasso. The German poet claims nevertheless the originality, and believes that he himself was called to enjoy the first inspiration. In order that this high aspiration might have been realized, a mass of learning very difficult to find would have been necessary. I will explain briefly this idea. I believe that the one who, disdaining to follow in the footsteps of Homer or of Vergil, would wish to open another road to epopœia, should be well acquainted with the ground over which he ventures to trace it, and the goal toward which he aspires to conduct it; I think he should make himself master of his subject so that nothing might remain obscure or unknown to him; so that if he should choose either the downfall of Man, as Milton, or his rehabilitation, after the example of Klopstock, he would be able to acquaint himself with the inner meaning of these mysteries, to explain all the conditions, to comprehend the beginning and the end, and, raising himself to the intellectual nature where they had birth, to spread light upon physical nature. This is the first attainment that I deem indispensable to the epic poet; I say that he should understand what he would sing. Homer knew what Ilium was, what Ithaca was; he could explain to himself the nature of Achilles and Helen, of Penelope and Ulysses; consequently he could depict them. I do not wish to investigate here whether Milton has understood in the same manner the beginning of the World and the nature of Satan; nor whether Klopstock has well understood the mystery of the incarnation of the Messiah. I only say that if they have not understood these things, they cannot sing them in a manner really epic.

A defect which is common to these two poets, and which is even noticeable in the Jerusalem Delivered of Tasso, is, that everything which does not pertain to the part of the celebrated hero, is by its impure, unfaithful, impious nature, governed by the Principle of evil, and as such consigned to eternal damnation. An insurmountable barrier separates the personages and makes them not alone enemies, but opposed, as much as good and evil, light and darkness. However, the passions act unknown even to the poet; the reader is hurried along, he forgets the fatal line of demarcation, and is deceived into becoming interested in Satan, into finding great, beautiful, and terrible, this enemy of mankind; he trusts in Armida, he is moved by her troubles, and seconds with his vows those of a notorious magician, instrument of the Infernal Spirit. Matters go not thus with

Homer. The Greeks see in the Trojans, enemies, and not reprobates. Paris is culpable but not impious. Hector is a hero in whom one can be interested without shame, and the interest that one devotes to him reflects upon Achilles and can even be increased. The gods are divided; but Venus and Juno, Minerva and Mars, Vulcan and Neptune are of a like nature; and although divided in the epic action, they are none the less venerated by both parties, equal among each other and all equally subject to Jupiter, who excites or checks their resentment. I know not whether any one has already made this observation; but be that as it may, it is very important. One can attain to the sublimity of epopœia only if like Homer one knows how to oppose the Powers which serve the hero with the Powers which persecute him. For if everything which serves the hero is good, holy, and sacred, and everything which is harmful to him wicked, impious, and reprobate, I do not see the glory of his triumph.

The principal defect in Milton's poem is that his hero succumbs, although he has to combat only the evil things within himself, whilst everything which is good protects him: the poem of Klopstock does not hold the reader's interest, because the perils of his hero are illusory and as soon as he is represented as God, and when he himself knows his divinity, his downfall is absolutely impossible.

But it is too much to dwell upon points of criticism which do not belong to my subject. I have touched upon them only slightly so that you may feel, Messieurs, notwithstanding the pretensions of three rival peoples, that the epic career remains none the less wholly open to the French nation. Some out-of-the-way paths have been traced here and there; but no poet since Vergil, has left the imprint of his steps upon the true path. The moment is perhaps at hand for gathering the palms that time has ripened. Must this century, great in prodigies, remain without an impassioned and enchanting voice to sing of them? Assuredly not. Whoever may be the poet whose genius raises itself to this noble task, I have wished from afar to lend him my feeble support; for I have often enough repeated, that talent alone will aspire to this in vain. Epopœia will only be the portion of the one who thoroughly understands the essence of poetry and who is able to apply to it a proper form. I have penetrated this essence as far as has been possible for me, and I have revealed my ideas, Messieurs, as clearly as the insufficiency of my means has permitted. I trust that their development may have appeared satisfactory and useful to you; I trust equally that the new form which I offer you merits your attention. I have applied it before you, to ideas, to intentions and to very different harmonies: it adapts itself here, for of itself it is nothing. Subject wholly to poetic essence, it receives therefrom all its lustre. If the ideas that it would render have grandeur and sublimity, it will easily become grand and sublime; but nothing would be poorer and more void, than that it should serve trivial thoughts or that it should conceal an absolute want of ideas. Do not imagine, Messieurs, that the absence of rhyme makes easy the French verse; it is precisely this absence which makes the great difficulty: for there is not then the means of writing without thinking. One can, with the aid of talent and practice, compose pleasing rhymed verse, without a great expenditure of ideas; the enormous quantity that is made today proves that it is not very difficult. The elegance of form supplies the sterility of substance. But this form becomes at last worn out; the rhymes are not inexhaustible; one word attracts another, forces it to unite with it, making understood the sounds that one has heard a thousand times, repeating the pictures which are everywhere; one repeats unceasingly the same things: the enjambment which gives so much grace to the Greek and Latin verse and without which real epic impulse cannot exist, is opposed to the rhyme and destroys it. You can see, Messieurs, that it constitutes one of the principal qualities of eumolpique verse; nothing here constrains the enthusiasm of the poet.

After some impassioned verses that I have believed ecessary for you to hear, I shall now pass on to verses, philosophical and devoid of passion, which form the subject of this writing and to which I desire above all to call your attention.

THE GOLDEN VERSES OF PYTHAGORAS

THE GOLDEN VERSES OF PYTHAGORAS
ΤΆ ΤΩ͂Ν ΠΥΘΑΓΟΡΕΙΩΝ ἜΠΗ ΤΆ ΧΡΥΣΆ

ΠΑΡΑΣΚΕΥΝ.

GOLDEN VERSES OF THE PYTHAGO-REANS (1)
PREPARATION

ΑΘΑΝΑΤΟΥΣ μὲν πρῶτα Δεοὺς, νόμῳ ὡς διάκεινται,
Τίμα· καὶ σέβου ὅρκον. ἔπειθ᾽ Ἥρωας ἀγαυούς.
Τοὺς τε κατα χθονίους σέβε Δαίμονας, ἔννομα ῥέζων.
ΚΆΘΑΡΣΙΣ

Render to the Immortal Gods the consecrated cult;
Guard then thy faith (2): Revere the memory
Of the Illustrious Heroes, of Spirits demi-Gods (3).

PURIFICATION

Τοὺς τε γονεῖς τίμα, τοὺς τ᾽ ἄγχις᾽ ἐχγεγαῶτας.
Τῶν δ᾽ ἄλλων ἀρετη ποιεὺ φίλον ὅςις ²²⁷ ἄριστος.
Πραέσι δ᾽ ἔικε λόγοις, ἔργοισί τ᾽ επωφελίμοισι.
Μὴδ᾽ ἔχθαιρε φίλον σὸν ἁμαρτάδος εἴνεκα μικρῆς,
Ὄφρα δύνῃ δύναμις γὰρ ἀνάγχης ἐγγύθι ναίει.
Ταῦτα μὲν οὕτως ἴσθι. κρατεῖν δ᾽ εἰθίζεο τῶν δε·
Γαστρὸς μὲν πρώπιστα, καὶ ὕπνου, λαγνείης τε,
Καὶ θυμοῦ. Πρήξεις δ᾽ αἰσχρὸν ποτε

Be a good son, just brother, spouse tender and good father (4)
Choose for thy friend, the friend of virtue;
Yield to his gentle counsels, profit by his life,
And for a trifling grievance never leave him (5);
If thou canst at least: for a most rigid law
Binds Power to Necessity (6).
Still it is given thee to fight and overcome
Thy foolish passions: learn thou to subdue them (7).
Be sober, diligent, and chaste; avoid

μήτε μετ' ἄλλου,
Μήτ' ἰδίη. Πάντων δὲ μάλιστα αἰσχύνεο σαυτόν.

Εἶτα διχαιοσύνην ἀσκεῖν ἔργῳ τε, λόγῳ τε.
Μηδ' ἀλογίστως σαυτὸν ἔχειν περὶ μηδὲν ἔθιζε.
Ἀλλὰ γνῶθι μὲν ὡς θανέειν πέπρωται ἅπασι.
Χρήματα δ'ἄλλοτε μὲν κτᾶσθαι φιλέῖ, ἄλλοτ' ὀλέσθαι.
Ὅσσα τε δαιμονίῃσι τύχαις βροτοὶ ἄλγε ἔχουσιν,
Ὧν ἄν μοῖραν ἔχῃς πρᾴως φέρε, μηδ' ἀγανάκτει.
Ἰᾶσθαι δὲ πρέπει καθόσον δυνὴ· Ὧδε δὲ φράζεν.
Οὐ πάνυ τοῖς ἀγαθοῖς τουτῶν πολὺ μοῖρα δίδωσι.

Πολλοὶ δ'ἀνθρώποισι λόγοι δειλοί τε, καὶ ἐσθλοὶ
Πορσπίπτους, ὧν μήτ' ἐκπλήσσεο, μήτ' ἄρ ἐάσῃς
Ἔιργεσθαι σαυτόν. Ψεῦδος δ' ἤν πὲρ τι λέγηται,
Πρᾴως εἶχ'· Ὃ δὲ τοι ἐρέω, επὶ παντὶ τελείσθω.
Μηδεὶς μήτε λόγῳ σε παρείπῃ, μήτε τι ἔργῳ
Πρῆξαι, μηδ' ἐιπεῖν, ὅ τι τοὶ μὴ βέτερὸν ἐστί.
Βουλεύου δὲ πρὸ ἔργου, ὅπως μὴ μωρὰ πέληεται.
Δειλοῦ τοι πρήσσειν τε λέγειν

all wrath.
In public or in secret ne'er permit thou
Any evil; and above all else respect thyself (8).

Speak not nor act before thou hast reflected.
Be just (9). Remember that a power invincible
Ordains to die (10); that riches and the honours
Easily acquired, are easy thus to lose (11).
As to the evils which Destiny involves,
Judge them what they are: endure them all and strive,
As much as thou art able, to modify the traits:
The Gods, to the most cruel, have not exposed the Sage (12).

Even as Truth, does Error have its lovers:
With prudence the Philosopher approves or blames;
If Error triumph, he departs and waits (13).
Listen and in thine heart engrave my words;
Keep closed thine eye and ear 'gainst prejudice;
Of others the example fear; think always for thyself (14):
Consult, deliberate, and freely choose (15).
Let fools act aimlessly and without cause.

τ'ἀνόητα πρὸς ἀνδρὸς.
Ἀλλὰ τάδ' ἐκτελέειν, ἅ σε μὴ
μετέπειτ' ἀνιήση.

Πρῆσσε δὲ μηδὲν τῶν μὴ
πίστασσι· ἀλλὰ διδάσκευ
Ὅσσα χρεὼν, καὶ τερπνότατον βίον
ὧδε διάξεις.
Οὐδ' ὑγιείης τῆς περὶ σῶμ'
ἀμέλειαν ἔχειν χρή.
Ἀλλὰ ποτοῦ τε μέτρον, καὶ σίτου,
γυμνασίων τε
Ποιεῖσθαι. μέτρον δὲ λέγω τό δ', ὃ
μὴ σ' ἀνιήσει.
Ἐιθίζου δε δίαιταν ἔχειν
καθάρειον, ἄθφρυπτον.
Καὶ πεφύλαξὸ γε ταῦτα ποιεῖν,
ὁπόσα φθόνον ἴσχει
Μη δαπανᾶν παρὰ καιρὸν, ὁποῖα
καλῶν ἀδαήμων.
Μη δ' ἀνελεύθερος ἴσθι· μέτρον
δ'ἐπὶ πᾶσιν ἄριστον.
Πρῆσσε δὲ ταῦθ', ἃ σε μὴ βλάψη·
λόγισαι δὲ πρὸ ἔργου.

Thou shouldst, in the present, contemplate the future (16).

That which thou dost not know, pretend not that thou dost.
Instruct thyself: for time and patience favour all (17).
Neglect not thy health (18): dispense with moderation,
Food to the body and to the mind repose (19).
Too much attention or too little shun; for envy
Thus, to either excess is alike attached (20).
Luxury and avarice have similar results.
One must choose in all things a mean just and good (21).

ΤΕΛΕΑΌΤΗΣ.

PERFECTION

Μὴδ' ὕπνον μαλακοῖσιν ἐπ'
ὄμμασι προσδέξασθαι,
Πρὶν τῶν ἡμερινῶν ἔργῶν τρὶς
ἕκαστον ἐπελθεῖν·
Πῆ παρέβην; τὶ δ'ἔρεξα; τὶ μοι δέον
οὐκ ἐτελέσθη;
Ἀρξάμενος δ'ἀπὸ πρώτου ἐπέξιθι·
καὶ μετέπειτα
Δεινὰ μὲν ἐκπρήξας ἐπιπλήσσεο·
χρηστὰ δὲ, τέρπου.

Let not sleep e'er close thy tired eyes
Without thou ask thyself: What have I omitted and what done? (22).
Abstain thou if 'tis evil; persevere if good (23).
Meditate upon my counsels; love them; follow them;
To the divine virtues will they know how to lead thee (24).
I swear it by the one who in our

Ταῦτα πόνει· ταῦτ᾽ ἐκμελέτα·
τούτων χρὴ ἐρᾶν σε.
Ταῦτά σε τῆς θείης ἀρετῆς εἰς ἴχνια
θήσει.

hearts engraved
The sacred Tetrad, symbol immense and pure,
Source of Nature and model of the Gods (25).
But before all, thy soul to its faithful duty,
Invoke these Gods with fervour, they whose aid,
Thy work begun, alone can terminate (26).
Instructed by them, naught shall then deceive thee:

Ναὶ μὰ τὸν ἡμετέρᾳ ψυχᾷ παραδόντα τετρακτὺν,
Παγὰν ἀενάοῦ φύσεως. Ἀλλ᾽ ἔρχευ ἐπ᾽ ἔργον
Θεοῖσιν ἐπευξάμενος τελέσαι.
Τούτων δὲ κρατήσας,
Γνώσῃ ἀθανάτων τε θεῶν, θνητῶν τ᾽ ἀνθρώτων
Σύστασιν, ἧ τε ἕκαστα διέρχεται, ἧ τε κρατεῖται.
Γνώσῃ δ᾽, ᾗ θέμις ἐστὶ, φύσιν περὶ παντὸς ὁμοίην
Ὥστε σε μήτ᾽ ἄελπτ᾽ ελπίζεῖν, μήτε τι λήθειν.
Γνώσῃ δ᾽ ἀνθρώπους αὐθαίρετα πήματ᾽ ἔχοντας
Τλήμονας, οἵ τ᾽ἀγαθῶν πέλας ὄντων οὔτ᾽ ἐσορῶσιν.
Οὔτε κλύουσι· λύσιν δὲ κακῶν πᾶυροι συνίσασι.
Τοίη μοίρα βροτῶν βλάπτει φρένας· οἱ δὲ κυλίνδροις
Ἄλλοτ᾽ ἐπ᾽ ἄλλα φέρονται ἀπείρονα πήματ᾽ ἔχοντες.

Of diverse beings thou shalt sound the essence;
And thou shalt know the principle and end of All (27).
If Heaven wills it, thou shalt know that Nature,
Alike in everything, is the same in every place (28):
So that, as to thy true rights enlightened,
Thine heart shall no more feed on vain desires (29).
Thou shalt see that the evils which devour men
Are of their choice the fruit (30); that these unfortunates
Seek afar the goodness whose source within they bear (31).
For few know happiness: playthings of the passions,
Hither, thither tossed by adverse waves,
Upon a shoreless sea, they blinded roll,

Λυγρὴ γὰρ συνοπαδὸς ἔρις
βλάπτουσα λέληθε
Σύμφυτος· ἣ οὗ δεῖ προσάγειν,
εἴκοντα δὲ φεύγειν.

 Ζεῦ πάτερ, ἦ πολλῶν τε κακῶν
λύσειας ἅπαντας.
Ἤ πᾶσιν δείξαις ²²⁸ οἵῳ τῷ δαίμονι
χρῶνται.
Ἀλλὰ σὺ θάρσει· ἐπεὶ θεῖον γένος
ἐστὶ βροτοῖσιν
Οἷς ἱερὰ προφέρουσα φύσις
δείκνυσιν ἕκαστα.
Ὧν εἰ σοί τι μέτεστι, κρατήσεῖς ὧν
σε κελεύω,
Ἐξακέσας, ψυχὴν δὲ πόνων ἀπὸ
τῶν δὲ σαώσεις.
Ἀλλ᾽ εἴεγου βρωτῶν, ὧ εἴπομεν, ἔν
τε καθάρμοῖς,
Ἔν τε λύσει ψυχῆς κρίνων·καὶ
ψράζευ ἕκαστα,
Ἡνίοχον γνώμην στήσας
καθύπερθεν ἀρίστην.
Ἢν δ᾽ἀπολείψας ²²⁹ σῶμα ἐς αἰθέρ
ἐλεύθερον ἔλθης,
Ἔσσεαι ἀθάνατος θεος, αμβροτος,
οὐκ ἔτι θνηός.

Unable to resist or to the tempest yield (32).

God! Thou couldst save them by opening their eyes (33).
But no: 'tis for the humans of a race divine
To discern Error and to see the Truth (34).
Nature serves them (35). Thou who fathomed it,
O wise and happy man, rest in its haven.
But observe my laws, abstaining from the things
Which thy soul must fear, distinguishing them well;
Letting intelligence o'er thy body reign, (36);
So that, ascending into radiant Ether,
Midst the Immortals, thou shalt be thyself a God.

EXAMINATIONS OF THE GOLDEN VERSES

THE GOLDEN VERSES OF THE PYTHAGOREANS

THE ancients had the habit of comparing with gold all that they deemed without defects and pre-eminently beautiful: thus, by the Golden Age they understood, the age of virtues and of happiness; and by the Golden Verses, the verses, wherein was concealed the most pure doctrine. They constantly attributed these Verses to Pythagoras, not that they believed that this philosopher had himself composed them, but because they knew that his disciple, whose work they were, had revealed the exact doctrine of his master and had based them all upon maxims issued from his mouth! [230] This disciple, commendable through his learning, and especially through his devotion to the precepts of Pythagoras, was called Lysis. [231] After the death of this philosopher and while his enemies, momentarily triumphant, had raised at Crotona and at Metaponte that terrible persecution which cost the lives of so great a number of Pythagoreans, crushed beneath the débris of their burned school, or constrained to die of hunger in the temple of the Muses, [232] Lysis, happily escaped from these disasters, retired into Greece, where, wishing to spread the sect of Pythagoras, to whose principles calumnies had been attached, he felt it necessary to set up a sort of formulary which would contain the basis of morals and the principal rules of conduct given by this celebrated man. It is to this generous movement that we owe the philosophical verses that I have essayed to translate into French. These verses, called golden for the reason I have given, contain the sentiments of Pythagoras and are all that remain to us, really authentic, concerning one of the greatest men of antiquity. Hierocles, who has transmitted them to us with a long and masterly Commentary, assures us that they do not contain, as one might believe, the sentiment of one in particular, but the doctrine of all the sacred corps of Pythagoreans and the voice of all the assemblies. [233] He adds that there existed a law which prescribed that each one, every morning upon rising and every evening upon retiring, should read these verses as the oracles of the Pythagorean school. One sees, in reality, by many passages from Cicero, Horace, Seneca, and other writers worthy of belief, that this law was still vigorously executed in their time. [234] We know by the testimony of Galen in his treatise on The Understanding and the Cure of the Maladies of the Soul, that he himself read every day, morning and evening, the Verses of Pythagoras; and that, after having read them, he recited them by heart. However, I must not neglect to say that Lysis, who is the author of them, obtained so much celebrity in Greece that he was honoured as the master and friend of Epaminondas. [235] If his name has not been attached to this work, it is because at the epoch when he wrote it, the ancient custom still existed of considering things and not individuals: it was with the doctrine of Pythagoras that one was concerned, and not with the talent of Lysis which had made it known. The disciples of a great man had no of her name than his. All their works were attributed to him. This is an observation sufficiently important to make and which explains how Vyasa in India, Hermes in Egypt, Orpheus in Greece, have been the supposed authors of such a multitude of books that the lives of many men would not even suffice to read them.

In my translation, I have followed the Greek text, such as is cited at the head of the Commentary of Hierocles, commentated on by the son of Casaubon, and interpreted into Latin by J. Curterius; London edition, 1673. This work, like all those which remain to us of the ancients, has been the subject of a great many critical and grammatical discussions: in the first place one must before everything else be assured of the material part. This part is today as authentic and as correct as it is possible to be, and although there exists still. several different readings, they are of too little importance for me to dwell upon. It is not my affair and besides, chacun doit faire son métier. That of the grammarian has ended where it ought to end. For how can man ever expect to advance if he never is willing to try some new thing which is offered. I shall not therefore make any criticizing remarks concerning the text, for I consider this text sufficiently examined; neither will I make any notes concerning the Commentaries, properly so-called, on these seventy-one lines, for I think it is sufficient having those of Hierocles, of Vitus Amerbachius, Theodore Marcilius, Henri Brem, Michel Neander, Jean Straselius, Guilhaume Diezius, Magnus-Daniel Omeis, André Dacier, etc. As I stated, I shall make examinations rather than commentaries, and I will give, regarding the inner meaning of the Verses, all the explanations that I believe useful for their complete development.

RENDER TO THE IMMORTAL GODS THE CONSECRATED CULT; GUARD THEN THY FAITH

PYTHAGORAS, of whom a modern savant, otherwise most estimable, has rather thoughtlessly reproached with being a fanatical and superstitious man, a begins his teaching, nevertheless, by laying down a principle of universal tolerance. He commands his disciples to follow the cult established by the laws, whatever this cult may be, and to adore the gods of their country, what ever these gods may be; enjoining them only, to guard afterwards their faith—that is, to remain inwardly faithful to his doctrine, and never to divulge the mysteries. Lysis, in writing these opening lines, adroitly conceals herein a double meaning. By the first he commended, as I have said, tolerance and reserve for the Pythagorean, and, following the example of the Egyptian priests, established two doctrines, the one apparent and vulgar, conformable to the law; the other mysterious and secret, analogous to the faith; by the second meaning, he reassures the suspicious people of Greece, who, according to the slanders which were in circulation might have feared that the new sect would attack the sanctity of their gods. This tolerance on the one hand, and this reserve on the other, were no more than what they would be today. The Christian Religion, exclusive and severe, has changed all our ideas in this respect: by admitting only one sole. doctrine in one unique church, this religion has necessarily confused tolerance with indifference or coldness, and reserve with heresy or hypocrisy; but in the spirit of polytheism these same things take on another colour. A Christian philosopher could not, without perjuring himself and committing a frightful impiety, bend the knee in China before Kong-Tse, nor offer incense to Chang-Ty nor to Tien; he could neither render, in India, homage to Krishna, nor present himself at Benares as a worshipper of Vishnu; he could not even, although recognizing the same God as the Jews and Mussulmans, take part in their ceremonies, or what is still more, worship this God with the Arians, the Lutherans, or Calvinists, if he were a Catholic. This belongs to the very essence of his cult. A Pythagorean philosopher did not recognize in the least these formidable barriers, which hem in the nations, as it were, isolate them, and make them worse than enemies. The gods of the people were in his eyes the same gods, and his cosmopolitan dogmas condemned no one to eternal damnation. From one end of the earth to the other he could cause incense to rise from the altar of the Divinity, under whatever name, under whatever form it might be worshipped, and render to it the public cult established by the law. And this is the reason. Polytheism was not in their opinion what it has become in ours, an impious and gross idolatry, a cult inspired by the infernal adversary to seduce men and to claim for itself the honours which are due only to the Divinity; it was a particularization of the Universal Being, a personification of its attributes and its faculties. Before Moses, none of the theocratic legislators had thought it well to present for the adoration of the people, the Supreme God, unique and uncreated in His unfathomable universality. The Indian Brahmans, who can be considered as the living types of all the sages and of all the pontiffs of the world, never permit themselves, even in this day when their great age has effaced the traces of their ancient science, to utter the name of God, principle of All. [236] They are content to meditate upon its essence in silence and to offer sacrifices to its sublimest emanations. The Chinese sages act the same with regard to the Primal Cause, that must be neither named nor defined [237]; the followers of Zoroaster, who believe that the two universal principles of good and evil, Ormuzd and Ahriman, emanate from this ineffable Cause, are content to designate it under the name of Eternity. [238] The Egyptians, so celebrated for their wisdom, the extent of their learning, and the multitude of their divine symbols, honoured with silence the God, principle and source of all things [239]; they never spoke of it, regarding it as inaccessible to all the researches of man; and Orpheus, their disciple, first author of the brilliant mythology of the Greeks, Orpheus, who seemed to announce the soul of the World as creator of this same God from which it emanated, said plainly: "I never see this Being surrounded with a cloud." [240]

Moses, as I have said, was the first who made a public dogma of the unity of God, and who divulged what, up to that time had been buried in the seclusion of the sanctuaries; for the principal tenets of the mysteries, those upon which reposed all others, were the Unity of God and the homogeneity of Nature. [241] It is true that Moses, in making this disclosure, permitted no definition, no reflection, either upon the essence or upon the nature of this unique Being; this is very remarkable. Before him, in all the known world, and after him (save in Judea where more than one cloud still darkened the idea of divine Unity, until the establishment of Christianity), the Divinity was considered by the theosophists of all nations, under two relations: primarily as unique, secondarily as infinite; as unique, preserved under the seal of silence to the contemplation and meditation of the sages; as infinite, delivered to the veneration and invocation of the people. Now the unity of God resides in His essence so that the vulgar can never in any way either conceive or understand. His infinity consists in His perfections, His faculties, His attributes, of which the vulgar can, according to the measure of their understanding, grasp some feeble emanations, and draw nearer to Him by detaching them from the universality—that is, by particularizing and personifying them. This is the particularization and the personification which constitutes, as I have said, polytheism. The mass of gods which result from it, is as infinite as the Divinity itself whence it had birth. Each nation, each people, each city adopts at its liking, those of the divine faculties which are best suited to its character and its requirements. These faculties, represented by simulacra, become so many particular gods whose variety of names augments the number still further. Nothing can limit this immense theogony, since the Primal Cause whence it emanates has not done so. The vulgar, lured by the objects which strike the senses, can become idolatrous, and he does ordinarily; he can even distinguish these objects of his adoration, one from another, and believe that there really exist as many gods as statues; but the sage, the philosopher, the most ordinary man of letters does not fall into this error. He knows, with Plutarch, that different places and names do not make different gods; that the Greeks and Barbarians, the nations of the North and those of the South, adore the same Divinity [242]; he restores easily that infinity of attributes to the unity of the essence, and as the honoured remnants of the ancient Sramanas, the priests of the Burmans, still do today, he worships God, whatever may be the altar, the temple, and the place where he finds himself! [243]

This is what was done by the disciples of Pythagoras, according to the commandment of their master; they saw in the gods of the nations, the attributes of the Ineffable Being which were forbidden them to name; they augmented ostensibly and without the slightest reluctance, the number of these attributes of which they recognized the Infinite Cause; they gave homage to the cult consecrated by the law and brought them all back secretly to the Unity which was the object of their faith.

REVERE THE MEMORY OF THE ILLUSTRIOUS HEROES, OF SPIRITS DEMI-GODS

PYTHAGORAS considered the Universe as an animated All, whose members were the divine Intelligences, each ranked according to its perfections, in its proper sphere, a He it was who first designated this All, by the Greek word Kosmos, in order to express the beauty, order, and regularity which reigned there [244]; the Latins translated this word by Mundus, from which has come the French word monde. It is from Unity considered as principle of the world, that the name Universe which we give to it is derived. Pythagoras establishes Unity as the principle of all things and said that from this Unity sprang an infinite Duality. [245] The essence of this Unity, and the manner in which the Duality that emanated from it was finally brought back again, were the most profound mysteries of his doctrine; the subject sacred to the faith of his disciples and the fundamental points which were forbidden them to reveal. Their explanation was never made in writing; those who appeared worthy of learning them were content to be taught them by word of mouth. [246] When one was forced, by the concatenation of ideas, to mention them in the books of the sect, symbols and ciphers were used, and the language of Numbers employed; and these books, all obscure as they were, were still concealed with the greatest care; by all manner of means they were guarded against falling into profane hands. [247] I cannot enter into the discussion of the famous symbol of Pythagoras, one and two, without exceeding very much the limits that I have set down in these examinations [248]; let it suffice for me to say, that as he designated God by 1, and Matter by 2, he expressed the Universe by the number 12, which results in the union of the other two. This number is formed by the multiplication of 3 by 4: that is to say, that this philosopher conceived the Universal world as composed of three particular worlds, which, being linked one with the other by means of the four elementary modifications, were developed in twelve concentric spheres. [249] The ineffable Being which filled these twelve spheres without being understood by any one, was God. Pythagoras gave to It, truth for soul and light for body. [250] The Intelligence which peopled the three worlds were, firstly, the immortal gods properly so-called; secondly, the glorified heroes; thirdly, the terrestrial demons. The immortal gods, direct emanations of the uncreated Being and manifestation of Its infinite faculties, were thus named because they could not depart from the divine life—that is, they could never fall away from their Father into oblivion, wandering in the darkness of ignorance and of impiety; whereas the souls of men, which produced, according to their degree of purity, glorified heroes and terrestrial demons, were able to depart sometimes from the divine life by voluntary drawing away from God; because the death of the intellectual essence, according to Pythagoras and imitated in this by Plato, was only ignorance and impiety. [251] It must be observed that in my translation I have not rendered the Greek word δαίμονες by the word demons, but by that of spirits, on account of the evil meaning that Christianity has attached to it, as I explained in a preceding note. [252]

This application of the number 12 to the Universe is not at all an arbitrary invention of Pythagoras; it was common to the Chaldeans, to the Egyptians from whom he had received it, and to the principal peoples of the earth [253]: it gave rise to the institution of the zodiac, whose division into twelve asterisms has been found everywhere existent from time immemorial. [254] The distinction of the three worlds and their development into a number, more or less great, of concentric spheres inhabited by intelligences of different degrees of purity, were also known before Pythagoras, who in this only spread the doctrine which he had received at Tyre, at Memphis, and at Babylon. [255] This doctrine was that of the Indians. One finds still today among the Burmans, the division of all the created beings established in three classes, each of which contains a certain number of species, from the material beings to the spiritual, from the sentient to the intelligible. [256] The Brahmans, who count fifteen spheres in the universe, [257] appear to unite the three primordial worlds with the twelve concentric spheres which result from their development. Zoroaster, who admitted the dogma of the three worlds, limited the inferior world to the vortex of the moon. There, according to him, the empire of evil and of matter comes to an end. [258] This idea thus conceived has been general; it was that of all the ancient philosophers [259]; and what is very remarkable, is that it has been adopted by the Christian theosophists who certainly were not sufficiently learned to act through imitation. [260] The followers of Basil, those of Valentine, and all the gnostics have imbibed from this source the system of emanations which has enjoyed such a great renown in the school of Alexandria. According to this system, the Absolute Unity, or God, was conceived as the spiritual Soul of the Universe, the Principle of existence, the Light of lights; it was believed that this creative Unity, inaccessible to the understanding even, produced by emanation a diffusion of light which, proceeding from the centre to the circumference, losing insensibly its splendour and its purity in proportion as it receded from its source, ended by being absorbed in the confines of darkness; so that its divergent rays, becoming less and less spiritual and, moreover, repulsed by the darkness, were condensed in commingling with it, and, taking a material shape, formed all the kinds of beings that the world contains. Thus was admitted, between the Supreme Being and man, an incalculable chain of intermediary beings whose perfections decreased proportionably with their alienation from the Creative Principle. All the philosophers and all the sectarians who admired this spiritual hierarchy considered, under the relations peculiar to them, the different beings of which it was composed. The Persian magians who saw there genii, more or less perfect, gave them names relative to their perfections, and later made use of these same names to evoke them: from this came the Persian magic, which the Jews, having received by tradition during their captivity in Babylon, called Kabbala. [261] This magic became mixed with astrology among the Chaldeans, who regarded the stars as animated beings belonging to the universal chain of divine emanations; in Egypt, it became linked with the mysteries of Nature, and was enclosed in the sanctuaries, where it was taught by the priests under the safeguard of symbols and hieroglyphics. Pythagoras, in conceiving this spiritual hierarchy as a geometrical progression, considered the beings which compose it under harmonious relations, and based, by analogy, the laws of the universe upon those of music. He called the movement of the celestial spheres, harmony, and made use of numbers to express the faculties of different beings, their relations and their influences. Hierocles mentions a sacred book attributed to this philosopher, in which he called the divinity, the Number of numbers. [262] Plato, who, some centuries later, regarded these same beings as ideas and types, sought to penetrate their nature and to subjugate them by dialectics and the force of thought. Synesius, who united the doctrine of Pythagoras to that of Plato, sometimes called God, the Number of numbers, and sometimes the Idea of ideas. [263] The gnostics gave to the intermediary beings the name of Eons. [264] This name, which signifies, in Egyptian, a principle of the will, being developed by an inherent, plastic faculty, is applied in Greek to a term of infinite duration. [265] One finds in Hermes Trismegistus the origin of this change of meaning. This ancient sage remarks that the two faculties, the two virtues of God, are the understanding and the soul, and that the two virtues of the Eon are perpetuity and immortality. The essence of God, he said again, is the good and the beautiful, beatitude and wisdom; the essence of Eon, is being always the same. [266] But, not content with assimilating beings of the celestial hierarchy to ideas, to numbers, or to the plastic principle of the will, there were philosophers who preferred to designate them by the name of Words. Plutarch said on one occasion that words, ideas, and divine emanations reside in heaven and in the stars. [267] Philo gives in more than one instance the name of word to angels; and Clement of Alexandria relates that the Valentiniansoften called their Eons thus. According to Beausobre, the philosophers and theologians, seeking for terms in which to express substances, designated them by some one of their attributes or by some one of their operations, naming them Spirits, on account of the subtlety of their substance; Intelligences, on account of the thought; Words, on account of the reason; Angels, on account of their services; Eons, on account of their manner of subsisting, always equal, without change and without alteration. Pythagoras called them Gods, Heroes, Demons, relative to their respective elevation and the harmonious position of the three worlds which they inhabit. This cosmogonic ternary joined with Creative Unity, constitutes the famous Quaternary, or Sacred Tetrad, the subject of which will be taken up further on.

BE A GOOD SON, JUST BROTHER, SPOUSE TENDER, AND GOOD FATHER

THE aim of the doctrine of Pythagoras was to enlighten men, to purify them of their vices, to deliver them from their errors, and to restore them to virtue and to truth; and after having caused them to pass through all the degrees of the understanding and intelligence, to render them like unto the immortal gods. This philosopher had for this purpose divided his doctrine into two parts: the purgative part and the unitive part. Through the first, man became purified of his uncleanness, emerged from the darkness of ignorance, and attained to virtue: through the second, he used his acquired virtue to become united to the Divinity through whose means he arrived at perfection. These two parts are found quite distinct in the Golden Verses. Hierocles, who has clearly grasped them, speaks of it in the beginning of his Commentaries and designates them by two words which contain, he said, all the doctrine of Pythagoras, Purification and Perfection. [268] The Magians and the Chaldeans, all of whose principles Pythagoras had adopted, were agreed on this point, and in order to express their idea, made use of a parabolical phrase very celebrated among them. "We consume," they said, "the refuse of matter by the fire of divine love." [269] An anonymous author who has written an history of Pythagoras, preserved by Photius, said that the disciples of this great man taught that one perfects oneself in three ways: in communing with the gods, in doing good in imitation of the gods, and in departing from this life to rejoin the gods. [270] The first of these ways is contained in the first three lines of the Golden Verses which concern the cult rendered, according to the law and according to the faith, to the Gods, to the glorified Heroes, and to the Spirits. The second, that is, the Purification, begins at the fourth line which makes the subject of this Examination. The third, that is, the union with the Divinity, or Perfection, begins at the fortieth line of my translation:

Let not sleep e'er close thy tired eyes.

Thus the division that I have believed ought to be made of this short poem is not at all arbitrary, as one sees the judicious Bay le had remarked it before me. [271]

It is worthy of observation, that Pythagoras begins the purgative part of his doctrine by commending the observance of natural duties, and that he places in the rank of primary virtues, filial piety, paternal and conjugal love. Thus this admirable philosopher made it his first care to strengthen the ties of blood and make them cherished and sacred; he exhorts respect to children, tenderness to parents, and union to all the members of the family; he follows thus the profound sentiment which Nature inspires in all sentient beings, very different in this from certain legislators, blinded by false politics, who in order to conduct men to I know not what power and what imaginary welfare, have wished, on the contrary, to break those ties, annihilate those relationships of father, son, and brother, to concentrate, they said, upon a being of reason called Country the affection that the soul divides among those objects of its first love. [272] If the legislators had cared to reflect a moment, they would have seen that there existed no country for the one who had no father, and that the respect and love that a man in his virile age feels for the place of his birth, holds its principle and receives its force from those same sentiments that he felt in his infancy for his mother. Every effect proclaims a cause; every edifice rests upon a foundation: the real cause of love of country is maternal love; the sole foundations of the social edifice are paternal power and filial respect. From this sole power issues that of the prince, who, in every well-organized state, being considered as father of the people, has right to the obedience and respect of his children.

I am going to make here a singular comparison which I beg the reader to observe. Moses, instructed in the same school as Pythagoras, after having announced the Unity of God in the famous Decalogue which contains the summary of his law, and having commanded its adoration to his people, announces for the first virtue, filial piety [273]: "Honour," he said, "thy father and thy mother, that thy days may be multiplied in this country of Adam, that Jhôah, thy Gods, has given thee." [274]

The theocratic legislator of the Hebrews in making this commandment places recompense by the side of precept: he declares formally that the exercise of filial piety draws with it a long existence. Now, it must be remarked that Moses being content with enclosing in his doctrine the sole purgative part, doubtless judging his people not in a condition to support the unitive part, spoke to them nowhere of the immortality which is its consequence; contenting himself with promising the joys of temporal blessings, among which he carefully placed in the first rank a long life. Experience has proved, relative to people in general, that Moses spoke with a profound understanding of the causes which prolong the duration of empires. Filial piety is the national virtue of the Chinese, the sacred foundation upon which reposes the social edifice of the greatest and the most ancient people of the world. [275] This virtue has been to China, for more than four thousand years, what love of country was to Sparta or to Rome. Sparta and Rome have fallen notwithstanding the sort of fanaticism with which their children were animated, and the Chinese Empire which existed two thousand years before their foundation, still exists two thousand years after their downfall. If China has been able to preserve herself in the midst of the flux and reflux of a thousand revolutions, to save herself from her own wrecks, to triumph over her own defects, and to subjugate even her conquerors, she owes it to this virtue which, raising itself from the humblest citizen to the Son of heaven seated upon the imperial throne, animates all the hearts with a sacred fire, of which Nature herself provides the nourishment and eternalizes the duration. The Emperor is the father of the state; two hundred million men, who regard themselves as his children, compose his immense family; what human effort could overthrow this colossus? [276]

CHOOSE FOR THY FRIEND, THE FRIEND OF VIRTUE; YIELD TO HIS GENTLE COUNSELS, PROFIT BY HIS LIFE, AND FOR A TRIFLING GRIEVANCE NEVER LEAVE HIM

AFTER the duties which have their source directly in Nature, Pythagoras commends to his disciples those which proceed from the social state; friendship follows immediately filial piety, paternal and fraternal love; but this philosopher makes a distinction full of meaning: he ordains to honour one's relations; he says to choose one's friends. This is why: it is Nature that presides at our birth, that gives us a father, a mother, brothers, sisters, relations of kinship, a position upon the earth, and a place in society; all this depends not upon us: all this, according to the vulgar, is the work of hazard; but according to the Pythagorean philosopher these are the consequences of an anterior order, severe and irresistible, called Fortune or Necessity. Pythagoras opposed to this restrained nature, a free Nature, which, acting upon forced things as upon brute matter, modifies them and draws as it wills, good or bad results. This second nature was called Power or Will: it is this which rules the life of man, and which directs his conduct according to the elements furnished him by the first. Necessity and Power are, according to Pythagoras, the two opposed motives of the sublunary world where man is relegated. These two motives draw their force from a superior cause that the ancients named Nemesis, the fundamental decree, that we name Providence. Thus then, Pythagoras recognized, relative to man, things constrained and things free, according as they depend upon Necessity or the Will: he ranked filial piety in the first and friendship in the second. Man not being free to give himself parents of his choice, must honour them such as they are, and fulfil in regard to them all the duties of nature, whatever wrong they might do towards him; but as nothing constrains him from giving his friendship, he need give it only to the one who shows himself worthy of it by his attachment to virtue.

Let us observe an important point. In China where filial piety is regarded as the root of all virtues and the first source of instruction, [277] the exercise of the duties which it imposes admits of no exception. As the legislator

teaches there that the greatest crime is to lack in filial piety, he infers that he who has been a good son will be a good father and that thus nothing will break the social tie [278]; for he first establishes this virtue which embraces all, from the emperor to the lowliest of his subjects, and that it is for the peoples what the regularity of the celestial movements is for the ethereal space: but in Italy and in Greece where Pythagoras established his dogmas, it would have been dangerous for him to give the same extension, since this virtue not being that of the State, would necessarily involve abuses in the paternal authority, already excessive among certain peoples. That is the reason the disciples of this philosopher, in distinguishing between forced and voluntary actions, judged wisely that it would be necessary to apply here the distinction: therefore they urged to honour one's father and mother and to obey them in all that concerns the body and mundane things, but without abandoning one's soul to them [279]; for the divine law declares free what has not been received from them and delivers it from their power. Pythagoras furthermore had favoured this opinion by saying, that after having chosen a friend from among the men most commended for their virtues, it was necessary to learn by his actions and to be guided by his discourse: which testified to the lofty idea that he had of friendship. "Friends," he said, "are like companions of travel who reciprocally assist each other to persevere in the path of the noblest life.[280]"
It is to him that we owe that beautiful expression, so often quoted, so little felt by the generality of men, and which a victorious king, Alexander the Great, felt so keenly and expressed so felicitously by the following: "My friend is another myself. [281]" It is also from him that Aristotle had borrowed that beautiful definition: "The real friend is one soul that lives in two bodies." [282] The founder of the Lyceum, in giving such a definition of friendship, spoke rather by theory than by practice, he who reasoning one day upon friendship, cried ingenuously: "Oh, my friends! there are no friends." [283]

Yet Pythagoras did not conceive friendship as a simple individual affection, but as an universal benevolence which should be extended to all men in general, and to all good people. [284] At that time he gave to this virtue the name of philanthropy. It is the virtue which, under the name of charity, serves as foundation for the Christian religion. Jesus offers it to his disciples immediately after divine love, and as equal to piety. [285] Zoroaster places it after sincerity [286]; he wished that man might be pure in thought, speech, and action; that he might speak the truth, and that he might do good to all men. Kong-Tse as well as Pythagoras commended it after filial piety. [287] "All morals," he said, "can be reduced to the observation of three fundamental laws, of the relations between sovereigns and subjects, between parents and children, between husbands and wives; and to the strict practice of the five capital virtues, of which the first is humanity, that is to say, that universal charity, that expansion of the soul which binds man to man without distinction."

IF THOU CANST AT LEAST: FOR A MOST RIGID LAW BINDS POWER TO NECESSITY

HERE is the proof of what I said just now, that Pythagoras recognized two motives of human actions, the first, issuing from a constrained nature, called Necessity; the second emanating from a free nature, called Power, and both dependent upon an implied primordial law. This doctrine was that of the ancient Egyptians, among whom Pythagoras had imbibed it. "Man is mortal with reference to the body," they said, "but he is immortal with reference to the soul which constitutes essential man. As immortal he has authority over all things; but relative to the material and mortal part of himself, he is subject to destiny."

One can see by these few words that the ancient sages did not give to Destiny the universal influence that certain philosophers and particularly the Stoics gave to it later on; but they considered it only as exercising its empire over matter. It is necessary to believe that since the followers of the Porch had defined it as a chain of causes, by virtue of which the past has taken place, the present exists, and the future is to be realized [288]; or still better, as the rule of the law by which the Universe is governed [289]; one must believe, I say, that these philosophers confounded Destiny with Providence, and did not distinguish the effect from its cause, since these definitions conform only with the fundamental law of which destiny is but an emanation. This confusion of words had to produce and in fact did produce, among the Stoics, an inversion of ideas which was the most unfortunate result [290]; for, as they established, according to their system, a chain of good and evil that nothing could either alter or break, one easily inferred that the Universe being subject to the attraction of a blind fatality, all actions are here necessarily determined in advance, forced, and thereafter indifferent in themselves; so that good and evil, virtue and vice, are vain words, things whose existence is purely ideal and relative.

The Stoics would have evaded these calamitous results if, like Pythagoras, they had admitted the two motives of which I have spoken, Necessity and Power; and if, far from instituting Necessity alone as absolute master of the Universe, under the name of Destiny or Fatality, they had seen it balanced by the Power of the Will, and subject to the Providential Cause whence all emanates. The disciples of Plato would also have evaded many errors, if they had clearly understood this concatenation of the two opposed principles, from which results universal equilibrium; but following certain false interpretations of the doctrine of their master regarding the soul of matter, they had imagined that this soul was no other than Necessity by which it is ruled [291]; so that, according to them, this soul being inherent in matter, and bad in itself, gave to Evil a necessary existence: a dogma quite formidable, since it makes the world to be considered as the theatre of a struggle without beginning or end, between Providence, principle of Good, and the soul of matter, principle of Evil. The greatest mistake of the Platonists, exactly contrary to that of the Stoics, was in having confused the free power of the Will with the divine Providence, in having instituted it for the principle of good and thus being put in position of maintaining that there are two souls in the world, a beneficent one, God, and a malefic one, Matter. This system, approved of by many celebrated men of antiquity and which Beausobre assures was the most widely received, [292] offers, as I have observed, the very great disadvantage of giving to Evil a necessary existence, that is to say, an independent and eternal existence. Now, Bayle has very well proved, by attacking this system through that of Manes, that two opposed Principles cannot exist equally eternal and independent of one another, because the clearest ideas of order teach us that a Being which exists by itself, which is necessary, which is eternal, must be unique, infinite, all-powerful, and endowed with all manner of perfections. [293]

But it is not at all certain that Plato may have had the idea that his disciples have attributed to him, since far from considering matter as an independent and necessary being, animated by a soul essentially bad, he seems even to doubt its existence, going so far as to regard it as pure nothingness, and calls the bodies which are formed of it, equivocal beings holding the medium between what is always existing and what does not exist at all [294]; he affirms sometimes that matter has been created and sometimes that it has not been [295]; and thus falls into contradictions of which his enemies have taken advantage. Plutarch, who has clearly seen it, excuses them by saying that this great philosopher has fallen into these contradictions designedly, in order to conceal some mystery; a mind constructed like his not being made to affirm two opposites in the same sense. [296] The mystery that Plato wished to conceal, as he makes it sufficiently understood, [297] was the origin of Evil. He himself declares that he has never revealed and that he never will reveal, in writing, his real sentiments in this respect. Thus what Chalcidius and after him André Dacier have given concerning the doctrine of Plato are only conjectures or very remote inferences drawn from certain of his dogmas. One has often made use of this means, with regard to celebrated men whose writings one comments upon and particularly when one has certain reasons for presenting one's ideas sous un côté which outlines or which favours an opinion either favourable or unfavourable. It is this which happened more to Manes than to any other; his doctrine concerning the two Principles has been greatly calumniated, and without knowing just what he meant by them, one hastened to condemn him without investigating what he had said; adopting as axioms that he had laid down, inferences the most bizarre and most ridiculous that his enemies had drawn from certain equivocal phrases. [298] What persuades me to make this observation, is because it has been proved that Manes had indeed admitted two opposed Principles of Good and Evil, eternal independents, and holding of themselves their proper and absolute existence, since it is easy to see that Zoroaster, whose doctrine he had principally imitated, had not admitted them as such, but as equally issued from a superior Cause, concerning the essence of which he was silent. [299] I am very much inclined to believe that the Christian doctors who have transmitted to us the ideas of this mighty heresiarch, blinded by their hatred or by their ignorance, have travestied them as I find that the Platonist philosophers, bewildered by their own opinions, have entirely disfigured those of the illustrious founder of the Academy. The errors of both have been, taking for absolute beings, what Zoroaster and Pythagoras, Plato or Manes, had put down as emanations, results, forces, or even the simple abstractions of the understanding. Thus Ormuzd and Ahriman, Power and Necessity, the Same and the Other, Light and Darkness, are, in reality, only the same things diversely expressed, diversely sensed, but always drawn from the same origin and subject to the same fundamental Cause of the Universe.

It is not true therefore, as Chalcidius has stated, that Pythagoras may have demonstrated that evil exists necessarily, [300] because matter is evil in itself. Pythagoras never said that matter might be an absolute being whose essence might be composed of evil. Hierocles, who had studied the doctrine of this great man and that of Plato, has denied that either the one or the other had ever declared matter as a being existing by itself. He has proved, on the contrary, that Plato taught, following the steps of Pythagoras, that the World was produced from Nothing, and that his followers were mistaken when they thought that he admitted an uncreated matter. [301] Power and Necessity (mentioned in the lines at the head of this Examination) are not, as has been believed, the absolute source of good and evil. Necessity is not more evil in itself than Power is not good; it is from the usage that man is called to make of them, and from their employment which is indicated by wisdom or ignorance, virtue or vice, that results Good or Evil. This has been felt by Homer who has expressed it in an admirable allegory, by representing the god of gods himself, Jupiter, opening indifferently the sources of good and evil upon the universe.

Beside Jove's threshold stand two casks of gifts for man.
One cask contains the evil, one the good, . . . [302]

Those who have rejected this thought of Homer have not reflected enough upon the prerogatives of poetry, which are to particularize what is universal and to represent as done what is to be done. Good and Evil do not emanate from Jupiter in action, but in potentiality, that is to say, that the same thing represented by Jupiter or the Universal Principle of the Will and the Intelligence, becomes good or evil, according as it is determined by the particular operation of each individual principle of the Will and the Intelligence. [303] Now, man is to the Being called Jupiter by Homer, as the particular is to the Universal. [304]

STILL IT IS GIVEN THEE TO FIGHT AND OVERCOME THY FOOLISH PASSIONS: LEARN THOU TO SUBDUE THEM

IT seems that Lysis, foreseeing the wrong inductions that would be drawn from what he had said, and as if he had a presentiment that one would not fail to generalize the influence of Necessity upon the actions of men, may have wished beforehand to oppose himself to the destructive dogma of fatality, by establishing the empire of the Will over the passions. This is in the doctrine of Pythagoras the real foundation of the liberty of man: for, according to this philosopher, no one is free, only he who knows how to master himself, and the yoke of the passions is much heavier and more difficult to throw off than that of the most cruel tyrants. Pythagoras, however, did not, according to Hierocles, prescribe destroying the passions, as the Stoics taught in late times; but only to watch over them and repress excess in them, because all excess is vicious. [305] He regarded the passions as useful to man, and although produced in principle by Necessity, and given by an irresistible destiny, as nevertheless submissive in their use to the free power of the Will. Plato had well realized this truth and had forcibly indicated it in many passages of his works: one finds it chiefly in the second dialogue of Hippias, where this philosopher shows, evidently without seeming to have the design, that man good or bad, virtuous or criminal, truthful or false, is only such by the power of his will, and that the passion which carries him to virtue or to vice, to truth or falsehood, is nothing in itself; so that no man is bad, only by the faculty which he has of being good; nor good, only by the faculty which he has of being bad.

But has man the faculty of being good or bad at his pleasure, and is he not irresistibly drawn toward vice or virtue? This is a question which has tried all the great thinkers of the earth, and which according to circumstances has caused storms of more or less violence. It is necessary, however, to give close attention to one thing, which is, that before the establishment of Christianity and the admission of original sin as fundamental dogma of religion, no founder of sect, no celebrated philosopher had positively denied the free will, nor had taught ostensibly that man may be necessarily determined to Evil or to Good and predestined from all time to vice or virtue, to wickedness or eternal happiness. It is indeed true that this cruel fatality seemed often to follow from their principles as an inevitable consequence, and that their adversaries reproached them with it; but nearly all rejected it as an insult, or a false interpretation of their system. The first who gave place to this accusation, in ancient times, was a certain Moschus, a Phœnician philosopher, who, according to Strabo, lived before the epoch in which the war of Troy is said to have taken place, that is to say, about twelve or thirteen centuries before our era. [306] This philosopher detaching himself from the theosophical doctrine, the only one known at that time, and having sought the reason of things in the things themselves, can be considered as the real founder of Natural Philosophy: he was the first who made abstraction from the Divinity, and from the intelligence, and assumed that the Universe existing by itself was composed of indivisible particles, which, endowed with figures and diverse movements, produced by their fortuitous combinations an infinite series of beings, generating, destroying, and renewing themselves unceasingly. These particles, which the Greeks named atoms, [307] on account of their indivisibility, constituted the particular system which still bears this name. Leucippus, Democritus, and Epicurus adopted it, adding to it their own ideas; and Lucretius having naturalized it among the Romans, favoured its passage down to these modern times, when the greater part of our philosophers have done nothing but renovate it under other forms. [308] Assuredly there is no system whence the fatal necessity of all things issues more inevitably than from that of atoms; also it is certain that Democritus was accused of admitting a compulsory destiny, [309] although, like Leibnitz, he admitted to each atom an animated and sentient nature. [310] It is not known if he replied to this accusation; but there are certain proofs that Epicurus, who had less right than he to reject it, since he regarded atoms as absolutely inanimate, [311] rejected it nevertheless, and not wishing to admit a dogma subversive of all morals, he declared himself against it, and taught the liberty of man. [312] A singular thing is, that this fatality which appears attached to the system of atoms, whence the materialist promoters, true to their principle, banished the influence of Divine Providence, [313] followed still more naturally from the opposed system, wherein the spiritualist philosophers admitted this Providence to the full extent of its power. According to this last system, a sole and same spiritual substance filled the Universe, and by its diverse modifications produced there all the phenomena by which the senses are affected. Parmenides, Melissus, and Zeno of Elea, who adopted it, sustained it with great success: they asserted that matter was only pure illusion, that there is nothing in things, that bodies and all their variations are only pure appearances, and that therefore nothing really exists outside of spirit. [314] Zeno of Elea particularly, who denied the existence of movement, brought against this existence some objections very difficult to remove. [315] The Stoic philosophers became more or less strongly attached to this opinion. Chrysippus, one of the firmest pillars of the Porch, taught that God is the soul of the world, and the world, the universal extension of that soul. He said that by Jupiter, should be understood, the eternal law, the fatal necessity, the immutable truth of all future things. [316] Now, it is evident that if, in accordance with the energetic expression of Seneca; this unique principle of the Universe has ordained once to obey always its own command, [317] the Stoics were not able to escape from the reproach that was directed toward them, of admitting the most absolute fatality, since the soul of man being, according to them, only a portion of the Divinity, its actions could have no other cause than God Himself who had willed them. [318] Nevertheless Chrysippus rejected the reproach in the same manner as did Epicurus; he always sustained the liberty of man, notwithstanding the irresistible force that he admitted in the unique Cause [319]; and what seemed a manifest contradiction, he taught that the soul sins only by the impulse of its own will, and therefore that the blame of its errors should not be put upon destiny. [320]

But it suffices to reflect a moment upon the nature of the principles set down by Epicurus, by Chrysippus, and by all those who have preceded them or followed them in their divergent opinions, to see that the inferences drawn by their adversaries were just, and that they could not refute them without contradicting themselves. [321] Every time that one has claimed to found the Universe upon the existence of a sole material or spiritual nature, and to make proceed from this sole nature the explanation of all phenomena, one has become exposed and always will be, to insurmountable difficulties. It is always in asking what the origin of Good and Evil is, that all the systems of this sort have been irresistibly overthrown, from Moschus, Leucippus, and Epicurus, down to Spinoza and Leibnitz; from Parmenides, Zeno of Elea, and Chrysippus, down to Berkeley and Kant. For, let there be no misunderstanding, the solution of the problem concerning free will depends upon preliminary knowledge of the origin of evil, so that one cannot reply plainly to this question: Whence comes Evil? Neither can one reply to this one: Is man free? And that one be not still further deceived here, the knowledge of the origin of evil, if it has been acquired, has never been openly divulged: it has been profoundly buried with that of the Unity of God in the ancient mysteries and has never emerged except enveloped in a triple veil. The initiates imposed upon themselves a rigid silence concerning what they called the sufferings of God [322]: his death, his descent into the infernal regions, and his resurrection. [323] They knew that the serpent was, in general, the symbol of evil, and that it was under this form that the Python had fought with and been slain by Apollo. [324] The theosophists have not made a public dogma of the Unity of God, precisely on account of the explanation that it would be necessary to give to the origin of good and evil; for without this explanation, the dogma in itself would have been incomprehensible. Moses realized it perfectly, and in the plan which he had conceived of striking the people whose legislator he was, with a character as extraordinary as indelible, by founding his cult upon the publicity of a dogma hidden, until that time in the depths of the sanctuaries and reserved for the initiates alone, he did not hesitate to divulge what he knew pertaining to the creation of the world and the origin of evil. It is true that the manner in which he gave it, under a simplicity and apparent clarity, concealed a profundity and obscurity almost unfathomable; but the form which he gave to this formidable mystery sufficed to support, in the opinion of the vulgar, the Unity of God and this was all that he wished to do.

Now it is the essence of theosophy to be dogmatic, and that of natural philosophy to be skeptical; the theosophist speaks by faith, the physicist speaks by reason; the doctrine of the one excludes the discussion that the system of the other admits and even necessitates. Up to that time, theosophy dominating upon the earth had taught the influence of the will, and the tradition which was preserved in it among all the nations of the earth during an incalculable succession of centuries gave it the force of demonstration. Among the Indians, Krishna; among the Persians, Zoroaster; in China, Kong-Tse; in Egypt, Thoth; among the Greeks, Orpheus; even Odin, among the Scandinavians; everywhere the lawgivers of the people had linked the liberty of man with the consoling dogma of Divine Providence. [325] The peoples accustomed to worship in polytheism the Divine Infinity and not its Unity, did not find it strange to be guided, protected, and watched over on the one side, whereas they remained, on the other, free in their movements; and they did not trouble themselves to find the source of good and evil since they saw it in the objects of their cult, in these same gods, the greater part of whom being neither essentially good nor essentially bad were reputed to inspire in them the virtues or the vices which, gathered freely by them, rendered them worthy of recompense or chastisement. [326] But when Natural Philosophy appeared, the face of things was changed. The natural philosophers, substituting the observation of nature and experience for mental contemplation and the inspiration of theosophists, thought that they could make sentient what was intelligible, and promised to prove by fact and reasoning whatever up to that time had had only proofs of sentiment and analogy. They brought to light the great mystery of Universal Unity, and transforming this Intellectual Unity into corporal substance placed it in water, [327] in infinite space, [328] in the air, [329] in the fire, [330] whence they draw in turn the essential and formal existence of all things. The one, attached to the school of Ionia, established as fundamental maxim, that there is but one principle of all; and the other, attached to that of Elea, started from this axiom that nothing is made from nothing. [331] The former sought the how, and the latter the why of things; and all were united in saying that there is no effect without cause. Their different systems, based upon the principles of reasoning which seemed incontestable, and supported by a series of imposing conclusions, had, at first, a prodigious success; but this éclat paled considerably when soon the disciples of Pythagoras, and a little later those of Socrates and Plato, having received from their masters the theosophical tradition, stopped these sophistical physicists in the midst of their triumphs, and, asking them the cause of physical and of moral evil, proved to them that they knew nothing of it; and that, in whatever fashion they might deduce it by their system, they could not avoid establishing an absolute fatality, destructive to the liberty of man, which by depriving it of morality of actions, by confounding vice and virtue, ignorance and wisdom, made of the Universe no more than a frightful chaos. In vain these had thrust back the reproach and claimed that the inference was false; their adversaries pursuing them on their own ground cried out to them: If the principle that you admit is good, whence comes it that men are wicked and miserable? [332] If this unique principle is bad, whence emerge goodness and virtue? [333] If nature is the expression of this sole principle, how is it not constant and why does its government sow goodness and evil? [334] The materialists had recourse vainly to a certain deviation in atoms, [335] and the spiritualists, to a certain adjuvant cause quite similar to efficacious grace [336]; the theosophists would never have renounced them if they had not enclosed them in a syllogistic circle, by making them admit, sometimes that the unique and all-powerful Principle cannot think of everything, [337] sometimes that vice is useful and that without it there would be no virtue [338]; paradoxes of which they had no trouble demonstrating the absurdity and the revolting inferences. [339]

Take a survey of all the nations of the world, peruse all the books that you please, and you will find the liberty of man, the free will of his actions, the influence of his will over his passions, only in the theosophical tradition. Wherever you see physical or metaphysical systems, doctrines of whatever kind they may be, founded upon a sole principle of the material or spiritual Universe, you can conclude boldly that absolute fatality results from it and that their authors find themselves in need of making two things one: or of explaining the origin of good and evil, which is impossible; or of establishing the free will a priori, which is a manifest contradiction of their reasonings. If you care to penetrate into metaphysical depths, examine this decisive point upon this matter. Moses founded his cult upon the Unity of God and he explained the origin of evil; but he found himself forced by the very nature of this formidable mystery to envelop his explanation with such a veil, that it remained impenetrable for all those who had not received the traditional revelation; so that the liberty of man existed in his cult only by favour of theosophical tradition, and that it became weaker and disappeared entirely from it with this same tradition, the two opposed sects of the Pharisees and Sadducees which divided the cult prove this. [340] The former, attached to the tradition and allegorizing the text of the Sepher, [341] admitted the free will [342]; the others, on the contrary, rejecting it and following the literal meaning, established an irresistible destiny to which all was subjected. The most orthodox Hebrews, and those even who passed as seers or prophets of the nation, had no difficulty in attributing to God the cause of Evil. [343] They were obviously authorized by the history of the downfall of the first man, and by the dogma of original sin, which they took according to the meaning attached to it by the vulgar. It also happened, after the establishment of Christianity and of Islamism, that this dogma, received by both cults in all its extent and in all its literal obscurity, has necessarily drawn with it predestination, which is, in other words, only the fatality of the ancients. Mohammed, more enthusiast than learned, and stronger in imagination than in reasoning, has not hesitated a moment, admitting it as an inevitable result of the Unity of God, which he announced after Moses. [344] It is true that a few Christian doctors, when they have been capable of perceiving the inferences in it have denied this predestination, and have wished, either by allegorizing the dogma of original sin, as Origen, or rejecting it wholly, as Pelagius, to establish the free will and the power of the will; but it is easy to see, in reading the history of the church, that the most rigid Christians, such as Saint Augustine and the ecclesiastical authority itself, have always upheld predestination as proceeding necessarily from the divine Prescience and from the All-

Powerful, without which there is no Unity. The length of this examination forces me to suspend the proofs that I was going to give regarding this last assertion; but further on I will return to it.

BE SOBER, DILIGENT, AND CHASTE; AVOID ALL WRATH. IN PUBLIC OR IN SECRET NE'ER PERMIT THOU ANY EVIL; AND ABOVE ALL ELSE RESPECT THYSELF

PYTHAGORAS considered man under three principal modifications, like the Universe; and this is why he gave to man the name of the microcosm or the small world. [345] Nothing was more common among the ancient nations than to compare the Universe to a grand man, and man, to a small Universe. [346] The Universe, considered as a grand and animated All, composed of intelligence, soul and body, was called Pan or Phanes. [347] [348] Man, or microcosm, was composed in the same way but in an inverse manner, of body, soul, and intelligence; and each of these three parts was, in its turn, considered under three modifications, so that the ternary ruling in the whole ruled equally in the least of its subdivisions. Each ternary, from that which embraced Immensity, to that which constituted the weakest individual was, according to Pythagoras, included in an absolute or relative Unity, and formed thus, as I have already said, the Quaternary or Sacred Tetrad of the Pythagoreans. This Quaternary was universal or particular. Pythagoras was not, however, the inventor of this doctrine: it was spread from China to the depths of Scandinavia. [349] One finds it likewise expressed in the oracles of Zoroaster. [350]

In the Universe a Ternary shines forth,
And the Monad is its principle.

Thus, according to this doctrine, Man, considered as a relative unity contained in the absolute Unity of the Grand All, presents himself as the universal ternary, under three principal modifications, of body, soul, and spirit or intelligence. The soul, considered as the seat of the passions, is presented in its turn, under the three faculties of the rational, irascible or appetent soul. Now, in the opinion of Pythagoras, the vice of the appetent faculty of the soul is intemperance or avarice; that of the irascible faculty is cowardice; and that of the rational faculty is folly. The vice which reaches these three faculties is injustice. In order to avoid these vices, the philosopher commends four principal virtues to his disciples: temperance for the appetent faculty, courage for the irascible faculty, prudence for the rational faculty, and for these three faculties together, justice, which he regards as the most perfect virtue of the soul. [351] I say the soul, because the body and the intelligence, being equally developed by means of three faculties instinctive or spiritual, as well as the soul, were susceptible of the vices and the virtues which were peculiar to them.

SPEAK NOT NOR ACT BEFORE THOU HAST RE-FLECTED; BE JUST

BY the preceding lines, Lysis, speaking in the name of Pythagoras, had commended temperance and diligence; he had prescribed particularly watching over the irascible faculty, and moderating its excesses; by these, he indicates the peculiar character of prudence which is reflection and he imposes the obligation of being just, by binding, as it were, the most energetic idea of justice with that of death, as may be seen in the subsequent lines:

REMEMBER THAT A POWER INVINCIBLE ORDAINS TO DIE

THAT is to say, remember thou that the fatal necessity to which thou art subjected in reference to the material and mortal part of thyself, according to the sentence of the ancient sages, [352] will strike thee particularly in the objects of thy cupidity, of thy intemperance, in the things which will have excited thy folly, or flattered thy cowardice; remember thou that death will break the frail instruments of thy wrath, will extinguish the firebrands that it will have lighted; remember thou finally,

THAT RICHES AND THE HONOURS EASILY ACQUIRED, ARE EASY THUS TO LOSE

BE just: injustice has often easy triumphs; but what remains after death of the riches that it has procured? Nothing but the bitter remembrance of their loss, and the nakedness of a shameful vice uncovered and reduced to impotency. I have proceeded rapidly in the explanation of the foregoing lines, because the morals which they contain, founded upon the proofs of sentiment, are not susceptible of receiving others. I do not know if this simple reflection has already been made, but in any case it ought to draw with it one more complicated, and serve to find the reason for the surprising harmony which reigns, and which has always reigned, among all the peoples of the earth upon the subject of morals. Man has been allowed to disagree upon subjects of reasoning and opinion, to differ in a thousand ways in those of taste, to dispute upon the forms of cult, the dogmas of teachings, the bases of science, to build an infinity of psychological and physical systems; but Man has never been able, without belying his own conscience, to deny the truth and universality of morals. Temperance, prudence, courage, and justice, have always been considered as virtues, and avarice, folly, cowardice, and injustice, as vices; and this, without the least discussion. Never has any legislator said that it was necessary to be a bad son, a bad friend, a bad citizen, envious, ungrateful, perjured. The men most beset with these vices have always hated them in others, have concealed them at home, and their very hypocrisy has been a new homage rendered to morals.

If certain sectarians, blinded by a false zeal and furthermore systematically ignorant and intolerant, have circulated that the cults differing from theirs lacked morals, or received impure ones, it is because they either misunderstood the true principles of morals, or they calumniated them; principles are the same everywhere; only their application is more or less rigid and their consequences are more or less well applied in accordance with the times, the places, and the men. The Christians extol, and with reason, the purity and the sanctity of their morals; but if it must be told them with frankness they have nothing in their sacred books that cannot be found as forcibly expressed in the sacred books of other nations, and often even, in the opinion of impartial travellers, one has seen it much better practised. For example, the beautiful maxim touching upon the pardon of offences is found complete in the Zend-Avesta. It is written: "O God! greater than all that which is great! if a man provoke you by his thoughts, by his speech, or by his actions, if he humbles himself before you, pardon him; even so, if a man provoke me by his thoughts by his speech or by his actions may I pardon him." [353] One finds in the same book, the precept on charity, such as is practised among the Mussulmans, and that of agriculture placed in the rank of virtues, as among the Chinese. "The King whom you love, what desire you that he shall do, Ormuzd? Do you desire that, like unto you, he shall nourish the poor?" [354] "The purest point of the law is to sow the land. He who sows the grain and does it with purity is as great before me as he who celebrates ten thousand adorations. . . ." [355] "Render the earth fertile, cover it with flowers and with fruits; multiply the springs in the places where there is no grass." [356] This same maxim of the pardon of offences and those which decree to return good for evil, and to do unto others what we would that they should do unto us, is found in many of the Oriental writings. One reads in the distichs of Hafiz this beautiful passage:

Learn of the sea-shell to love thine enemy, and to fill with pearls the hand thrust out to harm thee. Be not less generous than the hard rock; make resplendent with precious stones, the arm which rends thy side. Mark thou yonder tree assailed by a shower of stones; upon those who throw them it lets fall only delicious fruits or perfumed flowers. The voice of all nature calls aloud to us: shall man be the only one refusing to heal the hand which is wounded in striking him? To bless the one who offends him? [357]

The evangelical precept paraphrased by Hafiz is found in substance in a discourse of Lysias; it is clearly expressed by Thales and Pittacus; Kong-Tse taught it in the same words as Jesus; finally one finds in the Arya, written more than three centuries before our era, these lines which seem made expressly to inculcate the maxim and depict the death of the righteous man:

The duty of a good man, even at the moment of his destruction, consists not only in forgiving but even in a desire of benefiting his destroyer; as the Sandal-tree, in the instant of its overthrow sheds perfume on the ax which fells; and he would triumph in repeating the verse of Sadi who represents a return of good for good as a slight reciprocity, but says to the virtuous man, "confer benefits on him who has injured thee." [358]

Interrogate the peoples from the Boreal pole to the extremities of Asia, and ask them what they think of virtue: they will respond to you, as Zeno, that it is all that is good and beautiful; the Scandinavians, disciples of Odin, will show you the Hâvamâl, sublime discourse of their ancient legislator, wherein hospitality, charity, justice, and courage are expressly commended to them [359]: You will know by tradition that the Celts had the sacred verses of their Druids, wherein piety, justice, and valour were celebrated as national virtues [360]; you will see in the books preserved under the name of Hermes [361] that the Egyptians followed the same idea regarding morals as the Indians their ancient preceptors; and these ideas, preserved still in the Dharma-Shastra, [362] will strike you in the Kings of the Chinese. It is there, in those sacred books whose origin is lost in the night of time, [363] that you will find at their source the most sublime maxims of Fo-Hi, Krishna, Thoth, Zoroaster, Pythagoras, Socrates, and Jesus. Morals, I repeat, are everywhere the same; therefore it is not upon its written principles that one should judge of the perfection of the cult, as has been done without reflection, but upon their practical application. This application, whence results the national spirit, depends upon the purity of the religious dogmas upon the sublimity of the mysteries, and upon their more or less great affinity with the Universal Truth which is the soul, apparent or hidden, of all religion.

AS TO THE EVILS WHICH DESTINY INVOLVES

Judge them what they are; endure them all and strive,
As much as thou art able, to modify the traits.
The Gods, to the most cruel, have not exposed the sage.

I have said that Pythagoras acknowledged two motives of human actions, the power of the Will and the necessity of Destiny, and that he subjected both to one fundamental law called Providence from which they emanated alike. The first of these motives was free, and the second constrained: so that man found himself placed between two opposed, but not injurious natures, indifferently good or bad, according as he understood the use of them. The power of the Will was exercised upon the things to be done, or upon the future; the necessity of Destiny, upon the things done, or upon the past: and the one nourished the other unceasingly, by working upon the materials which they reciprocally furnished each other; for according to this admirable philosopher, it is of the past that the future is born, of the future that the past is formed, and of the union of both that is engendered the always existing present, from which they draw alike their origin: a most profound idea that the Stoics had adopted. Thus, following this doctrine, liberty rules in the future, necessity in the past, and Providence over the present. Nothing that exists happens by chance but by the union of the fundamental and providential law with the human will which follows or transgresses it, by operating upon necessity.[364] The harmony of the Will and Providence constitutes Good; Evil is born of their opposition. Man has received three forces adapted to each of the three modifications of his being, to be guided in the course that he should pursue on earth and all three enchained to his Will. The first, attached to the body, is instinct; the second, devoted to the soul, is virtue; the third, appertaining to intelligence, is science or wisdom. These three forces, indifferent in themselves, take this name only through the good usage that the Will makes of it; for, through bad usage they degenerate into brutishness, vice, and ignorance. Instinct perceives the physical good or evil resulting from sensation; virtue recognizes the moral good or evil existing in sentiment; science judges the intelligible good or evil which springs from assent. In sensation, good or evil is called pleasure or pain; in sentiment, love or hate; in assent, truth or error. Sensation, sentiment, and assent, dwelling in the body, in the soul, and in the spirit, form a ternary, which becoming developed under favour of a relative unity constitutes the human quaternary, or Man considered abstractly. The three affections which compose this ternary act and react upon one another, and become mutually enlightened or obscured; and the unity which binds them, that is to say, Man, is perfected or depraved, according as it tends to become blended with the Universal Unity or to become distinguished from it. The means that this ternary has of becoming blended with it, or of becoming distinguished from it, of approaching near or of drawing away from it, resides wholly in its Will, which, through the use that it makes of the instruments furnished it by the body, soul, and mind, becomes instinctive or stupefied; is made virtuous or vicious, wise or ignorant, and places itself in condition to perceive with more or less energy, to understand and to judge with more or less rectitude what there is of goodness, excellence, and justice in sensation, sentiment, or assent; to distinguish, with more or less force and knowledge, good and evil; and not to be deceived at last in what is really pleasure or pain, love or hatred, truth or error.

Indeed one feels that the metaphysical doctrine that I have just briefly set forth is nowhere found so clearly expressed, and therefore I do not need to support it with any direct authority. It is only by adopting the principles set down in the Golden Verses and by meditating a long time upon what has been written by Pythagoras that one is able to conceive the ensemble. The disciples of this philosopher having been extremely discreet and often obscure, one can only well appreciate the opinions of their master by throwing light upon them with those of the Platonists and Stoics, who have adopted and spread them without any reserve. [365]

Man, such as I have just depicted him, according to the idea that Pythagoras has conceived, placed under the dominion of Providence between the past and the future, endowed with a free will by his essence, and being carried along toward virtue or vice with its own movement, Man, I say, should understand the source of the evils that he necessarily experiences; and far from accusing this same Providence which dispenses good and evil to each according to his merit and his anterior actions, can blame only himself if he suffers, through an inevitable consequence of his past mistakes. [366] For Pythagoras admitted many successive existences, [367] and maintained that the present, which strikes us, and the future, which menaces us, are only the expression of the past which has been our work in anterior times. He said that the greater part of men lose, in returning to life, the remembrance of these past existences; but that, concerning himself, he had, by a particular favour of the gods, preserved the memory of them. [368] Thus according to his doctrine, this fatal Necessity, of which man unceasingly complains, has been created by himself through the use of his will; he traverses, in proportion as he advances in time, the road that he has already traced for himself; and according as he has modified it by good or evil, as he sows so to speak, his virtues or his vices, he will find it again more smooth or laborious. when the time will come to traverse it anew.

These are the dogmas by means of which Pythagoras established the necessity of Destiny, without harming the power of the Will, and left to Providence its universal empire, without being obliged either to attribute to it the origin of evil, as those who admitted only one principle of things, or to give to evil an absolute existence, as those who admitted two principles. In this, he was in accordance with the ancient doctrine which was followed by the oracles of the gods. [369] The Pythagoreans, however, did not regard pain, that is to say, whatever afflicts the body in its mortal life, as veritable evils; they called veritable evils only sins, vices, and errors into which one falls voluntarily. In their opinion, the physical and inevitable evils being illustrated by the presence of virtue, could be transformed into blessings and become distinguished and enviable. [370] These last evils, dependent upon necessity, Lysis commended to be judged for what they were; that is, to consider as an inevitable consequence of some mistake, as the chastisement or remedy for some vice; and therefore to endure them, and far from irritating them further by impatience and anger, on the contrary to modify them by the resignation and acquiescence of the will to the judgment of Providence. He does not forbid, as one sees in the lines cited, assuaging them by lawful means; on the contrary, he desires that the sage should apply himself to diverting them if possible, and healing them. Thus this philosopher did not fall into the excess with which the Stoics have been justly reproached. [371] He considered pain evil, not that it was of the same nature as vice, but because its nature, a purgative for vice, makes it a necessary consequence. Plato adopted this idea, and made all the inferences felt with his customary eloquence. [372]

As to what Lysis said, always following Pythagoras, that the sage was never exposed to the cruelest evils, this can be understood as Hierocles has understood it, in a simple and natural manner, or in a more mysterious manner as I stated. It is evident at once, in following the inferences of the principles which have been given, that the sage is not, in reality, subject to the severest evils, since, not aggravating by his emotions those which the necessity of destiny inflict upon him, and bearing them with resignation, he alleviates them; living happy, even in the midst of misfortune, in the firm hope that these evils will no more trouble his days, and certain that the divine blessings which are reserved for virtue, await him in another life. [373] Hierocles, after having revealed this first manner of explaining the verse in question, touches lightly upon the second, in saying that the Will of man can have an influence on Providence, when, acting in a lofty soul, it is assisted by succour from heaven and operates with it. [374] This was a part of the doctrine taught in the mysteries, whose divulgence to the profane was forbidden. According to this doctrine, of which sufficiently strong traces can be recognized in Plato, [375] the Will, exerting itself by faith, was able to subjugate Necessity itself, to command Nature, and to work miracles. It was the principle upon which was founded the magic of the disciples of Zoroaster. [376] Jesus saying parabolically, that by means of faith one could remove mountains, [377] only spoke according to the theosophical traditions known to all the sages. "The uprightness of the heart and faith triumphs over all obstacles," said Kong-Tse [378]; "all men can render themselves equal to the sages and to the heroes whose memory the nations revere," said Meng-Tse; "it is never the power which is lacking, it is the will; provided one desire, one succeeds." [379] These ideas of the Chinese theosophists are found in the writings of the Indians, [380] and even in those of some Europeans who, as I have already observed, had not enough erudition to be imitators. "The greater the will," said Boehme, "the greater the being and the more powerfully inspired." [381] "Will and liberty are the same thing." [382] "It is the source of light, the magic which makes something from nothing." [383]

The Will which goes resolutely forward is faith; it models its own form in spirit and overcomes all things; by it, a soul receives the power of carrying its influence in another soul, and of penetrating its most intimate essences. When it acts with God it can overthrow mountains, break the rocks, confound the plots of the impious, and breathe upon them disorder and dismay; it can effect all prodigies, command the heavens, the sea, and enchain death itself: it subjugates all. Nothing can be named that cannot be commanded in the name of the Eternal. The soul which executes these great things only imitates the prophets and the saints, Moses, Jesus, and the apostles. All the elect have a similar power. Evil disappears before them. Nothing can harm the one in whom God dwells." [384]

It is in departing from this doctrine, taught as I have said in the mysteries, that certain gnostics of the Alexandrian school assert that evils never attended the true sages, if there were found men who might have been so in reality; for Providence, image of divine justice, would never allow the innocent to suffer and be punished. Basil, who was one of those who supported this Platonic opinion, [385] was sharply reprimanded by the orthodox Christians, who treated him as a heretic, quoting to him the example of the martyrs. Basil replied that the martyrs were not entirely innocent, because there is no man exempt from faults; that God punishes in them, either evil desires, actual and secret sins, or sins that the soul had committed in a previous existence; and as they did not fail to oppose him again with the example of Jesus, who, although fully innocent, had, however, suffered the torture of the cross, Basil answered without hesitation that God had been just, in his opinion, and that Jesus, being man, was no more than another exempt from sin.

EVEN AS TRUTH, DOES ERROR HAVE ITS LOVERS

With prudence the Philosopher approves or blames;
If Error triumph, he departs and waits.

IT is sufficiently known that Pythagoras was the first who used the word Philosopher to designate a friend of wisdom. [386] Before him, the word Sophos, sage, was used. It is therefore with intention that I have made it enter into my translation, although it may not be literally in the text. The portrayal that Lysis gives of the philosopher represents everything in moderation and in that just mean, where the celebrated Kong-Tse placed also the perfection of the sage. [387] He commended to him tolerance for the opinions of others, instilling in him that, as truth and error have likewise their followers, one must not be flattered into thinking that one can enlighten all men, nor bring them to accept the same sentiments and to profess the same doctrine. Pythagoras had, following his custom, expressed these same ideas by symbolic phrases: "Exceed not the balance," he had said, stir not the fire with the sword," "all materials are not fitting to make a statue of Mercury." That is to say, avoid all excess; depart not from the golden mean which is the appanage of the philosopher; propagate not your doctrine by violent means; use not the sword in the cause of God and the truth; confide not science to a corrupt soul; or as Jesus forcibly said: "Give not that which is holy unto the dogs, neither cast ye your pearls before swine" [388]; for all men are not equally fitted to receive science, to become models of wisdom, nor to reflect the image of God.

Pythagoras, it must be said, had not always entertained these sentiments. While he was young and while he still burned unconsciously with the fire of passions, he abandoned himself to a blind and vehement zeal. An excess of enthusiasm and of divine love had thrown him into intolerance and perhaps he would have become persecutor, if, like Mohammed, he had had the weapons at hand. An incident opened his eyes. As he had contracted the habit of treating his disciples very severely, and as he generally censured men for their vices with much asperity, it happened one day that a youth, whose mistakes he had publicly exposed and whom he had upbraided with bitterest reproaches, conceived such despair that he killed himself. The philosopher never thought of this evil of which he had been the cause without violent grief; he meditated deeply, and made from this incident reflections which served him the remainder of his life. He realized, as he energetically expressed it, that one must not stir the fire with the sword. One can, in this regard, compare him with Kong-Tse and Socrates. The other theosophists have not always shown the same moderation. Krishna, the most tolerant among them had nevertheless said, abandoning himself to thoughtless enthusiasm: "Wisdom consists in being wholly for Me . . . in freedom from love of self . . . in loosening all bonds of attachment for one's children, wife, and home . . . in rendering to God alone a steadfast cult . . . disdaining and fleeing from the society of men" [389]: words remarkable for the connection that they have with those of Jesus: "If any man come to me and hate not his father, and mother, and wife, and children, and brethren, and sisters, yea, and his own life also, he cannot be my disciple." [390] Zoroaster seemed to authorize persecution, saying in an outburst of indignation: "He who does evil, destroy him; rise up against all those who are cruel. . . . Smite with strength the proud Turanian who afflicts and torments the just." [391] One knows to what pitch of wrath Moses was kindled against the Midianites and the other peoples who resisted him, [392] notwithstanding that he had announced, in a calmer moment, the God of Israel as a God merciful and gracious, long-suffering and abundant in goodness and truth. [393] Mohammed, as passionate as Moses, and strongly resembling the legislator of the Hebrews by his ability and firmness, has fallen into the same excess. He has often depicted, as cruel and inexorable, this same God whom he invokes at the head of all of his writings, as very good, very just, and very clement. [394] This proves how rare a thing it is to remain in the golden mean so commended by Kong-Tse and Pythagoras, how difficult it is for any pupil to resist the lure of the passions to stifle utterly their voice, in order to hear only the voice of the divine inspiration. Reflecting upon the discrepancies of the great men whom I have just cited, one cannot refrain from thinking with Basil, that, in effect, there are no men on earth veritably wise and without sin [395]; above all when one considers that Jesus expressed himself in the same details as Krishna, Zoroaster, and Moses; and that he who had exhorted us in one passage to love our enemies, to do good to those who hate us, and to pray even for those who persecute and calumniate us, [396] menaces with fire from heaven the cities that recognize him not, [397] and elsewhere it is written: "Do not think that I came to send peace upon earth: I came not to send peace, but the sword" [398]; "For there shall be from henceforth five in one house divided: three against two, and two against three. The father shall be divided against the son, and the son against the father, the mother against the daughter, and the daughter against the mother." [399] "He that is not with me, is against me: and he that gathereth not with me, scattereth." [400]

LISTEN, AND IN THINE HEART ENGRAVE MY WORDS

Keep closed both eye and ear 'gainst prejudice;
Of others the example fear; think for thyself.

LYSIS continues, in the name of Pythagoras, to trace for the philosopher the course that he must follow in the first part of his doctrine, which is the Purification. After having commended to him moderation and prudence in all things, having exhorted him to be as slow to censure as to approve, he seeks to put him on guard against prejudices and the routine of example, which are, in reality, the greatest obstacles that are encountered by science and truth. This is what Bacon, the regenerator of philosophy in modern Europe, so keenly felt, as I have already cited with praise at the opening of this work. This excellent observer, to whom we owe our freedom from scholastic leading-strings whose ignorance had stifled for us the name of Aristotle, having formed the difficult enterprise of disencumbering and, as it were, clearing the air belonging to the human understanding, in order to put it in a condition to receive an edifice less barbarous, remarked, that one would never attain to establishing there the foundation of true science, if one did not first labour to set aside prejudices. He displayed all his forces against these formidable enemies of human perfectibility, and if he did not overthrow them all, at least he indicated them in such a manner as to make it easier to recognize and destroy them. The prejudices which obsess the human understanding and which he calls idols, are, according to him, of four kinds: these are the idols of the tribe; the idols of the den; the idols of society; and the idols of theories. The first are inherent in human nature; the second are those of each individual; the third result from the equivocal definitions attached to words; the fourth and the most numerous are those that man receives from his teachers and from the doctrines which are current. [401] The last are the most tenacious and the most difficult to conquer. It seems even impossible wholly to resist them. The man who aspires to the perilous glory of improving the human mind, finds himself placed between two formidable dangers, which, like those of and Charybdis, threaten alternately to break his frail bark: upon one is irresistible routine, upon the other proud innovation. There is danger alike from both sides. He can save himself only by favour of the golden mean, so commended by all the sages and so rarely followed even by them.

This golden mean must needs be very difficult to hold in the course of life, since Kong-Tse himself, who has made it all his study, has lacked it in the most important part of his doctrine, in that concerning human perfectibility. Imbued unknowingly with the prejudices of his nation, he has seen nothing beyond the doctrine of the ancients and has not believed that anything might be added thereunto! [402] Instead of pushing the mind of the Chinese forward toward the goal where nature unceasingly tends, which is the perfection of all things, he has, on the contrary, thrown it backward and, inspiring it with a fanatical respect for works of the past, has prevented it from meditating upon anything great for the future. [403] Filial piety itself, pushed, to excess changed to a blind imitation, has also augmented the evil. So that the greatest people of the world, the richest in principles of all kinds, not daring to draw from these same principles any development, through fear of profaning them, continually on their knees before a sterile antiquity, have remained stationary, whereas all around is progression; and for nearly four thousand years have really not advanced a step more towards the civilization and perfection of the arts and sciences.

The side on which Bacon has departed from the juste milieu has been precisely the opposite from that which prevented Kong-Tse from remaining there. The Chinese theosophist had been led astray by his excessive veneration for antiquity and the English philosopher, by his profound disdain for it. Warned against the doctrine of Aristotle, Bacon has extended his prejudice to everything that came from the ancients. Rejecting in a moment the labour of thirty centuries and the fruit of the meditation of the greatest geniuses, he has wished to admit nothing beyond what experience could confirm in his eyes. [404] Logic to him has seemed useless for the invention of the sciences. [405] He has abandoned the syllogism, as an instrument too gross to penetrate the depths of nature. [406] He has thought that it could be of no avail either in expression of words or in the ideas which flow from it. [407] He has believed the abstract principles deprived of all foundation; and with the same hand with which he fights these false ideas he has fought the results of these principles, in which he has unfortunately found much less resistance. [408] Filled with contempt for the philosophy of the Greeks, he has denied that it had produced anything either useful or good [409]; so that after having banished the natural philosophy of Aristotle, which he called a jumble of dialectic terms, [410] he has seen in the metaphysics of Plato only a dangerous and depraved philosophy, and in the theosophy of Pythagoras only a gross and shocking superstition. [411] Here indeed is a case of returning again to the idea of Basil, and of exclaiming with him, that no man is without sin. Kong-Tse has been unquestionably one of the greatest men who has honoured the earth, and Bacon one of the most judicious philosophers of Europe; both have, however, committed grave mistakes whose effect is more or less felt by posterity: the former, filling the Chinese literati with an exaggerated respect for antiquity, has made of it an immobile and almost inert mass, that Providence, in order to obtain certain necessary movements, has had to strike many times with the terrible scourge of revolutions; the latter, inspiring, on the contrary, a thoughtless contempt for everything that came from the ancients, demanding the proof of their principles, the reason for their dogmas, subjecting all to the light of experience, has broken the scientific body, has deprived it of unity, and has transformed the assemblage of thinkers into a tumultuous anarchy from whose irregular movement has sprung enough violent storms. If Bacon had been able to effect in Europe the same influence that Kong-Tse had effected in China, he would have drawn philosophy into materialism and absolute empiricism. Happily the remedy is born of the evil itself. The lack of unity has taken away all force from the anarchical colossus. Each supposing to be in the right, no one was. A hundred systems raised one upon the other clashed and were broken in turn. Experience, invoked by all parties, has taken all colours and its opposed judgments were self-destructive.

If, after having called attention to the mistakes of these great men, I dared to hazard my opinion upon the point where both of them have failed, I would say that they have confused the principles of the sciences with their developments; it must be so, by drawing the principles from the past, as Kong-Tse; by allowing the developments to act throughout the future, as Bacon. Principles hold to the Necessity of things; they are immutable in themselves; finite, inaccessible to the senses, they are proved by reason: their developments proceed from the power of the Will; these developments are free, indefinite; they affect the senses and are demonstrated by experience. Never is the development of a principle finished in the past, as Kong-Tse believed; never is a principle created in the future, as Bacon imagined. The development of a principle produces another principle, but always in the past; and as soon as this new principle is laid down, it is universal and beyond the reach of experience. Man knows that this principle exists, but he knows not how. If he knew, he would be able to create it at his pleasure; which does not belong to his nature.

Man develops, perfects, or depraves, but he creates nothing. The scientific golden mean commended by Pythagoras, consists therefore, in seizing the principles of the sciences where they are and developing them freely without being constrained or driven by any false ideas. As to that which concerns morals, it is forcibly enough expressed by all that has preceded.

The man who recognizes his dignity, says Hierocles, is incapable of being prejudiced or seduced by anything. [412] Temperance and force are the two incorruptible guardians of the soul: they prevent it from yielding to the allurements of things pleasing and being frightened by the horrors of things dreadful. Death suffered in a good cause is illustrious and glorious.

CONSULT, DELIBERATE, AND FREELY CHOOSE

IN explaining this line from a moral standpoint as Hierocles has done, one readily feels that to deliberate and choose in that which relates to moral conduct, consists in seeking for what is good or evil in an action, and in attaching oneself to it or fleeing from it, without letting oneself be drawn along by the lure of pleasure or the fear of pain. But if one penetrates still deeper into the meaning of this line, it is seen that it proceeds from principles previously laid down regarding the necessity of Destiny and the power of the Will; and that Pythagoras neglected no opportunity for making his disciples feel that, although forced by Destiny to find themselves in such or such a condition, they remained free to weigh the consequences of their action, and to decide themselves upon the part that they ought to take. The following lines are, as it were, the corollary of his counsel.

LET FOOLS ACT AIMLESSLY AND WITHOUT CAUSE, THOU SHOULDST, IN THE PRESENT, CONTEMPLATE THE FUTURE

THAT is to say, thou shouldst consider what will be the results of such or such action and think that these results, dependent upon thy will (while the action remains in suspense and free, while they are yet to be born), will become the domain of Necessity the very instant when the action will be executed, and increasing in the past, once they shall have had birth, will coöperate in forming the plan of a new future.

I beg the reader, interested in these sorts of comparisons, to reflect a moment upon the idea of Pythagoras. He will find here the veritable source of the astrological science of the ancients. Doubtless he is not ignorant of what an extended influence this science exercised already upon the face of the globe. The Egyptians, Chaldeans, Phœnicians, did not separate it from that which regulated the cult of the gods. Their temples were but an abridged image of the Universe, and the tower which served as an observatory was raised at the side of the sacrificial altar. The Peruvians followed, in this respect, the same usages as the Greeks and Romans. [413] Everywhere the grand Pontiff united the science of genethlialogy or astrology with the priesthood, and concealed with care the principles of this science within the precincts of the sanctuary. [414] It was a Secret of State among the Etruscans and at Rome, [415] as it still is in China and Japan. [416] The Brahmans did not confide its elements except to those whom they deemed worthy to be initiated. [417] For one need only lay aside an instant the bandage of prejudice to see that an Universal science, linked throughout to what men recognize as the most holy, can not be the product of folly and stupidity, as has been reiterated a hundred times by a host of moralists. All antiquity is certainly neither foolish nor stupid, and the sciences it cultivated were supported by principles which, for us today, being wholly unknown, have none the less existed. Pythagoras, if we give attention here, revealed to us those of genethlialogy and of all the sciences of divination which relate thereunto.

Let us observe this closely. The future is composed of the past—that is to say, that the route that man traverses in time, and that he modifies by means of the power of his will, he has already traversed and modified; in the same manner, using a practical illustration, that the earth describing its annual orbit around the sun, according to the modern system, traverses the same spaces and sees unfold around it almost the same aspects: so that, following anew a route that he has traced for himself, man would be able not only to recognize the imprints of his steps, but to foresee the objects that he is about to encounter, since he has already seen them, if his memory preserved the image, and if this image was not effaced by the necessary consequence of his nature and the providential laws which rule him. Such is the doctrine of Pythagoras as I have already revealed. [418] It was that of the mysteries and of all the sages of antiquity. Origen, who has opposed it, attributes it to the Egyptians, to the Pythagoreans, and to the disciples of Plato. It was contained in the sacred books of the Chaldeans, cited by Syncellus, under the title of livres géniques. [419] Seneca and Synesius have supported it as wholly in accordance with the spirit of the initiations. [420] What the ancients called the great year, was a consequence of this doctrine; for it was taught in the mysteries, that the Universe itself traversed, after a sequence of incalculable centuries, the same revolutions that it had already traversed, and brought around in the vast unfolding of its concentric spheres, as much for it as for the worlds which compose it, the succession of the four ages, the duration of which, relative to the nature of each being, immense for the Universal Man, is limited in the individual to what is called infancy, youth, manhood, and old age, and is represented on the earth by the fleeting seasons of spring, summer, autumn, and winter. This great year, thus conceived, has been common to all the peoples of the earth. [421] Cicero has plainly seen that it constituted the veritable basis of genethlialogy or the astrological science. [422] Indeed if the future is composed of the past—that is, a thing already made, upon which the present is gradually unfolded as upon the circumference of a circle which has neither beginning nor end, it is evident that one can succeed, up to a certain point, to recognize it, whether by means of remembrance, by examining in the past, the picture of the whole revolution; or by means of prevision carrying the moral sight, more or less far, upon the route through which the Universe is passing. These two methods have grave disadvantages. The first appears even impossible. For what is the duration of the great year? What is the immense period, which, containing the circle of all possible aspects and of all corresponding effects, as Cicero supposes, is able, by observations made and set down in the genethliatic archives, to foresee, at the second revolution, the return of the events which were already linked there and which must be reproduced? [423] Plato exacts, for the perfection of this great year, that the movement of the fixed stars, which constitutes what we call the precession of the equinoxes, should coincide with the particular movement of the celestial bodies, so as to bring back the heavens to the fixed point of its primitive position. [424] The Brahmans carry the greatest duration of this immense period, which they name Kalpa, to 4,320,000,000 of years, and its mean duration, which they name Maha-Youg, to 4,320,000. [425] The Chinese appear to restrict it to 432,000 years, [426] and in this they agree with the Chaldeans; but when one reduces it again to a twelfth of this number, with the Egyptians, that is, to the sole revolution of the fixed stars, which they made, according to Hipparchus, 36,000 years, and which we make no more than 25,867, according to modern calculations, [427] we feel indeed that we would be still very far from having a series of observations capable of making us foresee the return of the same events, and that we could not conceive even, how men could ever attain to its mastery. As to the second method, which consists, as I have said, in carrying forward the moral sight upon the route which one has before him, I have no need to observe that it can be only very conjectural and very uncertain, since it depends upon a faculty which man has never possessed except as a special favour of Providence.

The principle by which it is claimed that the future is only a return of the past, did not therefore suffice to recognize even the plan of it; a second principle is necessary, and this principle, openly announced in the Golden Verses, as we shall see farther on, was that by which it was established that Nature is everywhere alike, and, consequently, that its action, being uniform in the smallest sphere as in the greatest, in the highest as in the lowest, can be inferred from both, and pronounced by analogy. This principle proceeded from the ancient dogma concerning the animation of the Universe, as much in general as in particular: a dogma consecrated among all nations, and following which it was taught that not only the Great All, but the innumerable worlds which are like its members, the heavens and the heaven of heavens, the stars and all the beings who people them even to the plants and metals, are penetrated by the same Soul and moved by the same Spirit. [428] Stanley attributes this dogma to the Chaldeans, [429] Kircher to the Egyptians, [430] and the wise Rabbi Maimonides traces it back to the Sabæans. [431] Saumaise has attributed to them the origin of astrological science, [432] and he is correct in one point. But of what use is it to consider the movement of the heavens and the respective position of the stars belonging to the same sphere as the earth, in order to form the genethliatical theme of the empires of nations, cities, and even of simple individuals, and conclude from the point of departure in the temporal route of existence, the aim of this route and the fortunate or unfortunate events with which they should be sown, if one had not established, primarily, that this route, being only some portion of an existing sphere and already traversed, it belonged thus to the domain of Necessity and could be known; and, secondarily, that the analogical rapport ruling between the sentient sphere that one examined and the intelligible sphere that one could not perceive, authorized drawing inferences from both and even deciding from the general to the particular? For, believing that the stars have an actual and direct influence upon the destiny of peoples and of men, and that they even determine this destiny by their good or evil aspects, is an idea as false as ridiculous, born of the darkness of modern times, and that is not found among the ancients, even among the most ignorant masses. The genethliatical science is supported by principles less absurd. These principles, drawn from the mysteries, were, as I have explained, that the future is a return of the past and that nature is everywhere the same.

It is from the union of these two principles that resulted genethlialogy, or the science by which the point of departure being known in any sphere whatever, they believed they had discovered, by the aspect and direction of the stars, the portion of this sphere which must immediately follow this point. But this union, outside of the enormous difficulty that it presented, still involved in its execution very dangerous consequences. This is why they concealed in the sanctuaries the science which was its object, and made of religion a secret and state affair. The prevision of the future, supposing it possible as the ancients did, is not, in effect, a science that one should abandon to the vulgar, who, being unable to acquire previously the learning necessary, and having but rarely the wisdom which regulates its use, risked debasing it, or making use of it wrongfully. Furthermore, the pontiffs, who were in sole charge, initiated in the great mysteries and possessing the ensemble of the doctrine, knew very well that the future, such even as they could hope to understand it in the perfection of the science, was never aught but a doubtful future, a sort of canvas upon which the power of the Will might exercise itself freely, in such a manner that, although the matter might be determined beforehand, its form was not, and that such an imminent event could be suspended, evaded, or changed by a coöperation of the acts of the will, inaccessible to all prevision. This is what was said with such profoundness by Tiresias, the most famous hierophant of Greece and whom Homer called the only sage, [433] these words so often quoted and so little understood: "Whatever I may see will come to pass, or it will not come to pass" [434]; that is to say, The event that I see is in the necessity of Destiny and it will come to pass, unless it is changed by the power of the Will; in which case it will not come to pass.

THAT WHICH THOU DOST NOT KNOW, PRETEND NOT THAT THOU DOST. INSTRUCT THYSELF: FOR TIME AND PATIENCE FAVOUR ALL

LYSIS has enclosed in these two lines the summary of the doctrine of Pythagoras regarding science: according to this philosopher, all science consists of knowing how to distinguish what one does not know and of desiring to learn that of which one knows nothing. [435] Socrates had adopted this idea, as simple as profound; and Plato has consecrated several of his dialogues to its development. [436]

But the distinction between what one does not know and the desire to learn that of which one is ignorant, is a thing much rarer than one imagines. It is the golden mean of science, as difficult to possess as that of virtue, and without which it is, however, impossible to know oneself. For, without knowledge of oneself, how can one acquire knowledge of others? How judge them if one cannot be one's own judge? Pursue this reasoning. It is evident that one can know only what one has learned from others, or what one has found from oneself: in order to have learned from others, one must have wished to receive lessons; in order to have found, one must have wished to seek; but one cannot reasonably desire to learn or to seek only for what one believes one does not know. If one imposes upon oneself this important point, and if one imagines oneself knowing that of which one is ignorant, one must judge it wholly useless to learn or to seek, and then ignorance is incurable: it is madness to style oneself doctor concerning things that one has neither learned nor sought after, and of which one can consequently have no knowledge. It is Plato who has made this irresistible reasoning, and who has drawn this conclusion: that all the mistakes that man commits come from that sort of ignorance which makes him believe that he knows what he does not know. [437]

From time immemorial this sort of ignorance has been quite considerable; but I believe that it will never again show itself to the extent it did among us some centuries ago. Men hardly free from the mire of barbarism, without being given the time either to acquire or to seek after any true knowledge of antiquity, have offered themselves boldly as its judges and have declared that the great men who have made it illustrious were either ignorant, imposters, fanatics, or fools. Here, I see musicians who seriously assure me that the Greeks were rustics in the way of music; that all that can be said of the wonders effected by this art is idle talk, and that we have not a village fiddler who could not produce as much effect as Orpheus, Terpander, or Timotheus, if he had similar auditors. [438] There, are the critics who tell me with the same phlegmatic air that the Greeks of the time of Homer knew neither how to read nor how to write; that this poet himself, assuming that he really existed, did not know the letters of the alphabet [439]; but that his existence is a fancy, [440] and that the works attributed to him are the crude productions of certain plagiarist rhapsodists. [441] Further on I see, to complete the singularity, a research worker who finds, doubtless to the support of all this, that the first editor of the poems of Homer, the virile legislator of Sparta, Lycurgus in short, was a man ignorant and unlettered, knowing neither how to read nor write [442]: quite an original idea and a comparison wholly bizarre, between the author and the editor of the Iliad! But this is nothing. Here is an archbishop of Thessalonica, who, animated by a righteous indignation, declared that Homer may have been an instrument of the devil, [443] and that one may be damned in reading him. That one shrugs the shoulders at the allegories of this poet, that one finds them not in the least interesting, that one falls asleep even, let all that pass; but to be damned! I have said that Bacon, drawn along unfortunately by that fatal prejudice which makes one judge without understanding, had calumniated the philosophy of the Greeks; his numerous disciples have even surpassed him upon this point. Condillac, the coryphée of modern empiricism, has seen in Plato only delirious metaphysics unworthy of occupying his time, and in Zeno only logic deprived of reasoning and principles. I would that Condillac, so great an amateur of analysis, had endeavoured to analyse the metaphysics of the one and the logic of the other, to prove to me that he understood at least what he found so unworthy of taking up his time; but that was the thing about which he thought the least. Open whatever book you will; if the authors are theologians, they will say to you that Socrates, Pythagoras, Zoroaster, Kong-Tse or Confucius, as they call him, are pagans, [444] whose damnation is, if not certain, at least very probable; they will treat their theosophy with the most profound contempt: if they are physicists, they will assure you that Thales, Leucippus, Heraclitus, Parmenides, Anaxagoras, Empedocles, Aristotle, and the others are miserable dreamers; they will jeer at their systems: if they are astronomers, they will laugh at their astronomy: if they are naturalists, chemists, botanists, they will make jest of their methods, and will take into consideration their credulity, their stupidity, their bad faith, the numerous wonders that they no longer understand in Aristotle and in Pliny. None will take the trouble to prove their assertions; hut, like people blinded by passion and ignorance, they state as fact what is in question, or putting their own ideas in place of those that they do not understand they will create phantoms for the sake of fighting them. Never going back to the principles of anything, stopping only at forms, adopting without examination the commonest notions, they will commit on all sides the same mistake that they have committed with respect to the genethliatical science, the principles of which I have shown in my last Examination; and confounding this science of the ancients with the astrology of the moderns, they will consider in the same light Tiresias and Nostradamus, and will see no difference between the oracle of Ammon, or of Delphi, and the lucky chance of the most paltry fortune-teller.

However, I do not pretend to say that all the modern savants indulge, in this same manner, in presumption and false notions with regard to antiquity; there have been many honourable exceptions among them: even those have been found who, drawn beyond the golden mean, by the necessity of effecting a useful reform or of establishing a new system, have returned there as soon as their passion or their interest have no longer commanded them. Such for example is Bacon, to whom philosophy has owed enough great favours to forget certain incidental prejudices; for I am, furthermore, far from attributing to him the errors of his disciples. Bacon, at the risk of contradicting himself, yielding to the sentiment of truth, although he subjected all to the light of experience, admitted, however, positive and real universals, which, by his method are wholly inexplicable. [445] Forgetting what he had said of Plato in one book, he declared in another: that this philosopher, endowed with a sublime genius, turning his attention upon all nature and contemplating all things from a lofty elevation, had seen very clearly, in his doctrine of ideas, what the veritable objects of science are. [446] Finally recognizing the principles of physics and the ensemble of things as the foremost to be considered, he made astrological science, which he likened to astronomy, depend upon it, in such a manner as to show that he did not confound it with vulgar astrology. This philosopher found that before his time, astronomy, well enough founded upon phenomena, utterly lacked soundness, and that astrology had lost its true principles. To be sure he agreed with astronomy presenting the exterior of celestial phenomena, that is to say, the number, situation, movement, and periods of the stars; but he accused it of lacking in understanding of the physical reasons of these phenomena. He believed that a single theory which contents itself with appearances is a very easy thing, and that one can imagine an infinity of speculations of this sort; also he wished that the science of astronomy might be further advanced.

Instead of revealing the reasons of celestial phenomena [he said], one is occupied only with observations and mathematical demonstrations; for these observations and these demonstrations can indeed furnish certain ingenious hypotheses to settle all that in one's mind, and to make an idea of this assemblage, but not to know precisely how and why all this is actually in nature: they indicate, at the most, the apparent movements, the artificial assemblage, the arbitrary combination of all these phenomena, but not the veritable causes and the reality of things: and as to this subject [he continues], it is with very little judgment that astronomy is ranked among the mathematical sciences; this classification derogates from its dignity. [447]

Regarding astrological science, Bacon wished that it might be regenerated completely by bringing it back to its real principles, that is to say, that one should reject all that the vulgar had added thereto, both narrow and superstitious, preserving only the grand revolutions of the ancients. These ideas, as is quite obvious, are not at all in accord with those that his disciples have adopted since; also the greater part of them refrain from citing similar passages.

NEGLECT NOT THY HEALTH

I had at first the intention of making here some allusion to the manner in which Pythagoras and the ancient sages considered medicine; and I had wished to reveal their principles, quite different from those of the moderns; but I have realized that an object so important requires developments that this work would not allow and I have left them for a time more opportune, and for a work more suitable. Moreover the line of Lysis has no need of explanation; it is clear. This philosopher commends each one to guard his health, to keep it by temperance and moderation, and if it becomes impaired, to put himself in condition of not confiding to another the care of its re-establishment. This precept was sufficiently understood by the ancients for it to have become a sort of proverb.

The Emperor Tiberius, who made it a rule of conduct, said that a man of thirty years or more who called or even consulted a physician was an ignoramus. It is true that Tiberius did not add to the precept the exercise of the temperance that Lysis did not forget to commend in the following lines, also he lived only seventy-eight years, notwithstanding the strength of his constitution promised him a much longer life. Hippocrates of Cos, the father of medicine in Greece and strongly attached to the doctrine of Pythagoras, lived one hundred and four years; Xenophile, Apollonius, Tyanæus, Demonax, and many other Pythagorean philosophers lived to one hundred and six and one-hundred and ten years; and Pythagoras himself, although violently persecuted towards the end of his life, attained to nearly ninety-nine years according to some and even to the century mark according to others. [448]

DISPENSE WITH MODERATION, FOOD TO THE BODY, AND TO THE MIND REPOSE

THE body, being the instrument of the soul, Pythagoras desired that one should take reasonable and necessary care of it in order to hold it always in condition to execute the behests of the soul. He regarded its preservation as a part of the purgative virtue. [449]

TOO MUCH ATTENTION OR TOO LITTLE SHUN; FOR ENVY THUS, TO EITHER EXCESS IS ALIKE ATTACHED

THE philosopher, firm in his principle of juste milieu, wished that his disciples should avoid excess in all things, and that they should not draw attention to themselves by an unusual way of living. It was a widespread opinion among the ancients, that envy, shameful for the one who felt it and dangerous for the one who inspired it, had fatal consequences for both. For envy is attached to all that tends to distinguish men too ostensibly. Thus, notwithstanding all that have been published of the extraordinary rules and severe abstinences that Pythagoras imposed upon his disciples and that he made them observe, it appears indubitable that they were only established after his death, and that his interpreters, being deceived regarding the mysterious meaning of these symbols, take in the literal sense, what he had said in the figurative. The philosopher blamed only the excess, and permitted besides, a moderate usage of all the foods to which men were accustomed. Even the beans, for which his disciples later conceived so much abhorrence, were eaten frequently. [450] He did not forbid absolutely either wine, or meat, or even fish, whatever may have been asserted at different times [451]; though, indeed, those of his disciples who aspired to the highest perfection abstained from them [452]; he represented drunkenness and intemperance only as odious vices that should be avoided. [453] He had no scruples about drinking a little wine himself, and of tasting the meats set before him at table, [454] in order to show that he did not regard them as impure, notwithstanding he preferred the vegetable régime to all others and that, for the most part, he restricted himself to it from choice. [455] Further on I will return to the mystic meaning of the symbols, by which he had the appearance of forbidding the use of certain foods and above all beans.

LUXURY AND AVARICE HAVE SIMILAR RESULTS. ONE MUST CHOOSE IN ALL THINGS A MEAN JUST AND GOOD

LYSIS terminates the purgative part of the doctrine of Pythagoras with the trait which characterizes it in general and in particular; he has shown the golden mean in virtue and in science; he has commended it in conduct, he states in full and says openly that extremes meet; that luxury and avarice differ not in their effects, and that philosophy consists in avoiding excess in everything. Hierocles adds that, to be happy, one must know how, where, when, and how much to take; and that he who is ignorant of these just limits is always unhappy and he proves it as follows:

Voluptuousness [he said] is necessarily the effect of an action: now, if the action is good the voluptuousness remains; if it is evil the voluptuousness passes and is corrupted. When one does a shameful thing with, pleasure, the pleasure passes and the shame remains. When one does an excellent thing with great trouble and labour the pain passes and the excellence alone remains. Whence it follows necessarily, that the evil life is also bitter and produces as much sorrow and chagrin as the good life is sweet and procures joy and contentment.

"As the flame of a torch tends always upward whichever way one turns it," said the Indian sages, "thus the man whose heart is afire with virtue, whatever accident befalls him, directs himself always toward the end that wisdom indicates." [456]

"Misfortune follows vice, and happiness virtue," said the Chinese, "as the echo follows the voice and the shadow him who moves."' [457]

O virtue! divine virtue! [exclaims Kong-Tse [458]] a celestial power presents thee to us, an interior force conducts us toward thee; happy the mortal in whom thou dwellest! he strikes the goal without effort, a single glance suffices for him to penetrate the truth. His heart becomes the sanctuary of peace and his very inclinations protect his innocence. It is granted to the sage only, to attain to so desirable a state. He who aspires to this must resolve upon the good and attach himself strongly to it; he must apply himself to the study of himself, interrogate nature, examine all things carefully, meditate upon them and allow nothing to pass unfathomed. Let him develop the faculties of his soul, let him think with force, let him put energy and firmness into his actions. Alas! how many men there are who seek virtue and science, and who stop in the middle of their course, because the goal keeps them waiting! My studies, they say, leave me with all my ignorance, all my doubts; my efforts, my labours enlarge neither my views nor my sagacity; the same clouds hover over my understanding and obscure it; I feel my forces abandoning me and my will giving way beneath the weight of the obstacle. No matter; guard yourself against discouragement; that which others have been able to attain at the first attempt, you may be able at the hundredth; that which they have done at the hundredth, you will do at the thousandth. [459]

LET NOT SLEEP E'ER CLOSE THY TIRED EYES, WITHOUT THOU ASK THYSELF; WHAT HAVE I OMITTED, AND WHAT DONE?

LYSIS, after having indicated the route by which Pythagoras conducted his disciples to virtue, goes on to teach them the use that this philosopher wished them to make of this celestial gift, once they had mastered it. Up to this point it is confined in the purgative part of the doctrine of his teacher; he now passes to the unitive part, that is to say, to that which has as object the uniting of man to the Divinity, by rendering him more and more like unto the model of all perfection and of all wisdom, which is God. The sole instrument capable of operating this union has been placed at his disposition by means of the good usage that he has made of his will: it is virtue which must serve him at present to attain truth. Now, Truth is the ultimate goal of perfection: there is nothing beyond it and nothing this side of it but error; light springs from it; it is the soul of God, according to Pythagoras, and God himself, according to the legislator of the Indians. [460]

The first precept that Pythagoras gave to his disciples on entering the course of perfection tended to turn their thoughts upon themselves, to bring them to interrogate their actions, their thoughts, their discourse, to question the motives, to reflect in short upon their exterior movements and seek thus to know themselves. Knowledge of self was the most important knowledge of al(, that which must conduct them to all others. I will not weary my readers by adding anything to what I have already said pertaining to the importance of this knowledge, and the extreme value set upon it by the ancients. They know unquestionably that the morals of Socrates and the philosophy of Plato were only the development of it and that an inscription in the temple of Greece, that of Delphi, commended it, after that of the golden mean, as the very teaching of the God whom they worshipped there [461]: Nothing in excess, and know Thyself, contained in few words the doctrine of the sages, and presented for their meditation the principles upon which reposed virtue and wisdom which is its consequence. Nothing further was necessary to electrify the soul of Heraclitus and to develop the germs of genius, which until the moment when he read these two sentences were buried in a cold inertia.

I will not pause therefore to prove the necessity of a knowledge without which all other is but doubt and presumption. I will only examine, in a brief digression, if this knowledge is possible. Plato, as I have said, made the whole edifice of his doctrine rest upon it; he taught, according to Socrates, that ignorance of one's self involves all ignorance, all mistakes, all vices, and all misfortunes; whereas knowledge of one's self, on the contrary, draws all virtue and all goodness [462]: so that it cannot be doubted that this knowledge might be considered possible, since its impossibility merely questioned would render its system null and void. However, as Socrates had said that he knew nothing, in order to distinguish himself from the sophists of his day who pretended to know everything; as Plato had constantly used in his teachings that sort of dialectic which, proceeding toward truth by doubt, consists in defining things for what they are, knowing their essence, distinguishing those which are real from those which are only illusory; and above all as the favourite maxim of these two philosophers had been that it was necessary to renounce all manner of prejudices, not pretending to know that of which one is ignorant, and giving assent only to clear and evident truths; it came to pass that the disciples of these great men, having lost sight of the real spirit of their doctrine, took the means for the end; and imagining that the perfection of wisdom was in the doubt which leads to it, established as fundamental maxim, that the wise man ought neither to affirm nor deny anything; but to hold his assent suspended between the pro and con of each thing. [463] Arcesilaus, who declared himself the chief of this revolution, was a man of vast intellect, endowed with much physical and moral means, an imposing presence, and very eloquent, [464] but imbued with that secret terror which prevents concentrating upon the things that one regards as sacred and forbidden; audacious and almost impious to all outward appearance, he was, in reality, timid and superstitious. [465] Impressed with the inadequacy of his researches to discover the certainty of certain principles, his vanity had persuaded him that this certainty was undiscoverable, since he, Arcesilaus, did not find it; and his superstition acting in accord with his vanity, he finally believed that the ignorance of man is an effect of the will of God; and that, according to the meaning of a passage from Hesiod that he cited unceasingly, the Divinity has spread an impenetrable veil between it and the human understanding. [466] Also he named the effect of this ignorance, Acatalepsy, that is to say incomprehensibility, or impossibility to raise the veil. [467] His disciples in great numbers adopted this incomprehensibility and applied it to all sorts of subjects; now denying, then affirming the same thing; placing a principle, and overthrowing it the next moment;

becoming entangled themselves in captious arguments in order to prove that they knew nothing, and making for themselves the calamitous glory of ignoring good and evil, and of being unable to distinguish virtue from vice. [468] Dismal effect of an early error! Arcesilaus became the convincing proof of what I have repeated touching the golden mean and the similitude of extremes: once having left the path of truth, he became through weakness and through superstition the head of a crowd of audacious atheists, who, after having called in question the principles upon which logic and morals repose, placed there those of religion and overthrew them. Vainly he essayed to arrest the movement of which he had been the cause by establishing two doctrines: the one public, wherein he taught skepticism; the other secret, wherein he maintained dogmatism [469]: the time was no longer favourable for this distinction. All that he gained was to let another usurp the glory and to give his name to the new sect of doubters. It was Pyrrho who had this honour. This man, of a character as firm as impassive, to whom living or dying was a matter of indifference, who preferred nothing to something, whom a precipice opening beneath his feet would be unable to swerve from his path, gathered under his colours all those who made a philosophical profession of doubting everything, of recognizing nowhere the character of truth, and he gave them a sort of doctrine wherein wisdom was placed in the most complete uncertainty, felicity in the most absolute inertia, and genius in the art of stifling all kinds of genius by the accumulation of contradictory reasonings. [470] Pyrrho had much contempt for men, as was obvious from the doctrine which he gave them. He had constantly on his lips this line of Homer: "Even as are the generations of leaves such are those likewise of men." [471]

I pause a moment here, in order that the reader may observe, that although the thought of Hesiod, concerning the veil that the gods had spread between them and men, and which gave rise to Arcesilaus establishing his acatalepsy, had originated in India, [472] it had never had the same results there; and this, because the Brahmans, in teaching that this veil existed and that it even bewildered the vulgar by a series of illusory phenomena, have never said that it was impossible to raise it; because this might have been an attack on the power of the will of man and its perfectibility, to which they put no limit. We shall see further on that such was also the idea of Pythagoras. Let us return to the Skeptics.

The writer to whom we owe a comparative history of the systems of philosophy, written with thought and impartiality, has felt keenly that skepticism ought to be considered under two relations: as skepticism of criticism and reform, necessary to correct the presumption of the human mind and to destroy its prejudices; as skepticism absolute and determined, which confounds in a common proscription both truth and error. [473] The first, of which Socrates gave the example, and which Bacon and Descartes have revived, is a sort of intellectual remedy that Providence prepares for healing one of the most fatal maladies of the human mind, that kind of presumptuous ignorance which makes one believe that he knows that which he does not know: the second, which is only the excess and abuse of the first, is this same remedy transformed into poison by an aberration of the human reason which transports it beyond the circumstances which invoke its action, and employs it to devour itself and to exhaust in their source all the causes which coöperate in the progress of human understanding. [474] Arcesilaus was the first to introduce it into the Academy by exaggerating the maxims of Socrates, and Pyrrho made a special system of destruction in it, under the name of Pyrrhonism. This system, welcomed in Greece, soon infected it with its venom, notwithstanding the vigorous resistance of Zeno the Stoic, whom Providence had raised up to oppose its ravages. [475] Carried to Rome by Carneades, the head of the third academy, it alarmed with its maxims subversive of public morals, Cato the Censor, who confounding it with philosophy conceived for it an implacable hatred. [476] This rigid republican, hearing Carneades speak against justice, denying the existence of virtues, attacking the Divine Providence, and questioning the fundamental verities of religion, held in contempt a science which could bring forth such arguments. [477] He urged the return of the Greek philosophy, so that the Roman youth might not be imbued with its errors; but the evil was done. The destructive germs that Carneades had left, fermented secretly in the heart of the State, developed under the first favourable conditions, increased and produced at last that formidable colossus, which, after taking possession of the public mind, having obscured the most enlightened ideas of good and evil, annihilated religion, and delivered the Republic to disorder, civil wars, and destruction; and raising itself again with the Roman Empire, withering the principles of the life it had received, necessitated the institution of a new cult and thus was exposed to the incursion of foreign errors and the arms of the barbarians. This colossus, victim of its own fury, after having torn and devoured itself was buried beneath the shams that it had heaped up; Ignorance seated upon its débris governed Europe, until Bacon and Descartes came and resuscitating, as much as was possible for them the Socratic skepticism, endeavoured by its means to turn minds toward the research of truth. But they might not have done so well, had they not also awakened certain remnants of Pyrrhonic skepticism, which, being sustained with their passions and their prejudices, soon resulted in bewildering their disciples. This new skepticism, naïve in Montaigne, dogmatic in Hobbes, disguised in Locke, masterly in Bayle, paradoxical but seductive in the greater number of the eighteenth-century writers, hidden now beneath the surface of what is called Experimental philosophy, lures the mind on toward a sort of empirical routine, and unceasingly denying the past, discouraging the future, aims by all kinds of means to retard the progress of the human mind. It is no more even the character of truth; and the proof of this character that the modern skeptics demand ad infinitum, [478] is the demonstration of the very possibility of understanding this character and of proving it: a new subtlety that they have deduced from the unfruitful efforts that certain thinkers have made recently in Germany, to give to the possibility of the knowledge of self, a basis which they have not given.

I will relate in my next Examination, what has hindered these savants from finding this basis. I must, before terminating this one, show to my readers how I believe one can distinguish the two kinds of skepticism of which I have just spoken. A simple question put to a skeptic philosopher will indicate whether he belongs to the school of Socrates or Pyrrho. He must before entering into any discussion reply clearly to this demand: Do you admit of any difference whatever between that which is and that which is not? If the skeptic belongs to the school of Socrates, he will necessarily admit a difference and he will explain it, which will make him recognized at once. If on the contrary, he belongs to that of Pyrrho, he will respond in one of three ways: either that he admits a difference, or that he admits none, or that he does not know whether one exists. If he admits it without explaining it, he is beaten; if he does not admit it, he falls into absurdity; if he pretends not to distinguish it, he becomes foolish and ridiculous.

He is beaten, if he admits a difference between that which is and that which is not; because that difference, admitted, proves the existence of being; the existence of being proves that of the skeptic who replies; and that existence proved, proves all the others, whether one considers them in him, or outside of him, which is the same thing for the moment.

He falls into absurdity, if he does not admit any difference between that which is and that which is not, for then one can prove to him that 1 is equal to 0, and that the part is as great as the whole.

He becomes foolish and ridiculous, if he dares to say that he does not know whether a difference really exists between that which is, and that which is not; for then one asks him what he did at the age of six months, at one year, two years, two weeks ago, yesterday? Whatever he replies, he will become the object of ridicule.

Behold the Pyrrhonian beaten, that is to say, the one who professes to doubt everything; since a single acknowledged difference bringing him irresistibly to a certainty, and since one certainty militates against all the others, there is no further doubt; and since, doubting no further, it is only a question then of knowing what he ought, or ought not to doubt: this is the true character of the skeptic of the Socratic School.

ABSTAIN THOU IF 'TIS EVIL; PERSEVERE IF GOOD

BUT although one may bring the absolute skeptic to agree that a difference between good and evil can indeed exist, as he is forced to agree that one does exist between that which is and that which is not, just as I have demonstrated in my preceding Examination; would he not be right in saying, that to know in general, that good and evil can differ and consequently exist separately, does not prevent confounding them in particular; and that he can doubt that man may be able to make the distinction, until one may have proved to him that not alone their knowledge, but that some sort of knowledge is possible? Assuredly, this is pushing doubt very far. One could dispense with replying to this, since the skeptic already interrogated concerning the difference existing between what is and what is not has been forced to admit it and to acquire thus some sort of knowledge of being; but let us forget this, in order to examine why the savants of Germany have inadequately removed a difficulty which they have imposed upon themselves.

It is Kant, one of the ablest minds that Europe has produced since the extinction of learning, who, resolved to terminate with a single blow the struggle springing up unceasingly between dogmatism and skepticism, has been the first to form the bold project of creating a science which should determine, a priori, the possibility, the principles, and the limits of all knowledge. This science, which he named Critical Philosophy, or method of judgment, [479] he has developed in several works of considerable length and very difficult of comprehension. I do not intend here to make an explanation of this science; for this labour, out of place in these Examinations, would carry me too far. My intention is only to show the point wherein it has given way, and how it has furnished new weapons for the skeptics, in not holding well to the promise that it had made of determining the principle of knowledge. Therefore, I will suppose the doctrine of Kant understood or partially so. Several works, circulated somewhat extensively in France, have unravelled it sufficiently to the savants. [480] I will only say what the authors of these works have been unable to say, and this will be the general result of the impression that the study of this doctrine has made upon me: it is that Kant, who pretends to found all his doctrine upon principles, a priori, abstraction being made of all the underlying notions of experience, and who, rising into an ideal sphere there to consider reason in an absolute way, independent of its effects so as to deduce from it a theory transcendental and purely intelligible, concerning the principle of knowledge, has done precisely the opposite from what he wished to do; for not finding what he sought, he has found what he has not sought, that is to say, the essence of matter. Let the disciples of this philosophy give attention to what I say. I have known several systems of philosophy and I have put considerable force into penetrating them; but I can affirm that there exists not a single one upon the face of the earth, wherein the primitive matter of which the Universe is composed may be characterized by traits as striking as in that of Kant. I believe it impossible either to understand it better or to depict it better. He uses neither figures, nor symbols; he tells what he sees with a candour which would have been appalling to Pythagoras and Plato; for what the Koenigsberg professor advances concerning both the existence and the non-existence of this matter,[481] and of its intuitive reality, and of its phenomenal illusion, and of its essential forms, time and space, and of the labour that the mind exercises upon this equivocal being, which, always being engendered, never, however, exists; all this, taught in the mysteries, was only clearly revealed to the initiate. Listen a moment to what has transpired in India: it is the fundamental axiom of the Vedantic school, the illustrious disciples of Vyasa and of Sankarâchârya, an axiom in accordance with the dogmas of the sacred books.

Matter exists [say these philosophers], but not of an existence such as is imagined by the vulgar; it exists but it has no essence independent of intellectual perceptions; for existence and perceptibility are, in this case, convertible terms. The sage knows that appearances and their exterior sensations are purely illusory and that they would vanish into nothingness, if the Divine energy which alone sustains them was for an instant suspended.[482]

I beg the disciples of Kant to give attention to this passage, and to remember what Plato has said of the same, that, sometimes matter exists and sometimes it does not exist[483]; as Justin the martyr, and Cyril of Alexandria have reproached him for it; and as Plutarch and Chalcidius have strongly remarked it,[484] in seeking to excuse this apparent contradiction.
Let us endeavour now to call attention to the point where Kant is led astray. This point, in the philosophical course that this savant meant to pursue, seemed at first of very slight importance; but the deviation that it

causes, although small and almost imperceptible at the first instant, determines none the less a divergent line, which, turning aside more and more from the right line proportionably as it is prolonged, is found to strike at an enormous distance from the mark where Kant hoped it would arrive. This deviating point—who would have believed it—is found in the misinterpretation and the misapplication of a word All the attention of the reader is required here. What I am about to say, in demonstrating the error of the German philosopher, will serve to supplement all that I have said pertaining to the doctrine of Pythagoras.

Kant, whether through imitation of the ancient philosophers or through the effect of his own learning which had made him desirous of knowing the truth, has considered man under three principal modifications which he calls faculties. In my twelfth Examination I have said that such was the doctrine of Pythagoras. Plato, who followed in everything the metaphysics of this great genius, distinguished in Man as in the Universe, the body, soul, and spirit; and placed, in each of the modifications of the particular or universal unity which constituted them, the analogous faculties which, becoming developed in their turn, gave birth to three new modifications whose productive unity they became [485]; so that each ternary is represented in its development, under the image of the triple Ternary, and formed by its union with the Unity, first the Quaternary and afterwards the Decade. [486] Now the German philosopher, without explaining the principle which led him to consider man under three principal faculties, states them; without saying to what particular modification he attributes them, that is, without foreseeing if these faculties are physical, animistic or intellectual; if they belong to the body, to the soul, or to the mind: a first mistake which leads him to a second of which I am about to speak.

In order to express these three faculties, Kant makes use of three words taken from his own tongue and concerning the meaning of which it is well to fix our attention. He has named the first of these faculties Empfindlich-keit, the second, Verstand, and the third, Vernunft. These three words are excellent; it is only a question of clearly understanding and explaining them.

The word Empfindlichkeit expresses that sort of faculty which consists in collecting from without, feeling from within, and finding good or bad. [487] It has been very well rendered in French by the word sensibilité.

The word Verstand designates that sort of faculty which consists in reaching afar, being carried from a central point to all other points of the circumference to seize them. [488] It has been quite well rendered in French by the word entendement.

The word Vernunft is applied to that sort of faculty, which consists in choosing at a distance, in wishing, in selecting, in electing that which is good. [489] It is expressed by the word raison; but this expresses it very poorly, whatever may be the real meaning given it by Kant.

This philosopher ought to have realized more fully the origin of this word and he should have made a more just application; then his system would have taken another direction and he would have attained his goal. He would have made us see, and he would have seen himself, the reality, namely, intelligence and not reason.

One can easily see that the faculty which Kant designates by the word Empfindlichkeit, sense perception, belongs to the physical part of man; and that which he expresses by the word Verstand, the understanding, resides in his animistic part; but one cannot see at all that what he names Vernunft, and which he continually confounds with reason, may be able in any manner to dominate in his intellectual part. For this, it would be necessary that he should consider it under the relation of the intelligence; which he has not done. It is very true that he has wished to place it constantly in the mind, by representing the three faculties of which man is composed as a sort of hierarchy, of which sense perception occupies the base, understanding the centre, and reason the summit; or as one of his translators said, imagining this hierarchy under the emblem of an empire, of which sense perception constitutes the subjects, understanding the agents or ministers, and reason the sovereign or legislator. [490] I cannot conceive how Kant, by giving the word Vernunft, the meaning of the Latin word ratio, has been able to say that it is the highest degree of the activity of a mind which has the power of all its liberty, and the consciousness of all its strength [491]: there is nothing more false. Reason does not exist in liberty, but on the contrary, in necessity. Its movement, which is geometric, is always forced: it is an inference from the point of departure, and nothing more. Let us examine this carefully. The Latin word ratio, whose meaning Kant has visibly followed, has never translated exactly the Greek word logos, in the sense of word; and if the Greek philosophers have substituted sometimes the logos for nous, or the word for the intelligence, by taking the effect for the cause, it is wrong when the Romans have tried to imitate them, by using ratio, in place of mens, or intelligentia. In this they have proved their ignorance and have disclosed the calamitous ravages that skepticism had already made among them. The word ratio springs from the root ra or rat, which in all the tongues where it has been received, has carried the idea of a ray, a straight line drawn from one point to another. [492] Thus reason, far from being free as Kant has pretended, is what is the most constrained in nature: it is a geometric line, always subject to the point whence it emanates, and forced to strike the point toward which it is directed under penalty of ceasing to be itself; that is to say, of ceasing to be straight. Now, reason not being free in its course, is neither good nor bad in itself; it is always analogous to the principle of which it is the inference. Its nature is to go straight; its perfection is nothing else. One goes straight in every way, in every direction, high, low, to right, to left; one reasons correctly in truth as in error, in vice as in virtue: all depends upon the principle from which one sets out, and upon the manner in which one looks at things. Reason does not give this principle; it is no more master of the end which it goes to attain, than the straight line drawn upon the ground is master of the point toward which it tends. This end and this point are determined beforehand, by the position of the reasoner or by geometry.

> 1 Reason exists alike in the three great human modifications, although its principal seat is in the soul, according to Plato. [493] There is a physical reason acting in the instinct, a moral reason acting in the soul, and an intellectual reason acting in the mind. When a hungry dog brings to his master a piece of game without touching it, he obeys an instinctive reason which makes him sacrifice the pleasure of gratifying his appetite, to the pain of receiving the blow of a stick. When a man dies at his post instead of abandoning it, he follows a moral reason which makes him prefer the glory of dying to the shame of living. When a philosopher admits the immortality of the soul, he listens to an intellectual reason which shows him the impossibility of its annihilation. All this, nevertheless, takes place only so far as the dog, the man, and the philosopher admit the real principles; for if they admitted false principles, their reasons, although equally well deduced, would conduct them to opposed results; and the piece of game would be eaten, the post would be abandoned, and the immortality of the soul would be denied.

One ought to feel now the mistake of Kant in all its extent. This philosopher having confounded one of the principal modifications of man, his intelligence, [494] whose seat is in the soul, with one of his secondary faculties, his reason, finds himself, in raising this reason outside of its place and giving it a dominance that it has not, ousting entirely the spiritual part; so that meditating constantly in the median part of his being, which he believed to be the superior, and descending, he found matter, understood it perfectly, and missed absolutely the spirit. What he assumed was, it was nothing else than the understanding, a neuter faculty placed between sense perception which is purely passive, and the intelligence which is wholly active. He had the weakness to fix his thought here and thenceforth was lost. Reason which he invoked to teach him to distinguish, in his ideas, the part which is furnished by the spirit, from that which is given by objects, was only able to show him the straight line that it described in his understanding. This line being buried in matter instead of rising in intelligible regions, taught him that everything that did not correspond to a possible experience could not furnish him the subject of a positive knowledge, and thus all the great questions upon the existence of God, the immortality of the soul, the origin of the Universe; all that pertains to theosophy, to cosmology; in short, all that which is intelligible, cannot take place in the order of his understanding. [495] This catastrophe, quite inevitable as it was, was none the less poignant. It was odd to see a man who seemed to promise to establish the possibility and the principles of all knowledge upon an incontestable basis, announce coldly that God, the Universe, and the Soul could not be subjects there, and soon discover, pushed by the force of his reasoning, that even the reality of physical subjects by which the senses are affected is only phenomenal, that one can in no way know what they are, but only what they appear to be [496]; and that even one's own Self, considered as a subject, is also for one only a phenomenon, an appearance, concerning the intimate essence of which one can learn nothing. [497] Kant felt indeed the terrible contradiction into which he had fallen; but instead of retracing courageously his steps, and seeking above reason for the principles of knowledge that it did not possess, he continued his descending movement which he called transcendental, and finally discovered beneath this pure Reason, a certain practical Reason, to which he confided the destinies of the greatest subjects with which man can be occupied: God, nature, and himself. This practical reason, which is no other than common sense, ought, according to him, to bring man to believe what is not given him to know, [498] and to engage him, through the need of his own felicity, to follow the paths of virtue, and to admit the system of recompense which proceeds from the existence of God and the immortality of the soul. Thus, this common sense, already invoked to aid the existence of the physical subjects which Berkeley reduced to nothingness, was called, under another name, to sustain that of the spiritual beings which Kant admitted baffling the action of his pure reason; but this faculty, vainly proposed by Shaftesbury, [499] by Hutcheson, [500] by Reid [501] by Oswald, [502] by the celebrated Pascal himself, [503] to give a support to the first truths, and to furnish the principles of our moral and physical knowledge; this faculty, I say, whose seat is in the instinct, has been easily challenged as incompetent to pronounce upon the subjects which are outside the jurisdiction of its judgments; for it has been keenly felt that it was abandoning these subjects to the prejudices of the vulgar, to their erroneous opinions, to their blind passions; and that practical philosophy or common sense, acting in each man according to the extent of his views, would only embarrass relative truths and would create as many principles as individuals. Furthermore was it not to run counter to common sense itself, to submit intelligence and reason to it? Was it not subverting Nature, and, as it were, causing light to spring upward from below, seeking in the particular, the law which rules the Universal?

The skeptics who saw all these things triumphed, but their triumph only proved their weakness; for Reason, by which they demonstrated nothingness, is the sole weapon of which they can make use. This faculty overthrown in Kant, leaves them powerless, and delivers them defenceless to the irresistible axioms that the intelligence places a priori upon the primordial truths and the fundamental principles of the Universe, even as the sequel of these Examinations will demonstrate.

MEDITATE UPON MY COUNSELS, LOVE THEM; FOLLOW THEM: TO THE DIVINE VIRTUES WILL THEY KNOW HOW TO LEAD THEE

I have spoken at considerable length of the skeptics; but I have believed it necessary in explaining a dogmatic work, whose esprit is wholly opposed to that of skepticism. When Lysis wrote in Greece, there had been no one as yet who doubted either the existence of the gods, or that of the Universe, or made the distinction between good and evil, virtue and vice. Arcesilaus and Pyrrho were not born, and the clouds that they raised afterwards concerning these great subjects of the meditation of the sages were not even suspected. The minds had inclined rather toward credulity than toward doubt; toward superstition than toward atheism; it was more necessary to limit their curiosity than to excite their indifference. At that epoch, the philosophers enveloped the truth with veils, and rendered the avenues of science difficult, so that the vulgar might not profane them. They knew what had been too long forgotten: that all kinds of wood are not fitting to make a Mercury. Also their writers were obscure and sententious: in order to dishearten, not those who might be able to doubt, but those who were not in a condition to comprehend.

Today, as the minds are changed, it is of more importance to attract those who are able to receive the truth, than to keep at a distance those who are unable to receive it; the latter, separating themselves, are persuaded that they either possess it or have no need of it. I have given the history of skepticism; I have shown its origin and the sorry effects of its absolute and disordered influence; not in order to bring back the skeptics of the profession, but to endeavour to prevent the men who are still drifting in uncertainty from becoming so. I have essayed to show them by the example of one of the greatest reasoners of Germany, by the example of Kant, that reason alone, with whatever talents it may be accompanied, cannot fail to lead them to nothingness. I have made them see that this faculty so lauded is nothing of itself. I am content with the example of the Koenigsberg professor; but had I not feared prolixities, I would have added the example of Berkeley and that of Spinoza. The varied catastrophes of these three savants form a striking contrast. Kant, following step by step his pure Reason, comes to see that the knowledge of intelligible things is impossible and finds matter; Berkeley, led by the same reason, proves that the existence of matter is illusory, and that all is spirit; Spinoza, drawing irresistible arguments from this same faculty, shows that there exists and can exist only one sole substance and that therefore spirit and matter are but one. And do not think that, armed with reason alone, you can combat separately Spinoza, Berkeley, or Kant: their contradictory systems will clash in vain; they will triumph over you and will push you into the dark and bottomless abyss of skepticism.

Now, how can this be done? I have told you: it is because man is not a simple being. Fix this truth firmly. Man is triple; and it is according as his volitive unity operates in one or the other of his modifications that he is led on to see, in such or such a way. Plato has said it, following Pythagoras, and I say it to you not only following Pythagoras and Plato, but following all the sages and all the theosophists of the world. Plato places in the superior and spiritual modification, composed of the same, that is to say of the indivisible substance of the universe, the hegemonicon, or the intellectual assent; in the inferior and material modification, composed of the other or the diverse, that is to say, of the divisible substance, the physicon, [504] or the physical sense perception; in the median modification or the soul, properly speaking, composed of essence, that is to say, of the most subtle parts of matter elaborated by the spirit, the logicon, [505] or the moral, logical, or reasonable sentiment. One finds in Plutarch the résumé of the doctrine of a philosopher named Sylla, who, admitting, as did Plato, that man is composed of spirit, soul, and body, said that the body drew its origin from the earth, the soul from the moon, and the spirit from the sun. [506] But without disturbing ourselves for the present, with the origin of these three parts, since assuredly the earth, the moon, and the sun, which this philosopher has assigned them for principles, are things very difficult to understand in themselves, let us be content with knowing, as I have already said, that these three great modifications which form the human Quaternary manifest themselves by sensation, sentiment, and assent, and develop the principal faculties of the instinct, the understanding, and the intelligence. The instinct is the seat of common sense; the understanding is that of reason; and the intelligence, that of sagacity or wisdom. Men can never acquire any science, any real knowledge, if the assent is not determined by favour of the intelligence which elects the principle and places it with sagacity; for one can really know or understand only that to which the intelligence has given consent. All the results that the understanding, deprived of intelligence, can procure by means of reason are only opinions, those of these results which are rigorously demonstrated in the manner of the geometricians are identities; common sense transported even into the understanding can give only notions, the certainty of which, however founded it may be upon experience, can never surpass that of physical sensation, whose transient and limited authority is of no weight in the assent of intelligible truths.

Let us venture now to divulge a secret of the mysteries to which Pythagoras made allusion when he said: that not all kinds of wood are fitting to make a Mercury; and notwithstanding the vulgar prejudice which is opposed to this truth, let us affirm that animistic equality among men is a chimera. I feel that here I am about to clash greatly with theological ideas and to put myself in opposition to many brilliant paradoxes that modern philosophers, more virtuous than wise, have raised and sustained with more talent and reason than sagacity; but the force of my subject draws me on and since I am explaining the doctrine of Pythagoras, it is indeed necessary that I should say why Lysis, after having examined and commended in detail all the human virtues in the purgative part of his teachings, begins again a new instruction in the unitive part and promises to lead one to divine virtues. This important distinction that he makes between these two kinds of virtues has been made by Plato, Aristotle, Galen, and many others of the philosophers of antiquity. [507] One of them, Macrobius, to whom we owe the knowledge and explanation of many of the mystic secrets, which, notwithstanding the extreme care exercised to conceal them, were rumoured outside of the sanctuaries, has made a comparison between the degrees of the initiation and those that one admits in the exercise of the virtues; and he enumerates four. [508] This number, which is related to the universal Quaternary, has been the most constantly followed, although it may have varied, however, from three to seven. The number three was regarded by the ancients as the principle of nature, and the number seven as its end. [509] The principal degrees of initiation were, to the number of three, as the grades of the apprentice, companion, and master are in Free Masonry today. From this comes the epithet of Triple, given to the mysterious Hecate, and even to Mithra, considered as the emblem of mystic knowledge. [510] Sometimes three secondary degrees were added to the three principal ones and were terminated by an extraordinary revelation, which raising the initiate to the rank of Epopt, or seer par excellence, gave him the true signification of the degrees through which he had already passed [511]; showed him nature unveiled, [512] and admitted him to the contemplation of divine knowledge. [513] It was for the Epopt alone that the last veil fell, and the sacred vestment which covered the statue of the Goddess was removed. This manifestation, called Epiphany, shed the most brilliant light upon the darkness which until then had surrounded the initiate. It was prepared, said the historians, by frightful tableaux with alternatives of both terror and hope. [514] The grade of Elect has replaced that of Epopt among the Free Masons, without in any sense offering the same results. The forms are indeed nearly preserved; but the substance has disappeared. The Epopt of Eleusis, Samothrace, or Hierapolis was regarded as the foremost of men, the favourite of the gods, and the possessor of celestial treasures; the sun shone, in his sight, with a purer brightness; and the sublime virtue that he had acquired in the tests, more and more difficult, and the lessons more and more lofty, gave him the faculty of discerning good and evil, truth and error, and of making a free choice between them. [515]

But if the various grades of initiation expressed symbolically the different degrees of virtue to which men in general can attain, the tests that one was made to pass through at each new grade, made known in particular, whether the man who presented himself to obtain it, was worthy or unworthy. These tests were at first sufficiently easy; but they became increasingly difficult to such an extent that the life of the new member was frequently in danger. One would know in that way to what sort of man this life belonged, and verify by the crucible of terror and of suffering, the temper of the soul and the claim of his right to the truth. It is known that Pythagoras owed to his extreme patience and to the courage with which he surmounted all the obstacles, his initiation into the Egyptian mysteries. [516] Those who attained as he did the last degree of initiation were very rare; the greater number went no further than the second grade and very few attained the third. Lessons proportionate to their strength and to those of the faculties that had been recognized as dominating in them were given; for this is the essential point in this Examination, one learned in the sanctuaries to divide the mass of humanity into three great classes, dominated by a fourth more elevated, according to the relations that were established between the faculties of men and the parts of the Universe to which they corresponded. In the first were ranged the material or instinctive men; in the second, the animistic, and in the third, the intellectual men. Thus all men were by no means considered as equal among them. The pretended equality which was made on the exterior was mere compliance to the errors of the vulgar, who, having seized the authority in most of the cities of Greece and Italy, forced the truth to conceal an exposure which would have injured it. The Christian cult, raised upon the extinction of all enlightenment, nourished in the hearts of slaves and lowly citizens, sanctified in the course of time a precedent favourable to its growth. Those, however, among the Christians who were called gnostics, [517] on account of the particular knowledge that they possessed, and especially the Valentinians who boasted that they had preserved the knowledge of the initiation, wished to make a public dogma of the secret of the mysteries in this respect, pretending that the corruption of men being only the effect of their ignorance and of their earthly attachment, it was only necessary in order to save them, to enlighten them regarding their condition and their original destination [518]; but the orthodox ones, who felt the danger into which this doctrine was drawing them, condemned the authors as heretics.

This condemnation, which satisfied the pride of the vulgar, did not prevent the small number of sages remaining silent, faithful to the truth. It is only necessary to open one's eyes, and detaching them a moment from Judea, to see that the dogma of inequality among men had served as basis for the civil and religious laws of all the peoples of the earth, from the orient of Asia to the occidental limits of Africa and Europe. Everywhere, four great established divisions under the name of Castes, recalled the four principal degrees of initiation and retraced upon humanity en masse, the Universal Quaternary. Egypt had, in this respect, in very ancient times, given example to Greece [519]; for this Greece, so proud of her liberty, or rather of her turbulent anarchy, had been at first subjected to the common division, even as it is seen in Aristotle and Strabo. [520] The Chaldeans were, relative to the peoples of Assyria, [521] only what the Magi were among the Persians, [522] the Druids among the Gauls, [523] and the Brahmans among the Indians. It is quite well known that this last people, the Brahmans, constitute the foremost and highest of the four castes of which the whole nation is composed. The allegorical origin that religion gives to these castes proves clearly the analogy of which I have spoken. The following is what is found relative to this in one of the Shastras. "At the first creation by Brahma, the Brahmans sprang from his mouth; the Kshatrys issued from his arms; the Vaisyas from his thighs, and the Soudras from his feet." It is said in another of these books containing the cosmogony of the Banians, that the first man, called Pourou, having had four sons named Brahma, Kshetri, Vaisa, and Souderi, God designated them to be chiefs of the four tribes which he himself instituted. [524] The sacred books of the Burmans, which appear anterior to those of the other Indian nations, establish the same division. The Rahans, who fill the sacerdotal offices among these peoples, teach a doctrine conformable to that of the mysteries. They say that inequality among men is a necessary consequence of their past virtues or past vices, and that they are born in a nation more or less enlightened, in a caste, in a family, more or less illustrious, according to their previous conduct. [525] This is very close to the thought of Pythagoras; but no one has expressed it with greater force and clearness than Kong-Tse. I think I have no need to say that these two sages did not copy each other. The assent that they gave to the same idea had its source elsewhere than in sterile imitation.

The Chinese people, from time immemorial, have been divided into four great classes, relative to the rank that men occupy in society, following the functions that they execute therein, [526] very nearly as do the Indians: but this division, that long custom has rendered purely political, is looked upon very differently by the philosophers. Man, according to them, constitutes one of the three productive powers which compose the median trinity of the Universe; for they consider the Universe, or the great All, as the expression of a triple Trinity enveloped and dominated by the primordial Unity: which constitutes for them a decade instead of a Quaternary. This third power called Yin, that is to say, mankind, is subdivided into three principal classes, which by means of the intermediary classes admitted by Kong-Tse, produces the five classes spoken of by this sage.

The first class, the most numerous, comprises [he said] that multitude of men who act only by a sort of imitative instinct, doing today what they did yesterday, in order to recommence tomorrow what they have done today; and who, incapable of discerning in the distance the real and substantial advantages, the interest of highest importance, extract easily a little profit, a base interest in the pettiest things, and have enough adroitness to procure them. These men have an understanding as the others but this understanding goes no further than the senses; they see and hear only through the eyes and the ears of their bodies. Such are the people.

The second class is composed [according to the same sage] of men instructed in the sciences, in letters and in the liberal arts. These men have an object in view in whatever they undertake, and know the different means by which the end can be accomplished; they have not penetrated into the essence of things, but they know them well enough to speak of them with ease and to give lessons to others; whether they speak or whether they act, they can give reason for what they say or what they do, comparing subjects among them and drawing just inferences concerning what is harmful or profitable: these are the artists, the literati, who are occupied with things wherein reasoning must enter. This class can have an influence on customs and even on the government.

The third class [continues Kong-Tse] comprises those who in their speech, in their actions, and in the whole of their conduct, never deviate from what is prescribed by right reason; who do good without any pretension whatsoever; but only because it is good; who never vary, and show themselves the same in adversity as in fortune. These men speak when it is necessary to speak, and are silent when it is necessary to be silent. They are not satisfied with drawing the sciences from the diverse channels destined to transmit them, but go back to the source. These are the philosophers.

Those who never digress from the fixed and immutable rule which they have traced out for themselves, who, with utmost exactness and a constancy always the same, fulfill to the very least, their obligations, who fight their passions, observe themselves unceasingly, and prevent vices from developing; those finally, who speak no word which is not measured and that may not be useful for instruction, and who fear neither trouble nor labour in order to make virtue prosper in themselves and in others, constitute the fourth class, which is that of virtuous men.

The fifth class, finally [adds Kong-Tse], which is the loftiest and sublimest, comprises the extraordinary men, who unite in their persons the qualities of the spirit and heart, perfected by the blessed habit of fulfilling voluntarily and joyfully, what nature and morals impose jointly upon reasonable beings living in society. Imperturbable in their mode of life, like unto the sun and the moon, the heavens and the earth, they never cease their beneficent operations; they act by intelligence and as spirits see without being seen. This class, very few in number, can be called that of the Perfect ones, the Saints. [527]

I have transcribed what has just been read without changing a single word. If the reader has given to this extract the attention that it merits, he will have seen the doctrine of Pythagoras such as I have revealed and the important distinction between Instinct, Reason, and Intelligence such as I have established; he will have seen the dogma of the mysteries concerning the animistic inequality of men, of which I have spoken, and will have easily recognized, in the right reason which constitutes the third class according to the Chinese theosophist, the pure reason which has directed the German philosopher in the establishment of critical philosophy. This right reason, being quite near to human virtues, is still very far from Wisdom which alone leads to Truth. Nevertheless it can reach there, for nothing is impossible for the Will of man, even as I have quite forcibly stated [528]; but it would be necessary for that, to make acquisition of the divine virtues, and in the same manner that one is raised from instinct to understanding by purification, to pass from understanding to intelligence by perfection. Lysis offers the means: it is by knowledge of oneself that he promises to lead one to this desired end; he assures it, he invokes the name of Pythagoras himself:

I SWEAR IT BY THE ONE WHO IN OUR HEARTS ENGRAVED THE SACRED TETRAD, SYMBOL IMMENSE AND PURE, SOURCE OF NATURE AND MODEL OF THE GODS

DRAWN on by my subject, I have forgotten to say that, according to Porphyry, there is lacking in the Golden Verses as given by Hierocles, two lines which ought to be placed immediately before those which open the unitive part of the doctrine of Pythagoras called perfection; these are

Πρῶτα μὲν ἐξ ὕπνοιο μελίφρονος ἐξ ὑπανίσας,
Ἐν μάλα ποιπνευέιν ὅσ᾽ ἐν ἤμαγι ἔργα τελέσσεις.

On the moment of awakening, consider calmly
What are thy duties, and what thou shouldst accomplish.

These lines, which express the general outline of this last part, are remarkable, and one cannot conceive how Hierocles could have overlooked or neglected them. Although, it is true, they add nothing in the literal sense, they say much, however, in the figurative sense; they serve as proof of the division of this poem, which Hierocles himself has adopted without explanation. Lysis indicates quite strongly that he is about to pass on to a new teaching: he calls the attention of the disciple of Pythagoras to the new career which is opened before him, and to the means of traversing it and of attaining to the divine virtues which must crown it. This means is the knowledge of oneself, as I have said. This knowledge, so commended by the ancient sages, so t exalted by them, which must open the avenues of all the others and deliver to them the key of the mysteries of nature and the doors of the Universe; this knowledge, I say, could not be exposed unveiled at the epoch when Pythagoras lived, on account of the secrets that it would of necessity betray. Likewise this philosopher had the habit of proclaiming it under the emblem of the sacred Tetrad or of the Quaternary. This is why Lysis, in invoking the name of his master, designates it on this occasion with the most striking characteristic of his doctrine. "I swear," he said, "by the one who has revealed to our soul the knowledge of the Tetrad, that source of eternal Nature": that is to say, I swear by the one who, teaching our soul to know itself, has put it in condition to know all nature of which it is the abridged image.

In many of my preceding Examinations I have already explained what should be understood by this celebrated Tetrad, and here would perhaps be the time to reveal its constitutive principles; but this revelation would lead me too far. It would be necessary in order to do this, to enter into details of the arithmological doctrine of Pythagoras which, lacking preliminary data, would become fatiguing and unintelligible. The language of Numbers of which this philosopher made use, following the example of the ancient sages, seems today entirely lost. The fragments which have come down to us serve rather to prove its existence than to give any light upon its elements; for those who have composed these fragments wrote in a language that they supposed understood, in the same manner as our modern writers when they employ algebraic terms. It would be ridiculous if one wished before having acquired any notion concerning the value and use of the algebraic signs, to explain a problem contained in these signs. This is, however, what has often been done relative to the language of Numbers. One has pretended, not only to explain it before having learned it, but even to write of it, and has by so doing rendered it the most lamentable thing in the world. The savants seeing it thus travestied have justly scorned it; as their contempt was not unreasonable they have made it reflect, by the same language upon the ancients who have employed it. They have acted in this as in many other things; they themselves creating the stupidity of ancient sciences and saying afterwards: antiquity was stupid.

One day I shall try, if I find the time and the necessary facilities, to give the true elements of the arithmological science of Pythagoras and I will show that this science was for intelligible things what algebra has become among us for physical things; but I shall only do so after having revealed what the true principles of music are; for otherwise I should run the risk of not being understood.

Without perplexing ourselves, therefore, with the constitutive principles of the Pythagorean Quaternary. let us content ourselves with knowing that it was the general emblem of anything moving by itself and manifesting by its facultative modifications; for according to Pythagoras, 1 and 2 represent the hidden principles of things; 3, their faculties, and 4, their proper essence. These four numbers which, united by addition produce the number 10, constituted the Being, as much universal as particular; so that the Quaternary, which is as its virtue, could become the emblem of all beings, since there is none which may not recognize the principles, and which does not manifest itself by faculties more or less perfect, and which may not enjoy an existence universal or relative; but the being to which Pythagoras applied it most commonly was Man. Man, as I have said, manifests himself as does the Universe, under the three principal modifications of body, soul, and spirit. The unknown principles of this first Ternary are what Plato calls the same, and the other, the indivisible and the divisible. The indivisible principle gives the spirit; the divisible the body; and the soul has birth from this last principle elaborated by the first. [529] Such was the doctrine of Pythagoras which was borrowed by Plato. It had been that of the Egyptians, as can be seen in the works which remain to us under the name of Hermes. Synesius, who had been initiated into their mysteries, said particularly, that human souls emanated from two sources: the one luminous, which flows from heaven on high; the other tenebrous, which springs from the earth in the abysmal depths of which it finds its origin. [530] The early Christians, faithful to theosophical tradition, followed the same teaching; they established a great difference between the spirit and the soul. They considered the soul as an issue of the material principle, and in consequence being neither enlightened nor virtuous in itself. The spirit, said Basil, is a gift of God: it is the soul of the soul, as it were; it is united to the soul; it enlightens it, it rescues it from earth and raises it to heaven. [531] Beausobre, who relates these words, observes that this sentiment was common to several Fathers of the primitive church, particularly to Tatian. [532]

I have spoken often of this first Ternary, and even of the triple faculties which are attached to each of its modifications; but as I have done many times, I believe it useful to present here the ensemble, so as to have the opportunity of uniting, under the same viewpoint, the volitive unity, from which results the human Quaternary, in general, and in the particular being, which is man.

The three faculties which, as I have said, distinguish each of the three human modifications are: sense perception for the body, sentiment for the soul, and assent for the spirit. These three faculties develop instinct, understanding, and intelligence, which produce by a common reaction, common sense, reason, and sagacity.

Instinct, placed at the lowest degree of the ontological hierarchy, is absolutely passive; intelligence, raised to the summit, is entirely active, and understanding placed in the centre, is neuter. Sense perception perceives the sensations, sentiment conceives the ideas, assent elects the thoughts; perception, conception, election are modes of acting, of the instinct, the understanding, and the intelligence. The understanding is the seat of all the passions that the instinct feeds continually, excites, and tends to make unruly; and that the intelligence purifies, tempers, and seeks always to put in harmony. The instinct, reacted upon by the understanding, becomes common sense: it perceives notions more or less clearly, following more or less, the influence that it accords to the understanding. The understanding, reacted upon by the intelligence, becomes reason: it conceives of opinions so much the more just, as its passions are the more calm. Reason cannot by its own movement attain to wisdom and find truth, because being placed in the middle of a sphere and forced from there, it describes, from the centre to the circumference, a ray always straight and subordinate to the point of departure; it has against it infinity, that is to say, that truth being one, and residing in a single point of the circumference, it cannot be the subject of reason, only as far as it is known beforehand, and as reason is placed in the direction convenient for its encounter. Intelligence, which can only put reason in this direction by the assent that it gives at the point of departure, would never know this point only by wisdom which is the fruit of inspiration: now, inspiration is the mode of acting of the will, which joining itself to the triple Ternary, as I have just described, constitutes the human ontological Quaternary. It is the will which envelops the primordial Ternary in its unity, and which determines the action of each of its faculties according to its own mode without the will it would have no existence. The three faculties by which the volitive unity is manifested in the triple Ternary, are memory, judgment, and imagination. These three faculties, acting in a homogeneous unity, have neither height nor depth and do not affect one of the modifications of the being, any more than another; they are all wherever the will is, and the will operates freely in the intelligence or in the understanding; in the understanding or in the instinct: where it wills to be there it is; its faculties follow it everywhere. I say that it is wherever it wills to be when the being is wholly developed; for following the course of Nature, it is first in the instinct and only passes into the understanding and into the intelligence successively and in proportion as the animistic and spiritual faculties are developed. But in order that this development may take place, the will must determine it; for without the will there is no movement. Be assured of this. Without the operation of the will, the soul is inert and the spirit sterile. This is the origin of that inequality among men of which I have spoken. When the will does not disengage itself from matter, it constitutes instinctive men; when it is concentrated in the understanding, it produces animistic men; when it acts in the spirit, it creates intellectual men. Its perfect harmony in the primordial Ternary, and its action more or less energetic in the uniformity of their faculties, equally developed, constitute the extraordinary men endowed with sublime genius; but the men of this fourth class which represents the autopsy of the mysteries, [533] are extremely rare. Often it suffices for a powerful will, acting either in the understanding or in the intelligence and concentrating wholly there, to astonish men by the strength of reasoning and outbursts of wisdom, which draws the name of genius without being wholly merited. Recently there has been seen in Germany the most extraordinary reasoning, in Kant, failing in its aim through lack of intelligence; one has seen in the same country the most exalted intelligence, in Boehme, giving way for want of reason. There have been in all times and among all nations men similar to Boehme and to Kant. These men have erred through not knowing themselves; they have erred, through a lack of harmony that they might have been able to acquire, if they had taken the time to perfect themselves; they have erred, but their very error attests the force of their will. A weak will, operating either in the understanding or in the intelligence, makes only sensible men and men of intellect. This same will acting in the instinct produces artful men; and if it is strong and violently concentrated through its original attraction in this corporal faculty, it constitutes men dangerous to society, miscreants, and treacherous brigands.

After having applied the Pythagorean Quaternary to Man, and having shown the intimate composition of this Being, image of the Universe, according to the doctrine of the ancients, I ought perhaps to use all the means in my power, in order to demonstrate with what facility the physical and metaphysical phenomena which result from their combined action can be deduced; but such an undertaking would necessarily draw me into details foreign to these examinations. I must again put off this point as I have put off many others; I will take them up in another work, if the savants and the thinkers to whom I address myself approve the motive which has put the pen in my hand.

BUT BEFORE ALL, THY SOUL TO ITS FAITHFUL DUTY, INVOKE THESE GODS WITH FERVOUR, THEY WHOSE AID, THY WORK BEGUN, ALONE CAN TERMINATE

ALL the cults established upon the face of the earth have made a religious duty of prayer. This alone would prove, if it were necessary, what I have advanced concerning the theosophical dogma of the volitive liberty of man; for if man were not free in his actions, and if an irresistible fatality led him on to misfortune and to crime, what use would be invoking the gods, imploring their assistance, begging them to turn aside from him the evils which must inevitably overwhelm him? If, as Epicurus taught, an impenetrable barrier separated gods and men; if these gods, absorbed in their beatitude and their impassive immortality, were such strangers to the evils of humanity that they neither troubled to alleviate them nor to prevent them, for what purpose then the incense burning at the foot of their altars?

It was, he said, on account of the excellence of their nature that he honoured them thus, and not from any motive of hope or fear, not expecting any good from them and not dreading any evil. [534] What miserable sophism! How could Epicurus say such a thing before having explained clearly and without amphibology, what the origin of good and evil is, so as to prove that the gods indeed do not cooperate either for the augmentation of the one, or the diminution of the other? But Epicurus had never dreamed of giving this explanation. However little he might have considered it, he would have seen that in whatever fashion he had given it, it would have overthrown the doctrine of atoms; for a sole principle, whatever it may be, cannot produce at the same time good and evil. Nevertheless, if he has not explained this origin, and if he has not shown in a peremptory way that we are in a sphere where absolute evil reigns, and that consequently we can have no sort of communication with that wherein good resides, it will remain always evident that if we are not in such a sphere, and if we possess a portion of good, this good must come to us from the sphere wherein absolute good has its source. Now, this sphere is precisely that in which Epicurus places the gods. [535] But, perhaps, a defender of Epicurus will say, the good that we possess comes to us only once from the divine sphere and thenceforth it comes to us no more. This is contrary to the most intimate and most general notion that we have of the Divinity, to that of its immutability upon which Epicurus himself leans most, and from which it results that the gods could never be what they have been, nor do what they have done.

In one word, just as well as in a thousand, any maker of a system is obliged to do one of two things, either to declare himself what the origin is of good and evil, or to admit a priori the theosophical dogma of the liberty of man. Epicurus knew this, and although this dogma might ruin his system completely, he preferred to admit it than expose himself to give an explanation beyond his capability and beyond that of all men. But if man is free, he can be counselled; if he can be counselled, it is evident that he can, even that he must, demand counsel. This is the rational principle of prayer. Now, common sense is the asking for counsel wiser than its own, and sagacity shows in the Gods the source of wisdom.

Epicurus, nevertheless, denied the intervention of divine Providence and pretended that the Gods, absorbed in their supreme felicity, do not mingle in any affair. [536] A single question, simple and naïve, would overthrow this assertion destitute of proofs, and besides, inconsistent with the conduct of Greek philosophy; but I prefer to leave this question to Bayle, who has expended much logic in sustaining this point. This French philosopher, under pretext of making Epicurus dispute with a polytheistic priest, advances against Providence an argument which he believes irresistible, and which is, indeed, one of the most subtle that one could possibly advance. "Are the gods satisfied with their administration or are they dissatisfied? Be mindful," he says, "of my dilemma: if they are satisfied with what comes to pass under their providence, they are pleased with evil; if they are dissatisfied, they are unhappy." [537] The manner in which Bayle throws himself into the midst of the question, without examining the principles of it, denounces him as a skeptic; it is necessary therefore to use against him the weapons that I have given against skepticism; that is, to bring him back abruptly to the principles, by interrogating him before replying to him. It is necessary to ask him, if he admits a difference between that which is and that which is not? He is forced to admit it, as I have said; for in whatever region of himself his will takes refuge, whether it exercises its judgment in the instinct, in the understanding or in the intelligence, you will pursue it in him opposing, in the first case, the axiom of common sense: nothing is made from nothing; in the second, that of reason: that which is, is; in the last, that of sagacity: everything has its opposite and can have only one. Nothing is made from nothing therefore that which is not, can never produce that which is. That which is, is; therefore, that which is not, is not that which is. Everything has its opposite and can have only one; therefore the absolute opposite of that which is, is that which is not. If the skeptic refuses himself the evidence of common sense, of reason and of sagacity united, he lies to his conscience, or he is mad and then one must leave him.

The difference admitted between that which is and that which is not, proceeds therefore against Bayle, or against those who resemble him; ask them if man is a prey to absolute evil, whether physical or moral? They will reply to you, no; for they will feel that if they should respond otherwise, you would prove to them that not having the faculty of making a difference between good and evil, nor of comparing them together, they could never draw from this comparison their strongest argument against Providence. They will, therefore, reply that man is not a prey to absolute evil, but to a very great relative evil; as great as they wish. You, nevertheless continue thus: if man is not a prey to absolute evil, he might be, since it would suffice for this to take away the sum of good which mitigates the evil, and which the difference, previously established between that which is and that which is not, teaches to distinguish. Now, this sum of good, whence comes it? Who dispenses it? Who? If the skeptics are silent, affirm for them that it emanates from the gods themselves and that Providence is the dispenser. Then reply to their dilemma, and say that the gods are content with their administration and that they have reason to be, since by it they procure a sum of good increasing more and more, for the beings which without Providence would never know it; and that their Providence, which has mitigated evil from its origin, mitigates it still and will mitigate it to its end; and if the astonished skeptics object that Providence takes a great deal of time to make what should be made in an instant, reply to them that it is not a question of knowing how nor why it makes things, but only that it makes them; which is proved by the overthrow of their dilemma; and which, after all, is saying with more reason in this circumstance than in any other, that time has nothing to do with the affair, since it is nothing to Providence, although for us it may be much.

And if, continuing to draw inferences from your reasoning, the skeptics say to you that, according to the continual effusion of good which you establish, the sum ought to be daily augmented, whilst that of evil, diminishing in the same proportion, ought at last to disappear wholly, which they cannot believe; reply, that the inferences of a reasoning which confounds theirs are at their disposal; that they can deduce from them as much as they wish; without engaging you, for that matter, to discuss the extent of their view, either in the past, or in the future, because each one has his own; that, besides, you owe it to truth to teach them that the dogma, by means of which you have ruined the laborious structure of their logic, is no other than a theosophical tradition, universally received from one end of the earth to the other, as it is easy to prove to them.

Open the sacred books of the Chinese, the Burmans, Indians, and Persians, you will find there the unequivocal traces of this dogma. Here, it is Providence represented under the traits of a celestial virgin, who, sent by the Supreme Being, furnished arms to combat and to subjugate the genius of evil, and to bring to perfection everything that it had corrupted. [538] There, it is the Universe itself and the Worlds which compose it, which are signalized as the instrument employed by this same Providence to attain this end. [539] Such was the secret doctrine of the mysteries. [540] Good and Evil were represented in the sanctuaries under the emblems of light and darkness: the formidable spectacle of the combat between these two opposed principles was given there to the initiate; and after many scenes of terror, the most obscure night was insensibly succeeded by the purest and most brilliant day. [541] It was exactly this that Zoroaster had publicly taught.

Ormuzd [said this theosophist] knew by his sovereign science that at first he could in no way influence Ahriman; but that afterwards he united with him and that at last he finished by subjugating him and changing him to such a degree that the Universe existed without evil for a duration of centuries. [542] When the end of the world comes [he said in another place] the wickedest of the infernal spirits will be pure, excellent, celestial: yes [he adds], he will become celestial, this liar, this evil doer; he will become holy, celestial, excellent, this cruel one: vice itself, breathing only virtue, will make long offerings of praise to Ormuzd before all the world. [543]

These words are the more remarkable when one considers that the dogma relating to the downfall of the rebellious angel has passed from the cosmogony of the Parsees into that of the Hebrews, and that it is upon this dogma alone, imperfectly interpreted by the vulgar, that the contradictory doctrine of the eternity of evil and the torments that follow it, have been founded. This doctrine, but little understood, has been sharply attacked. [544] Simon, very inappropriately surnamed the Magician, forced St. Peter himself, disputing with him, to acknowledge that the Hebraic writings had said nothing positive on this subject. [545] This is certain. These writings, interpreted as they have been by the Hellenic Jews and given out under the name of Version of the Septuagint, shed no light upon this important point; but it is well to know that these interpreters have designedly concealed this light, in order not to divulge the meaning of their sacred book. If one understood thoroughly the language of Moses, one would see that, far from setting aside the theosophical traditions which he had received in Egypt, this theocratic legislator remained constantly faithful to them. The passage in his Sepher where he speaks of the annihilation of Evil, in the meaning of Zoroaster, is in chapter iii., v. 15, of the part vulgarly called Genesis, as I hope one day to show. [546] But without entering at this time, into the discussion where the real translation of this passage would lead me, let it suffice to say that the early Christians were very far from admitting the eternity of evil; for without speaking of Manes and his numerous followers who shared the opinion of Zoroaster, [547] those who are versed in these sorts of matters know that Origen taught that torments will not be eternal, and that demons, instructed by chastisement, will be converted at last and will obtain their pardon. [548] He was followed in this by a great number of learned men, by the evidence of Beausobre who quotes, on this subject, the example of a philosopher of Edessa, who maintained that after the consummation of the ages, all creatures would become consubstantial with God. [549]

One thing worthy of notice is that Zoroaster, who has made prayer one of the principal dogmas of his religion, has been imitated in this by Mohammed, who, unknowingly, perhaps, has borrowed a great number of things from this ancient legislator of the Parsees. It is presumable that the followers of Manes, having retired to Arabia, were responsible for these borrowings, by the opinions that they circulated there. But, it must be frankly stated, this dogma, quite in its place in the Zend-Avesta, does not appear so consistent in the Koran, for, of what use is it in a cult where the predestination of men, necessitated by the Prescient and All-Powerful Divine, delivers irresistibly the greatest part of them to an eternal damnation, on account of the original stain imprinted upon mankind by the sin of the first man? One cannot be prevented, in reflecting upon this manifest contradiction, from believing that the theosophical tradition pertaining to the free will of man, and the influencing action of Providence operating the progressive augmentation of good and the gradual diminution of evil, announced openly by Zoroaster, must have acted secretly in the mind of the theocratic legislator of Arabia. If it had not been thus, the prayers that he ordered as one of the first and most essential duties of the religion, would have been without object.

According to the doctrine of Pythagoras revealed by Hierocles, two things agree in the efficacy of prayer: the voluntary movement of our soul, and aid from heaven. The first of these things is that which seeks goodness; and the other that which shows it. Prayer is a medium between our quest and the celestial gift. One seeks, one prays in vain, if one adds not prayer to research and research to prayer. Virtue is an emanation from God; it is like a reflected image of the Divinity, the resemblance of which alone constitutes the good and the beautiful. The soul which is attached to this admirable type of all perfection is aroused to prayer by its inclination to virtue, and it augments this inclination by the effusion of the goodness which it receives by means of prayer; so that it does precisely what it demands and demands what it does. [550] Socrates was not far from the doctrine of Pythagoras in this respect; he added only, that prayer exacted much precaution and prudence, lest, without perceiving it, one demand of God great evils, in thinking to ask great blessings.

The sage [he said] knows what he ought to say or do; the fool is ignorant of it; the one implores in prayer, what can be really useful to him; the other desires often things which, being granted him, become for him the source of greatest misfortunes. The prudent man [he adds], however little he may doubt himself, ought to resign himself to Providence who knows better than he, the consequences that things must have.

This is why Socrates cited as a model of sense and reason this prayer of an ancient poet:

Grant us good whether prayed for or unsought by us;
But that which we ask amiss, do thou avert. [551]

The prayer was, as I have said, one of the principal dogmas of the religion of Zoroaster [552]: the Persians also had the greatest confidence therein. Like the Chaldeans, they founded all magical power upon its efficacy. They still possess today certain kinds of prayers for conjuring maladies and driving away demons. These prayers, which they name tavids, are written upon strips of paper and carried after the manner of talismans. [553] It is quite well-known that the modern Jews use them in the same way. In this they imitate, as in innumerable other things, the ancient Egyptians whose secret doctrine Moses has transmitted to them. [554] The early Christians were inclined to theosophical ideas on this subject. Origen explains it clearly in speaking of the virtue attached to certain names invoked by the Egyptian sages and the most enlightened of the magians of Persia. Synesius, the famous Bishop of Ptolemais, initiated into the mysteries, declares that the science, by means of which one linked the intelligible essences to sentient forms, by the invocation of spirits, was neither vain nor criminal, but on the contrary quite innocent and founded upon the nature of things. Pythagoras was accused of magic. Ignorance and weakness of mind have always charged science with this banal accusation. This philosopher, rightly placed in the rank of the ablest physicians of Greece, was, according to his most devoted disciples, neither of the number of the gods, nor even of those of the divine heroes; he was a man whom virtue and wisdom had adorned with a likeness to the gods, by the complete purifying of his understanding which had been effected through contemplation and prayer. This is what Lysis expressed by the following lines:

INSTRUCTED BY THEM, NAUGHT SHALL THEN DECEIVE THEE; OF DIVERSE BEINGS THOU SHALT SOUND THE ESSENCE; AND THOU SHALT KNOW THE PRINCIPLE AND END OF ALL

THAT is to say, that the true disciple of Pythagoras, placed on rapport with the gods through contemplation, arrived at the highest degree of perfection, called in the mysteries, autopsy; saw fall before him the false veil which until then had hidden Truth, and contemplated Nature in its remotest sources. It is necessary, in order to attain to this sublime degree, that the intelligence, penetrated by the divine ray of inspiration, should fill the understanding with a light intense enough to dissipate all the illusions of the senses, to exalt the soul and release it wholly from things material. Thus it was explained by Socrates and Plato. [555] These philosophers and their numerous disciples put no limit to the advantages of autopsy, or theophany, as they sometimes named this highest degree of the telestic science. They believed that the contemplation of God could be carried so far during this same life, that the soul became not only united to this Being of beings, but that it was mingled and blended with it. Plotinus boasted having experienced the joy of this beatific vision four times, according to Porphyry, who himself claimed to have been honoured with it at the age of sixty-eight [556]. The great aim of the mysteries was to teach the initiates the possibility of this union of man with God, and to indicate to them the means. All initiations, all mythological doctrines, tended only to alleviate the soul of the weight of material things, to purify it, so that, desirous of spiritual welfare, and being projected beyond the circle of generations, it could rise to the source of its existence. [557] If one examines carefully the different cults which still dominate upon earth, one will see that they have not been animated by any other spirit. The knowledge of the Being of beings has been offered everywhere as the aim of wisdom; its similitude, as the crown of perfection; and its enjoyment, as the object of all desires and the goal of all efforts. The enumeration of its infinite faculties has varied; but when one has dared fix one's attention upon the unity of its essence, one has always defined it as has Pythagoras: the principle and the end of all things.

The Spirit whence proceed the created beings [say the Brahmans], by which they live after being emanated from it, toward which they aspire, and in which they are finally absorbed, this Spirit is that, to the knowledge of which thou shouldst aspire, the Great Being. [558]—The Universe is one of its forms. [559] —It is the Being of beings: without form, without quality, without passion; immense, incomprehensible, infinite, indivisible, irresistible: no intelligence can conceive of its operations and its will suffices to move all intelligences. [560]—It is the Truth and the Science which never perish. [561]—Its wisdom, its power, and its plan, are as an immense and limitless sea which no being is in condition either to traverse or to fathom. There is no other God than it. The Universe is filled with its immensity. It is the principle of all things without having principles. [562] God is one, [563] eternal, like unto a perfect sphere which has neither beginning nor end. He rules and governs all that exists by a general providence, resultant of fixed and determined principles. Man ought not to seek to penetrate the nature or the essence of this Ineffable Being: such a research is vain and criminal.—

Thus do the Hindu sages express themselves in sundry places. They commend aspiring to the knowledge of the Being of beings, making oneself worthy to be absorbed in its bosom; and forbid, at the same time, seeking to penetrate its nature. I have already said that such was the doctrine of the mysteries. I am about to add an important reflection in order to cast some light upon a doctrine which, at first glance, appears contradictory.

Man, who aspires by the inner movement of his will, to attain to the highest degree of human perfection, and who, by the purification of his understanding, and the acquisition of celestial virtues, puts himself in a state to receive the truth, must observe that the higher he rises in the intelligible sphere, the nearer he approaches to the unfathomable Being whose contemplation must make his happiness, the less he can communicate the knowledge of it to others; for truth, coming to him under intelligible forms more and more universalized, can never be contained in the rational or sentient forms that he might give it. Here is the point where many mystic contemplators have gone astray. As they had never adequately fathomed the triple modification of their being, and as they had not known the intimate composition of the human Quaternary, they were ignorant of the manner in which the transformation of ideas was made, as much in the ascendant progression as in the descendant progression; so that, confusing continually understanding and intelligence, and making no difference between the products of their will according as it acted in one or the other of its modifications, they often showed the opposite of what they intended to show; and instead of the seers that they might, perhaps, have been, they became visionaries. I could give a great many examples of these aberrations; but I will limit myself to a single one, because the man who furnishes it for me, immeasurably great on the side of intelligence, lacked understanding and felt keenly himself, the weakness of his reason. This man, whose audacious gaze has penetrated as far as the divine sanctuary, is a German shoemaker of obscure birth, called Jacob Boehme. The rusticity of his mind, the roughness of his character, and more than all that, the force and the number of his prejudices, render his works almost unintelligible and therefore repel the savants. But when one has the patience and talent necessary to separate the pure gold from its dross and from its alloy, one can find there things which are nowhere else. These things, which present themselves nearly always under the oddest and most absurd forms, have taken them by passing from his intelligence to his instinct, without his reason having had the force to oppose itself. This is how he artlessly expresses this transformation of ideas: "Now that I have raised myself so high, I dare not look back for fear that giddiness may seize me . . . for as long as I ascend, I am convinced of my impulse; but it is not the same when I turn my; head and when I wish to descend; then I am troubled, I am bewildered, it seems to me that I shall fall." [564] And in truth he fell so rapidly that he did not perceive, either the terrible disparity between his ideas and his expressions, nor the manifest contradictions into which his prejudices had drawn him.

These grave disadvantages, which do not strike the vulgar, were perfectly understood and appreciated by the sages. The institutors of the mysteries were not ignorant of them and it is for this that they had imposed the most absolute silence upon the initiates and particularly upon the epopts, to whom they gave their highest teachings. They made them feel readily that intelligible things can only become sentient by being transformed, and that this transformation requires a talent and an authority even, which cannot be the appanage of all men.

I am now at the close of my reflection. The diverse cults established upon earth are but the transformations of ideas; that is to say, particular forms of religion, by means of which a theocratic legislator or theosophic sage renders sentient that which is intelligible, and puts within reach of all men what, without these forms, would have been only within reach of a very small number; now, these transformations can only be effected in three ways, according to the three faculties of the human Ternary; the fourth, which concerns its Quaternary or its relative unity, being impossible. I beg the reader to recall what I have said, touching the intimate composition and movement of this Quaternary, and grant me a little attention.

The aim of all the cults being to conduct to the knowledge of the Divinity, they differ only by the route that they travel in its attainment, and this route depends always upon the manner in which the Divinity has been considered by the founder of the cult. If this founder has considered it in his intelligence, he has seen the Divinity in its universal modifications, and, therefore, triple, as the Universe; if he has considered it in his understanding, he has seen it in its creative principles, and, therefore, double as Nature; if he has considered it in his instinct, he has seen it in its faculties and its attributes, and, therefore, infinite, as Matter; if he has considered it, finally, in its proper volitive unity, acting at once in its three modifications, he has seen this same Divinity according to the force and movement of his thought, either in its absolute essence or in its universal essence; that is, One in its cause, or One in its effects. Examine closely what I have said and see if there exists a single cult upon the face of the earth that you may not connect with one of the kinds whose origin I have indicated.

I have said that the Divinity, considered in the human intelligence, is shown under the emblem of the universal Ternary; hence all the cults which are dominated by three principal gods as in India. [565] in Greece and in Italy, [566] three principal modifications in the same God, as in China, [567] in Japan, in Tibet and among the considerable followers of Fo-Hi or Buddha. [568] This cult, which has been called that of the Tritheists, is one of the most widespread on earth, and one which has mingled most easily with the others. It pleases the imagination and gives to wisdom great power to rise to intelligible truths.

I have said that the Divinity, considered in the human understanding, is manifest under the emblem of two natural principles: hence, all the cults wherein two opposed beings appear, as in the cult of Zoroaster. This cult, which is rarely encountered as pure as among the ancient Persians, or among the followers of Manes, mingles readily with tritheism and even polytheism: it was quite recognizable in Egypt and among the Scandinavians, and much more involved among the Indians, Greeks, and Latins. This cult could be considered as a natural Diarchy, and those who follow it,

Diarchists. Judgment and reason conform very well in it; one also sees ordinarily, profound reasoners and skeptics, inclining there nolens volens. [569] Its abuse leads to atheism; but it offers great means, when one knows how to make good use of it, to penetrate the essence of things and succeed to the explanation of natural phenomena.

Again I say, that the Divinity considered in the instinct is presented under the emblem of material infinity: hence, all cults where, by a contrary movement, the intelligible becomes sentient and the sentient intelligible; as when the attributes and faculties of the Divinity are particularized and personified, and as the agents of Nature, the parts of the Universe and the individual beings themselves, are deified. This cult, to which I have given the name of Polytheism, is everywhere, under different forms and under different names, the portion of the vulgar. More or less apparent it insinuates itself in the midst of the other two, multiplies the images of the intellectual modifications and the natural principles, and whatever attentions the theosophists bring to forestall its invasion, end by stifling utterly the spirit of it beneath the material covering which envelops them. This cult, the cradle of all religions, with which the other two can never entirely dispense, which nourishes and lives in their life, is also the tomb. It pleases singularly that faculty of man which is developed first, sense perception; it aids the development of instinct and can, by the sole medium of common sense, lead to the knowledge of the natural principles. Its abuse precipitates people into idolatry and superstition; its good use arouses the talents and gives birth to heroic virtues. One becomes artist or hero through the exaltation of Polytheism; savant or philosopher through that of Diarchy; and sage or theosophist through that of Tritheism. These three cults, whether pure or variously mixed, are the only ones in which transformation may be possible; that is to say, which may be clothed in ostensible forms and enclosed in any sort of ritual. The fourth cult, which is founded upon the absolute unity of God, is not transformable. This is the reason.

The Divinity considered in the volitive unity of man, acting at the same time in its principal faculties, is manifested finally, in its absolute essence, or in its universal essence; One in its cause, or One in its effects: thence, not only all public cults, but all secret mysteries, all doctrines mystic and contemplative; for how can that which has no likeness to anything be represented? How render sentient that which is beyond all intelligence? What expressions will be consistent with that which is inexpressible, with that which is more ineffable than silence itself? What temples will one raise to that which is incomprehensible, inaccessible, unfathomable? The theosophists and sages have realized these difficulties; they have seen that it was necessary to suppress all discourse, to set aside all simulacra: to renounce all enclosures, to annihilate finally all sentient objects or to be exposed to give false ideas of the absolute essence of a Being that neither time nor space can contain. Many have dared the undertaking. One knows, in delving into ages long since past, that the ancient Magians of Persia erected no temple and set up no statue. [570] The Druids acted in the same manner. [571] The former invoked the Principle of all things upon the summits of mountains; the latter, in the depths of the forests. Both deemed it unworthy of the divine Majesty to enclose it within precincts and to represent it by a material image. [572] It even appears that the early Romans shared this opinion. [573] But this cult, entirely intellectual and destitute of forms, could not subsist long. Perceptible objects were needed by the people, on which they might place their ideas. These objects, even in spite of the legislator who sought to proscribe them, insinuated themselves. [574] Images, statues, temples were multiplied notwithstanding the laws which prohibited them. At that time if the cult did not undergo a salutary reform, it was changed, either into a gross anthropomorphism, or into an absolute materialism: that is to say, that a man of the people being unable to rise to the divine Unity, drew it down to his level; and the savant, being unable to comprehend it and believing nevertheless to grasp it, confused it with Nature.

It was to evade this inevitable catastrophe that the sages and theosophists had, as I have said, made a mystery of the Unity of God, and had concealed it in the inmost recesses of the sanctuaries. It was only after many trials, and not until the initiate was judged worthy to be admitted to the sublime degree of autopsy, that the last veil was lifted to his gaze, and the principle and end of all things, the Being of beings, in all its unfathomable Unity, was delivered to his contemplation. [575]

IF HEAVEN WILLS IT, THOU SHALT KNOW THAT NATURE, ALIKE IN EVERYTHING, IS THE SAME IN EVERY PLACE

I have already said that the homogeneity of Nature was, with the unity of God, one of the greatest secrets of the mysteries. Pythagoras founded this homogeneity upon the unity of the spirit by which it is penetrated and from which, according to him, all our souls draw their origin. This dogma which he had received from the Chaldeans and from the priests of Egypt was admitted by all the sages of antiquity, as is proved at great length by Stanley and the astute Beausobre. [576] These sages established a harmony, a perfect analogy between heaven and earth, the intelligible and the sentient, the indivisible substance and the divisible substance; in such a manner that that which took place in one of the regions of the Universe or of the modifications of the primordial Ternary was the exact image of that which took place in the other. This idea is found very forcibly revealed by the ancient Thoth, called Hermes Trismegistus, [577] by the Greeks, in the table of Emerald which is attributed to him.

In truth, and without fiction, in truth, in truth, I say to you, that things inferior are like unto the superior; both unite their invincible forces to produce one sole thing, the most marvellous of all, and as all things are emanated by the will of one unique God, thus all things whatsoever must be engendered by this sole thing,—by a disposition of Universal nature. [578]

I must say, however, that it is upon the homogeneity of Nature that were founded in the principle all the so-called occult sciences of which the principal four, relating to the human Quaternary, were Theurgy, Astrology, Magic, and Chemistry. [579] I have already spoken of the astrological science, and I have given sufficient evidence of what I think regarding the ridiculous and petty ideas concerning it that the moderns have conceived. I will refrain from speaking of the other three, on account of the prolixities into which the discussions that they would provoke might lure me. In another work I will endeavour to show that the principles upon which they were supported differed greatly from those which superstition and blind credulity have given them in times of ignorance; and that the sciences taught to the initiates in the ancient sanctuaries, under the names of Theurgy, Magic, or Chemistry, differed much from what the vulgar have understood in later times by the same words.

SO THAT, AS TO THY TRUE RIGHTS ENLIGHTENED, THINE HEART SHALL NO MORE FEED ON VAIN DESIRES

THAT is to say, that the disciple of Pythagoras, having attained through knowledge of himself to that of truth, ought to judge sanely of the possibility or impossibility of things, and to find in wisdom itself that just mean which he has found in virtue and in science. Equally distant from that blind credulity which admits and seeks without reflection the things most incompatible with the laws of Nature, and from that presumptuous ignorance which rejects and denies without examination all those things which issue from the narrow circle of its empirical notions; he should understand with exactness the limits and the forces of Nature, know instantly what is contained therein or what exceeds them, and not form any vow, any project, or any enterprise beyond his power.

THOU SHALT SEE THAT THE EVILS WHICH DEVOUR MEN ARE OF THEIR CHOICE THE FRUIT

UNDOUBTEDLY one of the most important things for man to understand is the nearest cause of his evils, so that, ceasing from murmuring against Providence, he may blame only himself for the misfortunes of which he is the proper artisan. Ignorance, always weak and presumptuous, concealing its own mistakes, holds responsible, with their consequences, the things which are most foreign there: thus the child which hurts itself, threatens with his voice and strikes with his hand the wall against which he has stumbled. Of all errors this is the most common. Likewise he acknowledges with as much difficulty his own wrongs as he accuses with ease those of others. This baleful habit of imputing to Providence the evils which afflict humanity has furnished, as we have seen, the strongest arguments to the skeptics to attack its influence, and to undermine thus in its foundation the very existence of the Divinity. All peoples have been guilty of this; but the moderns are, as I believe, the only ones who coldly and without passion, in order to sustain certain opinions that they have embraced, have raised systematically their ignorance concerning the cause of evil, and made an irresistible fatality proceed from the All-Powerful and divine Prescience, which drawing man on to vice and misfortune, damns him by force; and by a consequence determined by the will of God, delivers him to eternal sufferings. [580] Such were those among the Christians of the fifth century, who were named Predestinarians on account of their terrible system. Their opinion, it is true, was condemned by the councils of Arles and Lyon [581]; but they declared that the church fell into inconsistency, since the sentiment in this respect, being exactly conformable with that which Saint Augustine had advanced against the Pelagians, this church could not condemn the one without condemning the other and therefore, without deciding in favour of the opposed doctrine which they had already condemned. It is certain that the Predestinarians were right on this last point, as well as Gotescalc, Baius, and Jansenius, who, with the book of Saint Augustine in hand, proved it later on, by causing in this church, at different times, troubles more or less violent on the subject.

This is the moment to complete the proofs of what I advanced in my Seventh Examination, that the liberty of man can be established only by the sole theosophical tradition, and the assent that all the sages of the earth have given to it; and that there is no doctrine, which, becoming separated, does not abandon the Universe to the irresistible impulse of an absolute fatality. I have shown sufficiently the emptiness of all the cosmogonical systems, whether their authors have founded them upon a sole principle or upon two, upon spirit or upon matter; I have sufficiently indicated the danger that would have ensued from divulging the secret dogma of divine Unity, since this disclosure drew with it the necessity of explaining the origin of Good and Evil, which was impossible; I have cited the example of Moses, and I have demonstrated as a decisive point in this matter that those of his followers who rejected the oral tradition of this great man, to attach themselves to the literal meaning only of his Sepher, fell into fatalism and were led to make God himself the author of Evil; finally I have announced that Christianity and Islamism, issuing alike from the Mosaic doctrine, have not been able to evade the dogma of predestination: this dogma, although often repulsed by the Christian and Mussulman doctors, alarmed at its consequences, is shown, none the less, from the facts. The Koran which teaches it openly exempts me from other proofs in defence of the Mussulmans. Let us turn to the Christians.

It is certain that one of the greatest men of the primitive church, Origen, perceiving to what consequences the explanation of the origin of Evil led, by the way in which it was vulgarly understood, according to the literal translation of the Sepher of Moses, undertook to bring all back to allegory, recalling Christianity being born to the theosophical tradition pertaining to the free will of man [582]; but his books, wherein he exposed this tradition according to the doctrine of Pythagoras and Plato, [583] were burned as heretical, by the order of Pope Gelasius. [584] The church at that time paid little attention to the blow dealt by Origen, occupied as it was with examining the principal dogmas of incarnation, of the divinity of Jesus, of the consubstantiality of the Word, of the Unity of its person and the duality of its nature; but when, following the energetic expression of Plucquet, the flame of conflagration had passed over all these opinions, and when the waves of blood had drenched the ashes, it was necessary to offer new food for its activity. An English monk named Pelagius, [585] born with an ardent and impetuous mind, was the foremost to attack this thorny question of the liberty of man, and, wishing to establish it, was led to deny original sin.

Man [he said] is free to do good or evil: he who tries to lay the blame of his vices on the weakness of nature, is unjust: for what is sin, in general? Is it a thing that one may evade, or not? If one cannot evade it, there is no evil in committing it and then it does not exist: if one can evade it, it must be evil to commit it and therefore it exists: its very existence is born of the free will, and proves it. [586] The dogma of original sin [continued Pelagius] is absurd and unjust to God; for a creature which does not exist would not be an accomplice of a bad action; and it outrages divine justice, to say that God punishes him as guilty of this action. [587] Man [added Pelagius] has therefore a real power of doing good and evil, and he is free in these two respects. But the liberty of doing a thing supposes necessarily the union of all causes and of all conditions requisite for doing that thing; and one is not free regarding an effect, every time that one of the causes or conditions naturally exigent for producing this effect is lacking. Therefore, to have the liberty of seeing the subjects, it is necessary not only that the sense of sight be well developed, but also that the subjects be discriminated, and placed at an equitable distance. [588]

This far, the doctrine of Pelagius was wholly similar to that of Pythagoras, as explained by Hierocles [589]; but it differs from it afterwards, in what the English monk asserted, that since man is born with the liberty of doing good and evil, he receives from nature and unites in him all the conditions and all the causes naturally necessary for good and evil; which robs him of his most beautiful prerogative,—perfectibility; whereas Pythagoras held, on the contrary, that these causes and these effects were only accorded to those who, on their part, concurred in acquiring them, and who, by the work that they have done for themselves in seeking to know themselves, have succeeded in possessing them more and more perfectly.

However mitigated the doctrine of Pelagius might be, it appeared still to accord too much with free will and was condemned by the ecclesiastical authorities, who declared, through the medium of several councils, that man can do nothing of himself without the aid of grace. Saint Augustine, who had been the soul of these councils, pressed by the disciple of Pelagius to explain the nature of this grace and to say how God accorded it to one man rather than to another without being induced by the difference of their merits, replied that man being in the masse de perdition, and God having no need of them, and being furthermore independent and all-powerful, he gave grace to whom he willed, without the one to whom he did not give it having the right to complain; everything coming to pass as a result of his will, which had foreseen all and determined all. [590] Assuredly one could not establish more forcibly the necessity of all things, nor submit men to a sterner fatality, since the want of grace deprived them, not only of virtue in the fleeting course of this life, but delivered them without hope to the torments of an eternal hell. But Saint Augustine, who obeyed a severe and consistent reason, felt very well that he could not speak otherwise, without renouncing the dogma of original sin and overthrowing the foundation of Christianity. All the rigid Christians, all those who, at different times, have undertaken to restore Christianity to its constitutive principles, have thought as Saint Augustine, and although the church, alarmed at the terrible inferences that were drawn from the canonical doctrine, may have essayed to temper it, by condemning, as I have said, the Predestinarians and by approving of the persecutions directed against Gotescalc; and, at the time when Luther drew in his reform a great part of Christendom toward the dogma of predestination, this did not prevent Baius, who remained faithful to orthodoxy, from preaching the same dogma; nor Calvin, soon after, from adding new lights to what Luther had left doubtful, and Jansenius, finally, corroborating what Baius had only outlined, from raising in the very midst of the church that formidable faction which all the united efforts of the Pope and the Jesuits have been unable to convict of erring in the doctrine of Saint Augustine, which it has sustained with a force worthy of a better cause.

According to Calvin, who of all of them expresses himself most clearly, the soul of man, all of whose faculties are infected with sin, lacks force to resist the temptation which lures him on toward evil. The liberty of which he prides himself is a chimera; he confounds the free with the voluntary, and believes that he chooses freely because there is no constraint, and that he wills to do the evil that he does. [591] Thus following the doctrine of this reformer, man, dominated by his vicious passions, can produce of himself only wicked actions; and it is to draw him from this state of corruption and impotence that it was necessary that God should send his son upon earth to redeem him and to atone for him; so that it is from the absence of liberty in man that Calvin draws his strongest proofs of the coming of Christ: "For," he said, "if man had been free, and if he had been able to save himself, it would not have been needful that God should offer up his Son in sacrifice." [592]

This last argument seems irresistible. Besides when the Jesuits had accused Calvin and his followers of making God the author of sin, and of destroying thus all idea of the Divinity [593] they knew better than to say how it can be otherwise accomplished. They would not have been able, without doing a thing impossible for them—that is, without giving the origin of evil. The difficulty of this explanation, which Moses, even as I have said, has enveloped with a triple veil, has in no wise escaped the fathers of the primitive church. They have well felt that it was the important point whereon depended the solution of all other questions. But how can one attempt even the explanation? The most enlightened among them had agreed that it is an abyss of nature that one would not know how to fathom. [594]

THAT THESE UNFORTUNATES SEEK AFAR THE GOODNESS WHOSE SOURCE WITHIN THEY BEAR

THE source of all goodness is wisdom, and wisdom begins with the knowledge of oneself. Without this knowledge, one aspires in vain to real goodness. But how is it obtainable? If you interrogate Plato upon this important point, he will respond to you, that it is in going back to the essence of things—that is to say, in considering that which constitutes man in himself. "A workman, you will say to this philosopher, is not the same thing as the instrument which he uses; the one who plays the lyre differs from the lyre upon which he plays. You will readily agree to this, and the philosopher, pursuing his reasoning, will add: And the eyes with which this musician reads his music, and the hands with which he holds his lyre, are they not also instruments? Can you deny, if the eyes, if the hands are instruments, that the whole body may likewise be an instrument, different from the being who makes use of it and who commands?" Unquestionably no, and you will comprehend sufficiently that this being, by which man is really man, is the soul, the knowledge of which you ought to seek. "For, "Plato will also tell you, "he who knows his body, only knows that it is his, and is not himself. To know his body as a physician or as a sculptor, is an art, to know his soul, as a sage, is a science and the greatest of all sciences."

From the knowledge of himself man passes to that of God; and it is in fixing this model of all perfection that he succeeds in delivering himself from the evils which he has attracted by his own choice. [595] His deliverance depends, according to Pythagoras, upon virtue and upon truth. The virtue, that he acquires by purification, tempers and directs the passions; the truth, which he attains by his union with the Being of beings, dissipates the darkness with which his intelligence is obsessed; and both of them, acting jointly in him, give him the divine form, according as he is disposed to receive it, and guide him to supreme felicity. But how difficult to obtain this desired goal!

FOR FEW KNOW HAPPINESS: PLAYTHINGS OF THE PASSIONS

> Hither, thither tossed by adverse waves,
> Upon a shoreless sea, they blinded roll,
> Unable to resist or to the tempest yield.

LYSIS shows in these lines what are the greatest obstacles to the happiness of man. They are the passions: not the passions in themselves, but the evil effects that they produce by the disordered movement that the understanding allows them to take. It is to this that the attention must be directed so that one should not fall into the error of the Stoics. Pythagoras, as I have said, did not command his disciples to destroy their passions, but to moderate their ardour, and to guide them well. "The passions," said this philosopher, "are given to be aids to reason; it is necessary that they be its servants and not its masters." This is a truth that the Platonists and even the Peripatetics have recognized, by the evidence of Hierocles. [596] Thus Pythagoras regarded the passions as instruments of which the understanding makes use in raising the intellectual edifice. A man utterly deprived of them would resemble a mass inert and immovable in the course of life; it is true that he might be able not to become depraved, but then he could not enjoy his noblest advantage, which is perfectibility. Reason is established in the understanding to hold sway over the passions; it must command them with absolute sovereignty, and make them tend towards the end that wisdom indicates. If it should not recognize the laws that intelligence gives it, and if, presumptuously, it wishes, instead of acting according to given principles, to lay down principles itself, it falls into excess, and makes man superstitious or skeptic, fanatic or atheist; if, on the contrary, it receives laws from the passions that it ought to rule, and if weak it allows itself to be subjugated by them, it falls into error and renders man stupid or mad, brutish in vice, or audacious in crime. There are no true reasonings except those admitted by wisdom; the false reasonings must be considered as the cries of an insensate soul, given over to the movements of an anarchical reason which the passions confuse and blind. [597]

Pythagoras considered man as holding the mean between things intellectual and sentient, the lowest of the superior beings and the highest of the inferior, free to move either toward the heights or the depths, by means of his passions, which bring into action the ascending or descending movement that his will possesses with potentiality; sometimes being united with the immortals and, through his return to virtue, recovering the lot which is his own, and other times plunging again into mortal kind and through transgression of the divine laws finding himself fallen from his dignity! [598] This opinion, which had been that of all the sages who had preceded Pythagoras, has been that of all the sages who have followed him, even of those among the Christian theosophists whose religious prejudices have removed them farthest from his doctrine. I shall not stop to give the proofs of its antiquity; they are to be found everywhere, and would be superfluous. Thomas Burnet, having vainly sought for the origin without being able to discover it, decided that it was necessary that it should descend from heaven. [599] It is certain that one can only with difficulty explain how a man without erudition, like Boehme, never having received this opinion from anyone, has been able to explain it so clearly. "When one sees man existing," says this theosophist, "one can say: Here all Eternity is manifested in one image." [600]

The abode of this being is an intermediate point between heaven and hell, love and anger; that, of the things to which he is attached, becomes his kind. . . . If he inclines toward the celestial nature, he assumes a celestial form, and the human form becomes infernal if he inclines toward hell; for as the mind is, so is the body. In whatever way the mind projects itself, it shadows forth its body with a similar form and a similar source. [601]

It is upon this principle, which one finds still everywhere diversely expressed, that the dogma of the transmigration of souls is founded. This dogma, explained in the ancient mysteries, [602] and received by all peoples, [603] has been to such an extent disfigured in what the moderns have called Metempsychosis, that it would be necessary to exceed considerably the limits of these Examinations in order to give an explanation which could be understood. Later I will endeavour to expose my sentiment upon this mystery, when I treat of Theurgy and other occult sciences to which it is allied.

GOD! THOU COULDST SAVE THEM BY OPENING THEIR EYES

LYSIS here approaches openly one of the greatest difficulties of nature, that which in all time has furnished to the skeptics and to the atheists the weapons that they have believed most formidable. Hierocles has not concealed it in his Commentaries, and he expresses it in these terms: "If God is able to bring back all men to virtue and to happiness, and if he does not will to do so, is God therefore unjust and wicked? Or if he wills to bring them back and if he is unable, is God therefore weak and impotent?" Long before Hierocles, Epicurus seized upon this argument to support his system, and had extended it without augmenting its force. His design had been to prove by its means that, according as he had advanced it, God does not interfere with the things of this world, and that there is, consequently, no Providence. [604] Lactantius, thinking that he was answering this, has quoted from Epicurus and has afforded Bayle, the most learned and the most formidable of modern skeptics, the occasion for demonstrating that, until now, this terrible argument had remained unrefuted notwithstanding all the efforts made for its overthrow.

This indefatigable reasoner said:

The evil exists; man is wicked and unhappy: everything proves this sad truth. History is, properly speaking, only a miscellany of the crimes and adversities of mankind. However, at intervals, there have been seen shining some examples of virtue and happiness. There is, therefore, a mixture of evils and of moral and physical goodness. . . . Now, if man is the work of a sole principle, sovereignly good, sovereignly holy, sovereignly potential, how is he exposed to the maladies of cold, heat, hunger, thirst, pain, and sorrow? How has he so many wicked inclinations? How does he commit so many crimes? Can the sovereign sanctity produce a criminal creature? Can the sovereign bounty produce an unfortunate creature? [605]

Bayle, content with his anti-providential declaration, believes that he has triumphed over all the dogmatists of the world; but whilst he recovers his breath, observe that he admits a mixture of good and evil, and allow him to continue.

"Origen," he said, "asserts that evil has come from the wicked use of the free will. And why has God allowed man to have so pernicious a free will?" "Because, "Origen answers, "an intelligent creature who had not enjoyed free will would have been immutable and immortal as God." What pitiable reason! Is it that the glorified souls, the saints, are equal to God, being predestined to good, and deprived of what is called free will, which, according to Saint Augustine, is only the possibility of evil when the divine grace does not incline man towards the good?" [606]

Bayle, after several outbursts of this sort, finishes by declaring that the way in which evil is introduced under the rule of a sovereign being, infinitely good, infinitely potential, infinitely holy, is not only inexplicable but even incomprehensible. [607] Bayle is right on this point; also I have always said, in the course of this work, that the origin of evil, comprehensible or not, could never be divulged. But the matter of the origin of evil is not the question here. Bayle was too good a reasoner not to have felt it, not to have seen that the argument of Epicurus, and all the elocution with which he furnished it, did not bear upon the cause of evil itself, but upon its effects; which is quite different. Epicurus did not demand that the origin of evil be explained to him, but the local existence of its effects—that is to say, one should state clearly to him, that if God was able and willing to take away the evil from the world, or to prevent it from penetrating there, why he did not do so. When any one's house is the prey of flames, one is not so insensate as to be concerned with knowing what the essence of the fire is, and why it burns in general, but why it burns in particular; and why, being able to extinguish it, one has not done so. Bayle, I repeat, was too clever a logician not to have perceived this. This distinction was too simple to have escaped him; but seeing that its very simplicity had concealed it from the doctors of the Christian church, he was content to affect an ignorance of it to his adversaries, to have the pleasure, so precious to a skeptic such as he, of seeing them one after another exhaust themselves upon the argument of Epicurus:

God, whether he wills to take away evil, and can not; whether he can and does not will to; whether he does not will it nor can; whether he wills it and can. If he wills it and can not, he is weak; which does not accord with God. If he can and does not will it, he is wicked; which accords with him no better. If he does not will it nor can, he is wicked and weak, which could not be. If he can and wills it, that which alone is worthy of his divinity, whence then come the evils? Or why does he not take them away? [608]

Lactantius, to whom Bayle owed his argument, had thought to overthrow it, by saying that God, being able to take away evil, did not will it; so as to give to men, by its means, wisdom and virtue. [609] But the skeptic philosopher had no trouble to prove that this answer was worth nothing, and that the doctrine that it contained was monstrous; since it was certain that God was able to give wisdom and virtue without the means of evil; since he had even given them, following the belief of Lactantius himself, and that it was because he had renounced them that man had become subject to evil. Saint Basil was no more fortunate than Lactantius. Vainly he asserted that the free will, whence results evil, had been established by God himself in the design that this All-powerful Being had for being loved and freely served. Bayle, attacking him in his own faith, asked him, if God is loved and served by force in Paradise, where the glorified souls do not enjoy the fatal privilege of being able to sin. [610] And with the same blow with which he struck him, he brought down Malebranche who had said the same thing. [611] The downfall of Malebranche, and the desire to avenge him, bestirred in vain a crowd of audacious metaphysicians. Bayle pierced them one after another with the weapons of Epicurus, whose steel they did not know, and died with the glory of their having said the greatest piece of stupidity which could be said upon a like matter: namely, that it was possible that God might prescribe another end, in creating the world, than to make his creatures happy. [612]

The death of Bayle did not extinguish the ardour that his works had excited. Leibnitz, justly displeased with all that had been said, thought he could answer the skeptic philosopher better; and raising himself with a great force of genius to that pristine moment when God formed the decree of producing the world, he represented the Being of beings choosing among an infinity of worlds, all possible, all present at his thought, the actual world, as most conformable to his attributes, the most worthy of him, the best finally, the most capable of attaining to the greatest and most excellent end that this all-perfect Being may have been able to purpose. [613] But what is this magnificent and worthy end which the Divinity has chosen, this goal which not alone constitutes the actual world such as it is, but which also presents it to the mind, according to the system of Leibnitz, as the best of possible worlds? This philosopher does not know.

We are not able [he said] to penetrate it, for we are too limited for this; we can only infer, by reasoning with the insight that God has given us, that his bounty only has been able to purpose, by creating the greatest possible number of intelligent creatures, by endowing them with as much knowledge, happiness, and beauty as the Universe might admit without going away from the immutable order established by his wisdom. [614]

Up to this point, the system of Leibnitz sustained itself, and was able even to lead to a relative truth; but its work was not accomplished. It was necessary to explain, following the demand of Epicurus so much repeated by Bayle, how in this immutable order established by the divine Wisdom in this best of worlds, that physical and moral evil make felt such severe effects. The German philosopher, instead of stopping at these effects, and stating the primordial cause, inaccessible to his researches, still scorned it, as had all the adversaries of Bayle, and asserted that physical and moral evils were necessary to maintain this immutable order, and entered into the plan of this best of worlds. Fatal assertion which overthrew his system instantly: for, how dares one to say that evil is necessary, and above all necessary not only in what is best, but in what is the best possible!

Now, whatever may be the primordial cause of Evil, concerning which I can not nor do I wish to explain myself, until the triple veil, extended over this formidable mystery by Moses, may have been raised, I will say, according to the doctrine of Pythagoras and Plato, that its effects can be neither necessary, nor irresistible since they are not immutable and I will reply to the much-lauded argument of Epicurus, that by this very thing they are neither necessary nor irresistible; God can and will remove them and he does remove them.

And if certain disciples of Bayle, astonished by a reply so bold and so new, asked me when and how God works so great a benefit, of which they have perceived no traces, I will say to them: by time and by means of perfectibility. Time is the instrument of Providence; perfectibility, the plan of its work; Nature, the object of its labour; and Good, its result. You know, and Bayle himself agrees, that there exists a mixture of good and evil: and I repeat to you here what I have already said [615]; and I maintain that this good emanates from Providence, and is its work, and replaces in the sphere where it has been transported, an equivalent amount of evil which it has transmuted into good; I maintain that this good continues augmenting itself unceasingly and the evil which corresponds to it, diminishing in an equal proportion; I maintain finally that, having left absolute evil and having arrived at the point where you now are, you will arrive by the same road and by the same means, that is, by favour of time and of perfectibility, from the point where you are to absolute Good, the crown of perfection. This is the answer to your question, When and how does God take away evils? Still if you claim you cannot see any of this, I will reply that it is not for you, arguing with the weakness of your view, to deny the progress of Providence, you whose imperfect senses mistake all the time even the subjects within your range, and for whom the extremes are touching so forcibly, that it is impossible for you to distinguish upon the same dial the movement of the needle which traverses it in a cycle, from the movement of that which traverses it in less than a second; one of these needles appearing to you immobile and the other not existing for you. [616]

If you deny what I affirm, bring other proofs of your denial than your weakness and cease, from the little corner where Nature has placed you, presuming to judge its immensity. Still if you lack negative proofs, wait a moment more, and you shall have from me affirmative proofs. But if, going back, and wishing to sustain the argument of Epicurus which is giving way, you believe that you will succeed by saying that this philosopher had not asked, in the case where God was able and willed to remove evils, how he removed them, but why he did not remove them; I will reply to you that this question is a pure sophism; that the how is implicitly contained in the why, to which I have replied in affirming that God, being able and willing to remove evils, removes them. And if you recall an objection that I have already overthrown concerning the manner in which he removes them, and that bringing you to judge of his ways, you would assume that he ought to remove them, not in a lapse of time so long that you would be unconscious of it, but in the twinkling of an eye; I would reply that this way would be to you quite as imperceptible as the other; and that furthermore, that which you demand exists, since the lapse of time of which you complain, however long it may appear to you, is less than the twinkling of an eye for the Being of beings who employs it, being absolutely nihil compared to Eternity. And from there I will take occasion to tell you that evil, in the way in which it is manifest in the world, being a sort of malady, God, who alone can cure it, knows also the sole remedy which may be applicable to it and that this sole remedy is time.

It seems to me that however little attention you may have given to what I have just said, you ought to be tempted to pass on from the knowledge of the remedy to that of the malady; but it is in vain that you would demand of me an explanation concerning its nature. This explanation is not necessary to overthrow the argument of Epicurus and that is all that I have wished to do. The rest depends upon you and I can only repeat with Lysis:

"God! Thou couldst save them by opening their eyes."

BUT NO: 'TIS FOR THE HUMANS OF A RACE DIVINE, TO DISCERN ERROR, AND TO SEE THE TRUTH

HIEROCLES who, as I have said, has not concealed the difficulty which is contained in these lines, has raised it, by making evident that it depends upon the free will of man, and by putting a limit upon the evils which he attracts to himself by his own choice. His reasoning coinciding with mine can be reduced to these few words. The sole remedy for evil, whatever may be the cause, is time. Providence, minister of the Most High, employs this remedy; and by means of perfectibility which results from it, brings back all to good. But the aptitude of the maladies for receiving it acts in proportion to this remedy. Time, always the same, and always nihil for the Divinity is, however, shortened or lengthened for men, according as their will coincides with the providential action or differs therefrom. They have only to desire good, and time which fatigues them will be lightened. But what if they desire evil always, will time therefore not be finished? Will the evils therefore have no limit? Is it that the will of man is so inflexible that God may not turn it towards the good? The will of man is free beyond doubt; and its essence, immutable as the Divinity whence it emanates, knows not how to be changed, but nothing is impossible for God. The change which is effected in it, without which its immutability may in no wise be altered, is the miracle of the All-Powerful. It is a result of its own liberty, and if I dare to say it, takes place by the coincidence of two movements, whose impulse is given by Providence; by the first, it shows to the will, goodness; by the second, it puts it in a fitting position to meet this same goodness.

NATURE SERVES THEM

LYSIS expresses it thus: Nature, by the homogeneity which, as I have stated, constitutes its essence, teaches men to see beyond the range of their senses, transports them by analogy from one region to another and develops their ideas. The perfectibility which is manifested through the grace of time is called perfection; for the more a thing is perfected the more perfect it becomes. The man who perceives this is struck by it, and if he reflect he finds truth, as I have openly stated, and to which Lysis was content with making allusion, on account of the secret of the mysteries that he was forced to respect.

It is this perfectibility manifested in Nature, which gives the affirmative proofs that I have promised, touching the way in which Providence removes with time the evils which afflict men. These are the proofs de facto. They cannot be challenged without absurdity. I know well that there have been men who, studying Nature within four walls, and considering its operations through the extremely narrow prism of their ideas, have denied that anything might be perfectible, and have asserted that the Universe was immobile because they have not seen it move; but there does not exist today a genuine observer, a naturalist whose learning is founded upon Nature, who does not invalidate the decision of these pretended savants, and who does not put perfectibility in the rank of the most rigorously demonstrated truths.

I shall not quote the ancients on a subject where their authority would be challenged; I shall even limit myself, to evade prolixities, to a small number of striking passages among the moderns. Leibnitz, who ought less than any other to admit perfectibility, since he had founded his system upon the existence of the best of worlds possible, has, however, recognized it in Nature, in advancing that all the changes which are operated there are the consequence of both; that everything tends toward its improvement, and that therefore the present is already teeming with the future. a Buffon, inclining strongly toward the system of atoms, ought also to be much opposed, and yet he has been unable to see that Nature, in general, tends far more toward life than toward death, and that it seems to be seeking to organize bodies as much as is possible. [617] The school of Kant has pushed the system of perfectibility as far as it could go. Schelling, the disciple of most consequence of this celebrated man, has followed the development of Nature with a force of thought which has perhaps passed the mark. The former, has ventured to say that Nature is a sort of Divinity in germ, which tends to apotheosis, and is prepared for existence with God, by the reign of Chaos, and by that of Providence. [618] But those are only speculative opinions. Here are opinions founded upon facts.

As soon as one considers the Earth observingly, the naturalists say, one perceives striking traces of the revolutions that it has sustained in anterior times. [619]

The continents have not always been what they are today, the waters of the globe have not always been distributed in the same manner. The ocean changes insensibly its bed, undermines the lands, divides them, rushes over some, and leaves others dry. The islands have not always been islands. The continents have been peopled, with living and vegetating beings, before the present disposition of the waters upon the globe. [620]

These observations confirm what Pythagoras and the ancient sages have taught upon this subject [621]:

Besides [these same naturalists continue], the greater part of the fossil bones that have been assembled and compared are those of animals different from any of the species actually known; has the kingdom of life therefore changed? This one cannot refuse to believe. [622] As Nature proceeds unceasingly from the simple to the composite, it is probable that the most imperfect animals should have been created before the tribes, higher in the scale of life. It even seems that each of the animal classes indicates a sort of suspension in the creative power, an intermission, an era of repose, during which Nature prepared in silence the germs of life which should come to light in the course of the cycles. One might thus enumerate the epochs of living Nature, epochs remote in the night of ages and which have been obliged to precede the formation of mankind. A time may have been when the insect, the shell, the unclean reptile, did not recognize the master in the Universe and were placed at the head of the organized bodies. [623]

These observers add: It is certain that most perfect beings come from less perfect, and that they are obliged to be perfected in the sequence of generations. All animals tend towards man; all vegetables aspire to animality; minerals seek to draw nearer to the vegetable. . . . It is evident that Nature, having created a series of plants and animals, and having stopped at man who forms the superior extremity, has assembled in him all the vital faculties that it had distributed among the inferior races. [624]

These are the ideas of Leibnitz. This celebrated man had said: "Men hold to animals; these to plants, and those to fossils. It is necessary that all the natural orders form only one sole chain, in which the different classes hold strictly as if they were its links." [625] Several philosophers have adopted them, [626] but none have expressed them with more order and energy than the author of the article Nature, in Le Nouveau Dictionnaire d'Histoire naturelle.

All animals, all plants are only the modifications of an animal, of a vegetable origin. . . . Man is the knot which unites the Divinity to matter, which links heaven and earth. This ray of wisdom and intelligence which shines in his thoughts is reflected upon all Nature. It is the chain of communication between all beings. All the series of animals [he adds in another place] present only a long degradation from the proper nature of man. The monkey, considered either in his exterior form or in his interior organization, resembles only a degraded man; and the same suggestion of degradation is observed in passing from monkeys to quadrupeds; so that the primitive trend of the organization is recognized in all, and the principal viscera, the principal members are identical there. [627]

Who knows [observes elsewhere the same writer] who knows if in the eternal night of time the sceptre of the world will not pass from the hands of man into those of a being more worthy of bearing it and more perfect? Perhaps the race of negroes, today secondary in the human specie, has already been queen of the earth before the white race was created. . . . If Nature has successively accorded the empire to the species that it creates more and more perfect, why should she cease today. . . . The negro, already king of animals, has fallen beneath the yoke of the European; will the latter bow the head in his turn before a race more powerful and more intelligent when it enters into the plans of Nature to ordain his existence? Where will his creation stop? Who will place the limits of his power? God alone raises it and it is His all-powerful hand which governs. [628]

These striking passages full of forceful ideas, which appear new, and which would merit being better known, contain only a small part of the things taught in the ancient mysteries, as I shall perhaps demonstrate later.

THOU WHO FATHOMED IT. O WISE AND HAPPY MAN, REST IN ITS HAVEN. BUT OBSERVE MY LAWS, ABSTAINING FROM THE THINGS WHICH THY SOUL MUST FEAR, DISTINGUISHING THEM WELL; LETTING INTELLIGENCE O'ER THY BODY REIGN

LYSIS, speaking always in the name of Pythagoras, addressed himself to those of the disciples of this theosophist, who had reached the highest degree of perfection, or autopsy, and the felicity of their welfare. I have said often enough in the course of these Examinations, what should be understood by this last degree, so that I need not refer to it here. I shall not even pause upon what has reference to the symbolic teachings of Pythagoras, the formularies and dietetics that he gave to his disciples, and the abstinences that he prescribed for them, my design being to give incidentally a particular explanation of it, for the purpose of not further prolonging this volume. It is well known that all of the eminent men, as many among the ancients as among the moderns, all the savants commendable for their labours or their learning, are agreed in regarding the precepts of Pythagoras as symbolical, that is, as containing figuratively, a very different meaning from that which they would seem to offer literally. It was the custom of the Egyptian priests from whom he had imbibed them, [629] to conceal their doctrine beneath an outer covering of parables and allegories. [630] The world was, in their eyes, a vast enigma, whose mysteries, clothed in a style equally enigmatical, ought never to be openly divulged. [631] These priests had three kinds of characters, and three ways of expressing and depicting their thoughts. The first manner of writing and of speaking was clear and simple; the second, figurative; and the third, symbolic. In the first, they employed characters used by all peoples and took the words in their literal meaning; in the second, they used hieroglyphic characters, and took the words in an indirect and metaphorical meaning; finally in the third, they made use of phrases with double meaning of historic and astronomical fables, or of simple allegories. [632] The chef-d'œuvre of the sacerdotal art was uniting these three ways, and enclosing under the appearance of a clear and simple style, the vulgar, figurative, and symbolic meaning. Pythagoras has sought this kind of perfection in his precepts and often he has succeeded; but the one of all the theosophists instructed in the sanctuaries of Thebes or of Memphis, who has pushed farthest this marvellous art, is beyond doubt Moses. The first part of his Sepher, vulgarly called Genesis, and that should be called by its original name of Bereshith, is in this style, the most admirable work, the most astounding feat of strength that is possible for a man to conceive and execute. This book, which contains all the science of the ancient Egyptians, is still to be translated and will only be translated when one will put oneself in a condition to understand the language in which it has primitively been composed.

SO THAT, ASCENDING INTO RADIANT ETHER, MIDST THE IMMORTALS, THOU SHALT BE THYSELF A GOD

HERE, said Hierocles, in terminating his commentaries, is the blissful end of all efforts: here, according to Plato, is the hope which enkindles, which sustains the ardour of him who fights in the career of virtue: here, the inestimable prize which awaits him. It was the great object of the mysteries, and so to speak, the great work of initiation. [633] The initiate, said Sophocles, is not only happy during his life, but even after his death he can promise himself an eternal felicity. [634] His soul purified by virtue, said Pindar, unfolds in those blessed regions where reigns an eternal springtime. [635] It goes on, said Socrates, attracted by the celestial element which has the greatest affinity with its nature, to become united with the immortal Gods and to share their glory and their immortality. [636] This deification was, according to Pythagoras, the work of divine love; it was reserved for him who had acquired truth through his intellectual faculties, virtue through his animistic faculties, and purity through his instinctive faculties. This purity, after the end of his material body, shone forth and made itself known in the form of a luminous body, that the soul had been given during its confinement in its gloomy body; for as I finish these Examinations, I am seizing the only occasion which may still be presented of saying that, this philosopher taught that the soul has a body which is given according to his good or bad nature, by the inner labour of his faculties. He called this body the subtle chariot of the soul, and said that the mortal body is only the gross exterior. He adds, "The care of the soul and its luminous body is, in practicing virtue, in embracing truth and abstaining from all impure things." [637]

This is the veritable aim of the symbolic abstinences that he prescribes, even as Lysis insinuates moreover quite clearly in the lines which make the subject of my preceding Examination, when he said that it is necessary to abstain from the things which are injurious to the development of the soul and to distinguish clearly these things.

Furthermore, Pythagoras believed that there existed celestial goodness proportionate to each degree of virtue, and that there is for the souls, different ranks according to the luminous body with which they are clothed. The supreme happiness, according to him, belongs only to the soul which has learned how to recover itself, by its intimate union with the intelligence, whose essence, changing its nature, has become entirely spiritual. It is necessary that this soul be raised to the knowledge of universal truths, and that it should have found, as far as it is possible for it, the Principle and the end of all things. Then having attained to this high degree of perfection, being drawn into this immutable region whose ethereal element is no more subjected to the descending movement of generation, it can be united by its knowledge to the Universal All, and reflect in all its being the ineffable light with which the Being of beings, God Himself, fills unceasingly the Immensity.

ENDNOTES

[1] Addressé à la Classe de la Langue et de la Littérature françaises, et à celle d'Histoire et de Littérature ancienne de l'Institut impérial de France. (p. 4)

[2] This expression will be explained in the progress of the discourse. (p. 4)

[3] De Dignit. et Increment. Scient., l. ii., c. 13. (p. 6)

[4] Ibid., l. ii., c. 1. (p. 6)

[5] Ibid., l. vi., c. 1. (p. 6)

[6] Plat., Dial. Ion. Aristotle, who was often opposed to Plato, did not dare to be on this point. He agrees that verse alone does not constitute poetry, and that the History of Herodotus, put into verse, would never be other than history. (p. 6)

[7] Ibid. (p. 6)

[8] De Dignit. et Increment. Scient., l. ii., c. 13. (p. 7)

[9] Leclerc, known by the multitude of his works; l'abbé Bannier, Warburton, etc. (p. 7)

[10] De Dignit. et Increment. Scient., l. ii., c. 13. Court de Gébelin cites Chancellor Bacon as one of the first defenders of allegory. (Génie allég.) (p. 7)

[11] Pausanias, l. iii., p. 93. (p. 8)

[12] Acron, In Epist. Horat., i., 2. Certain authors say that Penelope had conceived this son when Mercury disguised as a goat had forced her virginity. (Lucian, Dialog. Deor., t. i., p. 176.) (p. 8)

[13] Héraclides, entre les petits mythologues. (p. 8)

[14] Geogr., l. i. (p. 10)

[15] Antiq. rom., l. ii. (p. 10)

[16] In his book entitled Περὶ τῆς τῶν θεῶν φύσεως, ch. 17. (p. 10)

[17] In his book entitled Περὶ θεῶν καὶ κόσμον, ch. 3. Court de Gébelin cites these works. (Génie allég.) (p. 10)

[18] Præp. Evang., l. iii., c. 1. (p. 10)

[19] Court de Gébelin, Génie allég., p. 149. (p. 10)

[20] Strabo positively assures it. See Bannier, Mythol., ii., p. 252. (p. 10)

[21] Bailly, Essai sur les Fables, ch. 14. Pausanias, l. ix., p. 302. (p. 10)

[22] Poetry, in Greek ποίησις, derived from the Phœnician פאה (phohe), mouth, voice, language, discourse; and from יש (ish), a superior being, a principle being, figuratively God. This last word, spread throughout Europe, is found with certain change of vowels and of aspirates, very common in the Oriental dialects; in the Etruscan Æs, Æsar, in the Gallic Æs, in the Basque As, and in the Scandinavian Ase; the Copts still say Os, the lord, and the Greeks have preserved it in Αἶσα, the immutable Being, Destiny, and in ἅζω, I adore, and ἀξιόω, I revere.
Thrace, in Greek θρᾴκη, derived from the Phœnician רקיע (rakiwha), which signifies the ethereal space, or, as one translates the Hebrew word which corresponds to it, the firmament. This word is preceded in the Dorian θρακιᾴ, by the letter θ, th, a kind of article which the Oriental grammarians range among the hémantique letters placed at the beginning of words to modify the sense, or to render it more emphatic.
Olen, in Greek ὤλεν, is derived from the Phœnician עילן (whôlon), and is applied in the greater part of the Oriental dialects to all that which is infinite, eternal, universal, whether in time or space. I ought to mention as an interesting thing and but little known by mythologists, that it is from the word אפ (ab or ap) joined to that of whôlon, that one formed ap-whôlon, Apollon: namely, the Father universal, infinite, eternal. This is why the invention of Poetry is attributed to Olen or to Apollo. It is the same mythological personage represented by the sun. According to an ancient tradition, Olen was native of Lycia, that is to say, of the light; for this is the meaning of the Greek word λύκη. (p. 11)

[23] Strabo has judiciously observed that in Greece all the technical words were foreign. (Voyez Bailly, Essai sur les Fables, ch. 14, p. 136.) (p. 11)

[24] The Getæ, in Greek Γέται, were, according to Ælius Spartianus, and according to the author of le Monde primitif (t. ix., p. 49), the same peoples as the Goths. Their country called Getæ, which should be pronounced Ghœtie, comes from the word

Goth, which signifies God in most of the idioms of the north of Europe. The name of the Dacians is only a softening of that of the Thracians in a different dialect. Mœsia, in Greek Μοίσια, is, in Phœnician, the interpretation of the name given to Thrace. The latter means, as we have seen, ethereal space, and the former signifies divine abode, being composed from the word איש (aïsh), whose rendering I have already given, before which is found placed the letter מ (M), one of the hémantiques, which according to the best grammarians serves to express the proper place, the means, the local manifestation of a thing. (p. 11)

[25] Voyez Court de Gébelin, Monde primitif, t. ix., p. 49. (p. 11)

[26] This mountain was called Kô-Kajôn, according to d'Anville. This learned geographer has clearly seen that this name was the same as that of Caucasus, a generic name given to all the sacred mountains. It is known that Caucasus was for the Persians, what Mount Merou had been for the Indians and what Mount Parnassus became afterwards for the Greeks, the central place of their cult. The Tibetans have also their sacred mountain distinct from that of the Indians, upon which still resides the God-Priest, or immortal Man, similar to that of the Getæ. (Mém. de l'Acad. des Inscript., t. xxv., p. 45.) (p. 11)

[27] Bailly, Essai sur les Fables, ch. 14. Conférez avec Hérodote, l. iv.; et Pausanias, l. ix., p. 302, l. x., p. 320. (p. 12)

[28] Dionysus, in Greek Διονύσος, comes from the word Διός, irregular genitive of Ζεύς, the living God, and of Νόος, mind or understanding. The Phœnician roots of these words are אש, יש, or איש (ash, ish, or aïsh), Unique Being, and נו (nô) the motive principle, the movement. These two roots, contracted, form the word Nôos, which signifies literally the principle of being, and figuratively, the understanding.
Demeter, in Greek Δημήτερ, comes from the ancient Greek Δημ, the earth, united to the word μήτερ, mother. The Phœnician roots are דם (dam) and מות (môt), the former expressing all that which is formed by aggregation of similar parts; and the latter, all that which varies the form and gives it generative movement. (p. 12)

[29] Bailly, Essai sur les Fables, ch. 15. Court de Gébelin expressly says, that the sacred mountain of Thrace was consecrated to Bacchus. Monde prim., t. ix., p. 49. Now, it is generally known that Parnassus of the Greeks was consecrated to Apollo. (p. 12)

[30] Theog., V. 500. (p. 12)

[31] The Greek word Θράκη, Thrace, in passing into the Ionian dialect Θρήξ, has furnished the following expressions: θρῆσκος, a devotee, θρησκεία, devotion,

θρησκηύω, I adore with devotion. These words, diverted from their real sense and used ironically after the cult of Thrace had yielded to that of Delphi, were applied to ideas of superstition and even of fanaticism. The point of considering the Thracians as schismatics was even reached, and the word ἐθελοθρησκεία composed to express a heresy, a cult particular to those who practised it, and separated from orthodoxy. (p. 13)

[32] Œtolinos is composed, by contraction, of two words which appear to belong to one of the Thracian dialects. Œto-Kyros signifies the ruling sun, among the Scythians, according to Herodotus (l. iv., 59). Helena signified the moon, among the Dorian. It is from this last word, deprived of its article he, that the Latins have made Luna. (p. 13)

[33] Court de Gébelin, Monde primit., t. viii., p. 190. Pausanias, l. x. Conférez avec Æschyl. In Choephori, v. 1036; Eurip., In Orest., v. 1330; Plat., De Rep., l. iv., etc. (p. 13)

[34] Plut., De Music. Tzetzes, Chiliads, vii.; Hist., 108. (p. 15)

[35] Amphion, in Greek Ἀμφίων, comes from the Phœnician words אם (am), a mother-nation, a metropolis, פי (phi), a mouth, a voice, and יון (Jôn), Greece. Thence the Greeks have derived Ὀμφή, a mother-voice, that is, orthodox, legal, upon which all should be regulated.
Thamyris, in Greek Θάμυρις, is composed of the Phœnician words תאם (tham), twin, אור (aur), light, יש (ish), of the being. (p. 15)

[36] Plut., De Music. (p. 15)

[37] Diod. Sicul., l. iii., 35. Pausan., In Bœot., p. 585. (p. 15)

[38] Bibliotheca Græca, p. 4. (p. 15)

[39] Duhalde, t. iv., in-fol., p. 65. These Tartars had no idea of poetry before their conquest of China; also they imagined that it was only in China where the rules of this science had been formulated, and that the rest of the world resembled them. (p. 16)

[40] Kien-long, one of the descendants of Kang-hi, has made good verse in Chinese. This prince has composed an historical poem on the conquest of the Eleuth, or Oloth people, who, after having been a long time tributary to China, revolted. (Mém. concernant les Chin., t. i., p. 329.) (p. 16)

[41] The commencement of the Indian Kali-youg is placed 3101 or 3102 years before our era. Fréret has fixed it, in his chronological researches, at January 16, 3102, a half hour before the winter solstice, in the colure of which was then found the first star of Aries. The Brahmans say that this age of darkness and uncleanness must endure 432,000 years. Kali signifies in Sanskrit, all that which is black, shadowy, material, bad. From there, the Latin word caligo; and the French word galimatias; the last part of this word comes from the Greek word μῦθος, a discourse, which is itself derived from the Phœnician מיט (mot or myt), which expresses all that moves, stirs up; a motion, a word, etc. (p. 17)

[42] Asiat. Research., t. ii., p. 140. The Brahmans say that their imperial dynasties, pontifical as well as laic, or solar and lunar, became extinguished a thousand years after the beginning of the Kali-youg, about 2000 B.C. It was at this epoch that India was divided into many independent sovereignties and that a powerful reformer of the cult appeared in Magadha, who took the surname of Buddha. (p. 17)

[43] Herod., l. ii. This historian said that in the early times all Egypt was a morass, with the exception of the country of Thebes; that nothing was seen of the land, which one saw there at the epoch in which he was writing, beyond Lake Mœris; and that going up the river, during a seven days' journey, all seemed a vast sea. This same writer said in the beginning of book i., and this is very remarkable, that the Phœnicians had entered from the Red Sea into the Mediterranean, to establish themselves upon its shores, which they would have been unable to do if the Isthmus of Suez had existed. See what Aristotle says on this subject, Meteorolog., l. i., c. 54. (p. 17)

[44] Asiat. Research., t. iii., p. 321. The excerpts that Wilford has made from the Pourana, entitled Scanda, the God of War, prove that the Palis, called Philistines, on account of their same country, Palis-sthan, going out from India, established themselves upon the Persian Gulf and, under the name of Phœnicians, came afterwards along the coast of Yemen, on the borders of the Red Sea, whence they passed into the Mediterranean Sea, as Herodotus said, according to the Persian traditions. This coincidence is of great historical interest. (p. 17)

[45] Niebuhr, Descript. de l'Arab., p. 164. Two powerful tribes became divided in Arabia at this epoch: that of the Himyarites, who possessed the meridional part, or Yemen, and that of the Koreishites, who occupied the septentrional part, or Hejaz. The capital of the Himyarites was called Dhofar; their kings took the title of Tobba and enjoyed an hereditary power. The Koreishites possessed the sacred city of Arabia, Mecca, where was found the ancient temple still venerated today by the Mussulmans. (p. 17)

[46] Asiat. Research., t. iii., p. ii. (p. 17)

[47] Diodorus Siculus, l. ii., 12. Strabo, l. xvi. Suidas, art. Semiramis. (p. 17)

[48] Phot., Cod., 44. Ex. Diodor., l. xl. Syncell., p. 61. Joseph., Contr. Apion. (p. 17)

[49] Hérod., l. ii. Diod. Siculus, l. i., § 2. (p. 17)

[50] Diodor. Sicul., l. i., § 2. Delille-de-Salles, Hist. des Homm., Egypte, t. iii., p. 178. (p. 17)

[51] Plat., in Tim. Dial. Theopomp. apud Euseb., Præp. Evan., l. x., c. 10. Diod. Sicul., l. i., initio. (p. 17)

[52] Diodor. Sicul., l. i., initio. (p. 17)

[53] Pausan., Bœot., p. 768. (p. 18)

[54] This word is Egyptian and Phœnician alike. It is composed of the words אור (aur), light, and רפא (rophœ), cure, salvation. (p. 18)

[55] Eurydice, in Greek Εὐρυδίκη, comes from the Phœnician words ראה (rohe), vision, clearness, evidence, and דך (dich), that which demonstrates or teaches: these two words are preceded by the Greek adverb εὖ, which expresses all that is good, happy, and perfect in its kind. (p. 18)

[56] Plat., In Phædon. Ibid., In Panegyr. Aristot., Rhet., l. ii., c. 24. Isocr., Paneg. Cicero, De Leg., l. ii. Plutar., De Isid. Paus., In Phoc., etc. (p. 18)

[57] Théodoret, Therapeut. (p. 18)

[58] Philo, De Vitâ Mosis, l. i. (p. 18)

[59] Jamblic., De Vitâ Pythag., c. 2. Apul., Florid., ii. Diog. Laërt., l. viii. (p. 18)

[60] Voyage du jeune Anacharsis, t. i., Introd., p. 7. (p. 19)

[61] Meurs., De Relig. Athen., l. i., c. 9. (p. 19)

[62] Apollon., l. iii., p. 237. (p. 19)

[63] Hygin., Fabl., 143. (p. 19)

[64] Pausan., Arcad., p. 266, 268, etc. (p. 19)

[65] Strabo, l. x; Meurs., Eleus., c. 21 et seq.; Paus., Ath., c. 28; Fulgent., Myth., l. i.; Philostr., In Apollon., l. ii.; Athen., l. xi.; Procl., In Tim. Comment., l. v. (p. 20)

[66] Euseb., Præp. Evang., l. xiii., c. 52. (p. 20)

[67] The unity of God is taught in an Orphic hymn of which Justin, Tatian, Clement of Alexandria, Cyril, and Theodore have preserved fragments. (Orphei Hymn. Edente Eschenbach., p. 242.) (p. 20)

[68] Clem. Alex., Admon. ad Gent., p. 48; ibid., Strom., l. v., p. 607. (p. 20)

[69] Apoll., Arg., l. i., v. 496; Clem. Alex., Strom., l. iv., p. 475. (p. 20)

[70] Thimothée, cité par Bannier, Mythol., i., p. 104. (p. 20)

[71] Macrobius, Somm. Scip., l. i., c. 12. (p. 20)

[72] Eurip., Hippol., V. 948. (p. 20)

[73] Plat., De Leg., l. vi.; Jambl., De Vitâ Pythag. (p. 20)

[74] Acad. des Insc., t. v., p. 117. (p. 20)

[75] Procl., In Tim., l. v., p. 330; Cicero, Somm. Scip., c. 2, 3, 4, 6. (p. 20)

[76] Montesquieu and Buffon have been the greatest adversaries of poetry, they were very eloquent in prose; but that does not prevent one from applying to them, as did Voltaire, the words of Montaigne: "We cannot attain it, let us avenge ourselves by slandering it." (p. 20)

[77] Horat., De Arte poét.; Strab., l. x. (p. 20)

[78] Origen, Contr. Cels., l. i., p. 12; Dacier, Vie de Pythagore. (p. 21)

[79] Ἱερὸς λόγος. (p. 21)

[80] Θρονισμὸι μητρῶοι. (p. 21)

[81] Fabric., Bibl. græc., p. 120, 129. (p. 21)

[82] Fabric., Bibliot. græc., p. 4, 22, 26, 30, etc.; Voyag. d'Anach., ch. 80. (p. 23)

[83] From the Greek word κύκλος: as one would say circuit, the circular envelopment of a thing. (p. 23)

[84] Court de Gébelin, Gén. allég., p. 119. (p. 23)

[85] Casaubon, In Athen., p. 301; Fabric., Bibl. græc. l. i., c. 17. Voyag. d'Anach., ch. 80; Proclus, cité par Court de Gébelin, ibid. (p. 23)

[86] Arist., De Poët., c. 8, 16, 25, etc. (p. 23)

[87] It is needless for me to observe that the birthplace of Homer has been the object of a host of discussions as much among the ancients as among the moderns. My plan here is not to put down again en problème, nor to examine anew the things which have been a hundred times discussed and that I have sufficiently examined. I have chosen, from the midst of all the divergent opinions born of these discussions, that which has appeared to me the most probable, which agrees best with known facts, and which is connected better with the analytical thread of my ideas. I advise my readers to do the same. It is neither the birthplace of Homer nor the name of his parents that is the important matter: it is his genius that must be fathomed. Those who would, however, satisfy their curiosity regarding these subjects foreign to my researches, will find in La Bibliothèque grecque de Fabricius, and in the book by Léon Allatius entitled De Patriâ Homeri, enough material for all the systems they may wish to build. They will find there twenty-six different locations wherein they can, at their pleasure, place the cradle of the poet. The seven most famous places indicated in a Greek verse by Aulus Gellius are, Smyrna, Rhodes, Colophon, Salamis, Chios, Argos, and Athens. The nineteen indicated by divers authors, are Pylos, Chios, Cyprus, Clazomenæ, Babylon, Cumæ, Egypt, Italy, Crete, Ithaca, Mycenæ, Phrygia, Mæonia, Lucania, Lydia, Syria, Thessaly, and finally Troy, and even Rome.

However, the tradition which I have followed, in considering Homer as born not far from Smyrna, upon the borders of the river Meles, is not only the most probable but the most generally followed; it has in its favour Pindar; the first anonymous Life of Homer; the Life of this poet by Proclus; Cicero, in his oration for Archias; Eustathius in his Prolégoménes sur l'Iliade; Aristotle, Poétique, l. iii.; Aulus Gellius, Martial, and Suidas. It is known that Smyrna, jealous of consecrating the glory that it attributed to itself, of having given birth to Homer, erected to this great genius a temple with quadrangular portico, and showed for a long time, near the source of the Meles, a grotto, where a contemporaneous tradition supposes that he had composed his first works. Voyez La Vie d'Homère, par Delille-de-Sales, p. 49, et les ouvrages qu'il cite: Voyage de Chandeler, t. i., p. 162, et Voyages pittoresques de Choiseul-Gouffier, p. 200. (p. 24)

[88] Hérod., l. v., 42; Thucyd., l. i., 12. (p. 24)

[89] Marbres de Paros, Epoq. 28; Hérod., l. i., 142, 145, 149; Plat., De Leg., l. v.; Strab., l. xiv.; Pausan., l. vii., 2; Ælian., Var. Histor., l. viii., c. 5; Sainte-Croix, De l'état des Colon. des anc. Peuples, p. 65; Bourgainville, Dissert. sur les Métrop. et les Colon., p. 18; Spanheim, Præst., num. p. 580. (p. 24)

[90] Bible, Chron. ii., eh. 12 et suiv. (p. 24)

[91] Ibid., Chron. ii., ch. 32 et 36. (p. 24)

[92] Pausanias, passim. (p. 24)

[93] Strab., l. xiv.; Polyb., l. v.; Aulu-Gell., l. vii., c. 3; Meurs., In Rhod., l. i., c. 18 et 21; Hist. univ. des Anglais, in-8°, t. ii., p. 493. (p. 24)

[94] Diod. Sicul., l. i., 2. (p. 24)

[95] In Phœnician ארע-רלמ (Melich-ærtz), in Greek Μελικέρης: a name given to the Divinity whom the Thracians called Hercules, the Lord of the Universe: from חרר or שרר (harr or shar), excellence, dominance, sovereignty; and כל (col.), All. Notice that the Teutonic roots are not very different from the Phœnician: Herr signifies lord, and alles, all; so that Herr-alles is, with the exception of the guttural inflection which is effaced, the same word as that of Hercules, used by the Thracians and the Etruscans. The Greeks have made a transposition of letters in Ἡρακλῆς (Heracles) so as to evade the guttural harshness without entirely losing it. (p. 24)

[96] Goguet, Origine des Lois et des Arts, t. i., p. 359. (p. 24)

[97] Voyez Epiphane, Hæres, xxvi., et conférez avec Beausobre, Hist. du Manich., t. ii., p. 328. (p. 24)

[98] I have followed the tradition most analogous to the development of my ideas; but I am aware that, upon this point, as upon many others, I have only to choose. The historic fact, in that which relates to the sacerdotal archives which Homer consulted in composing his poems, is everywhere the same au fond; but the accessory details vary greatly according to the writers who relate them. For example, one reads in a small fragment attributed to Antipater of Sidon and preserved in Greece Anthology, that Homer, born at Thebes in Egypt, drew his epic subjects from the archives of the temple of Isis; from another source, Ptolemy Ephestion, cited by Photius, that the Greek poet had received from a priest of Memphis, named Thamitès, the original writings of an inspired damsel, named Phancy. Strabo, without mentioning any place in particular, said in general, speaking of the long journeys of Homer, that this poet went everywhere to consult

the religious archives and the oracles preserved in the temples; and Diodorus of Sicily gives evidence sometimes that he borrowed many things from a sibyl by the name of Manto, daughter of Tiresias; and sometimes that he appropriated the verse of a pythoness of Delphi, named Daphne. All these contradictory details prove, in reality, the truth; for whether it be from Thebes, Memphis, Tyre, Delphi, or elsewhere that Homer drew the subject of his chants, matters not with the subject which occupies me: the important point, serving as proof of my assertions, is, that they have been, in fact, drawn from a sanctuary; and what has determined me to choose Tyre rather than Thebes or Memphis, is that Tyre was the first mother city of Greece. (p. 25)

[99] I have said in the above that the name of Helena or Selena was that of the moon in Greek. The root of this word is alike Celtic and Phœnician. One finds it in Teutonic hell, which signifies clear, luminous, and in Hebrew חלל (hêll), which contains the same sense of splendour, glory, and elevation. One still says in German heilig, holy, and selig, blessed; also selle, soul, and seilen, souls. And this is worthy of the closest attention, particularly when one reflects that, following the doctrine of the ancients, the moon helenê or selenê was regarded as the reservoir of the souls of those who descend from heaven to pass into bodies by means of generation, and, purged by the fire of life, escape from earth to ascend to heaven. See, concerning this doctrine, Plutarch (De Facie in Orb. Lun.), and confer with Beausobre (Histoire du Manich., t. ii., p. 311). The name of Paris, in Greek Πάρις, comes from the Phœnician words בר or פר (bar or phar), all generation, propagation, extension, and (ish), the Being-principle.
The name of Menelaus, in Greek Μενέλαος, comes from the Phœnician words מן (men), all that which determines, regulates, or defines a thing, properly, the rational faculty, the reason, the measure, in Latin mens, mensura; and אוש (aôsh), the Being-principle acting, before which is placed the prefix ל (l), to express the genitive case, in this manner, מנח-ל-אוש (meneh-l-aôsh), the rational faculty or regulator of the being in general, and man in particular: for איש , יש , אוש , אש (ash, aôsh, ish, aîsh), signifies equally fire, principle, being, and man. The etymology of these three words can, as one sees, throw great light upon the fable of the Iliad. Here is another remarkable point on this subject. Homer has never used, to designate the Greeks, the name of Hellenes, that is to say, the resplendents, or the lunars: it was in his time quite a new name, which the confederated Greeks had taken to resist foreign attack; it is only in the Odyssey, and when he is already old, that he employs the name Hellas to designate Greece. The name which he gives constantly to this country, is that of Achaia (Ἀχαϊα), and he opposes it to that of Troy (Τρωία): now, Achaia signifies the strong, the igneous, the spiritual; and Troy, the terrestrial, the gross. The Phœnician roots are הוי (ehôi), the exhaling force of fire, and טרו (trô) the balancing power of the earth. Refer, in this regard, to Court de Gébelin (Mond. prim., t. vi., p. 64). Pomponius Sabinus, in his Commentaires sur

l'Enéïde, said that the name of the city of Troy signified a sow, and he adds that the Trojans had for an ensign a sow embroidered in gold. As to the word Ilion, which was the sacred name of Troy, it is very easy to recognize the name of the material principle, called ὕλε (ulè) by the Greeks and ylis by the Egyptians. Iamblichus speaks of it at great length in his Book on the Mysteries (§ 7), as the principle from which all has birth: this was also the opinion of Porphyry (Euseb., Præp. Evang., l. ix., c. 9 and 11). (p. 25)

[100] Metrodorus of Lampsacus cited by Tatian (Adver. Gent., § 37). Plato, In Alcibiad., ii., Cronius, Porphyry, Phurnutus, Iamblichus, cited by Court de Gébelin, Génie allég., p. 36, 43; Plato, In Ion.; Cicero, De Natur. Deor., l. ii.; Strabo, l. i.; Origen, Contr. Cels. Among the moderns can be counted Bacon, Blackwell, Basnage, Bergier, and Court de Gébelin himself, who has given a list of eighty writers who have this opinion. (p. 25)

[101] Dionys. Halic., De Comp. verb., t. v., c. 16, 26; Quintil., l. x., c. 1; Longin., De Sublim., c. 13; Ælian., Var. Hist., l. viii., c. 2; Plat., Alcibiad., i. (p. 25)

[102] Plat., In Vitâ Lycurg. (p. 25)

[103] Allat., De Patr. Homer., c. 5; Meurs., In Pisist., c. 9 et 12; Plat., In Hipparc. (p. 25)

[104] Senec., Epist., 117. (p. 25)

[105] Ibidem, 88. (p. 25)

[106] Dionys. Halic., In Vitâ Homer.; Eustath., In Iliad, l. i. (p. 25)

[107] Strabo, l. xiv., p. 646. (p. 25)

[108] Arist., De Poët., c. 2, cit. par Barth., Voyag. d'Anach., t. vii., c. 80, p. 44. (p. 26)

[109] The word Epopœia is taken from the Greek ἐπο-ποιός which designates alike a poet and an epic poem. It is derived from the Phœnician words אפא (apho) an impassioned transport, a vortex, an impulse, an enthusiasm; and פאה (phohe), a mouth, a discourse. One can observe that the Latin word versus, which is applied also to a thing which turns, which is borne along, and to a poetic verse, translates exactly the Greek word ἔπος, whose root אוף (aôph) expresses a vortex. The Hebrew אופן (aôphon) signifies properly a wheel. (p. 26)

[110] See in the collection of Meibomius, Aristides, Quintilianus, and Les Mém. de l'Acad. des Belles-Lettres, t. v., p. 552. (p. 26)

[111] Voltaire, Dict. philos., art. RIME. (p. 26)

[112] Refer to what I have already said in footnote 177 p. 41. (p. 27)

[113] Fréret said that the verses of the poet Eumelus engraven upon the arch of the Cypselidæ were thus represented. Voyez sa Dissert. sur l'Art de l'Equitation. Il cite Pausanias, l. v., p. 419. (p. 27)

[114] Court de Gébelin, Mond. primit., t. ix., p. 222. Conférez avec Aristotle, Poët., p. 20, 21, 22. (p. 27)

[115] Plat., Dial. Ion. (p. 28)

[116] Plat., ut suprà. (p. 29)

[117] Ælian., Var. Hist., l. xiii., c. 14; Diog. Laërt., In Solon., l. i., § 57. (p. 29)

[118] Plat., In Hipparc.; Pausan, l. vii., c. 26; Cicer., De Orat., l. iii. (p. 29)

[119] Eustath., In Iliad., l. i., p. 145; l. ii., p. 263. (p. 29)

[120] Dionys. Halle., De Comp. verb., t. v., c. 16 et 24; Quintil., Instit., l. x., c. 1. (p. 29)

[121] Athen., l. xv., c. 8; Aristot., De Poët., c. 16; Ælian., Var. Hist., c. 15. (p. 29)

[122] Barthel., Voyag. d'Anarchar., t. vii., ch. 80, p. 46, 52. (p. 30)

[123] It can be seen that I have placed in the word Stesi`chorus, an accent grave over the consonant c, and it will be noticed that I have used it thus with respect to many similar words. It is a habit I have contracted in writing, so as to distinguish, in this manner, the double consonant ch, in the foreign words, or in their derivatives, when it should take the guttural inflexion, in place of the hissing inflexion which we ordinarily give to it. Thus I accent the `c in Chio, `chæur, chorus, é`cho, `chlorose, `chiragre, `chronique, etc.; to indicate that these words should he pronounced Khio, khœur, khorus, ékho, khlorose, khiragre, khronique, with the aspirate sound of k, and not with that of the hissing c, as in Chypre, chaume, échope, chaire, etc. This accentuation has appeared to me necessary, especially when one is obliged to transcribe in modern characters many foreign words which, lacking usage, one knows not, at first, how to pronounce. It is, after all, a slight innovation in orthography, which I leave to the decision of the grammarians. I only say that it will be very difficult for them, without this accent, or any other sign which might be used, to know how one should pronounce with a different inflexion, A`chaïe

and Achéen; Achille and A`chilleïde; Achéron and a`chérontique; Bac`chus and bachique, etc. (p. 30)

[124] Vossius, De Inst. poët., l. iii., c. 15; Aristot., Rhet., l. ii., 23; Max. Tyr. Orat., viii., p. 86. (p. 30)

[125] Ælian., Var. Hist., l. xiii., c. 14, Court de Gébelin, Mond. prim., t. viii., p. 202. (p. 30)

[126] Plat., In Theæt.; ibid., De Republ., l. x.; Arist., De Poët., c. 4, etc. (p. 30)

[127] The name of Homeridæ, given at first to all the disciples of Homer, was afterwards usurped by certain inhabitants of Chios who called themselves his descendants (Strab., l. xiv.; Isocr., Hellen. encom.). Also I should state here that the name of Homer, Ὅμηρος, was never of Greek origin and has not signified, as has been said, blind. The initial letter O is not a negation, but an article added to the Phœnician word מלא (mœra), which signifies, properly speaking, a centre of light, and figuratively, a master, a doctor. (p. 30)

[128] The surname Eumolpidæ, given to the hierophants, successors of Orpheus, comes from the word Εὔμολπος, by which is designated the style of poetry of this divine man. It signifies the perfect voice. It is derived from the Phœnician words מלא (mola), perfected, and פאה (phoh), mouth, voice, discourse. The adverb ἔν, which precedes it, expresses whatever is beautiful, holy, perfect. (p. 30)

[129] Fabric., Bibl. Græc., p. 36, 505, 240, 469, passim; Arist., Probl., xix., 28; Meurs., Bibl. Græc., c. i. (p. 30)

[130] Arist., De Poët., c. 8. (p. 30)

[131] Porphyre, In Vitâ Pythagor., p. 21; Clem. Alex., l. vi., p. 658; Plato, De Leg., l. iii.; Plutar., De Music., p. 1141; Poll., l. iv., c. 9. (p. 30)

[132] I have placed the epoch of Orpheus, which coincides with that of the arrival of the Egyptian colony conducted into Greece by Cecrops, at 1582 B.C., according to the marbles of Paros. (p. 31)

[133] Schol. Aristoph., In Nub., v. 295. (p. 31)

[134] Athen., l. ii., c. 3. (p. 31)

[135] Voyez L'Hist. du Théâtre Français de Fontenelle. Voici les titres des premières pièces représentées dans le cours du XIVe siècle: L'Assomption de la glorieuse

Vierge Marie, mystère à 38 personnages; Le Mystère de la Sainte Hostie, à 26 personn.; Le Mystère de Monseigneur S. Pierre et S. Paul, à 100 personn.; Les Mystères de la Conception de la Passion, de la Résurrection de Notre Seigneur J. C.; etc. (p. 31)

[136] See Asiatic Researches, v. iii., p. 427-431, and 465-467. Also Grammar of the Bengal Language, preface, p. v. (p. 31)

[137] See Interesting Historical Events, by Holwell, ch. 7. (p. 31)

[138] Aristot., Probl., 15, c. 19; Pausan. l. i., c. 7. (p. 32)

[139] See Asiatic Researches, vol. vi., p. 300-308. (p. 32)

[140] Rama is, in Sanskrit, the name of that which is dazzling, elevated, white, sublime, protective, beautiful, excellent. This word has exactly the same sense in the Phœnician רם (ram). Its primitive root, which is universalized by the hémantique letter מ (m), is רא (ra), which has reference to the harmonic movement of good, of light, and of sight. The name of the adversary of Rama, Rawhan, is formed from the root ער (rawh) which expresses, on the contrary, the disordered movement of evil and of fire, and which, becoming united with the augmentative syllable ון (ôn), depicts whatever ravages and ruins; this is the signification which it has in Sanskrit. (p. 32)

[141] From the word רמא (rama) is formed in Phœnician the word דרמא (drama) by the adjunction of the demonstrative article ד (d'); that is to say, a thing which comes from Rama: an action well ordered, beautiful, sublime, etc. Notice that the Greek verb δραεῖν, to act, whence is drawn very inappropriately the word δρᾶμα, is always attached to the same root רא (ra) which is that of harmonic movement. (p. 32)

[142] Athen., l. ii., c. 3; Arist., De Poët., c. 3, 4, 5. (p. 32)

[143] Tragedy, in Greek τραγῳδία, comes from the words τραχίς, austere, severe, lofty, and ᾠδή chant.
Comedy, in Greek κωμῳδία, is derived from the words κῶμος, joyful, lascivious, and ᾠδή, chant.
It is unnecessary for me to say that the etymologists who have seen in tragedy a song of the goat, because τράγος signifies a goat in Greek, have misunderstood the simplest laws of etymology. Τράγος signifies a goat only by metaphor, because of the roughness and heights which this animal loves to climb; as caper, in Latin,

holds to the same root as caput; and chèvre, in French, to the same root as chef, for a similar reason. (p. 32)

[144] Diog. Laërt., l. i., § 59. (p. 32)

[145] Plutar. In Solon. (p. 32)

[146] Arist., De Mor., l. iii., c. 2; Ælian., Var. Hist., l. v., c. 59; Clem. Alex., Strom., l. ii., c. 14. (p. 33)

[147] Plato, De Legib., l. iii. (p. 33)

[148] Athen., l. viii., c. 8. (p. 33)

[149] Plutar., De Music. (p. 33)

[150] Horat., De Art. poët, v, 279; Vitruv., In Prefac., l. vii., p. 124. (p. 33)

[151] Æschylus, In Prometh., Act I., Sc. 1, et Act. V., Sc. ult. (p. 33)

[152] Æschylus, In Eumenid., Act V., Sc. 3. (p. 33)

[153] Aristoph. In Plut., v. 423; Pausan., l. i., c. 28; Vitâ Æschyl. apud., Stanley, p. 702. (p. 33)

[154] Dionys. Chrys., Orat., l. ii. (p. 34)

[155] Aristoph., In Ran.; Philostr., In Vitâ Apollon, l. vi., c. ii. (p. 34)

[156] Plutar., In Cimon.; Athen., l. viii., c. 8. (p. 34)

[157] Philostr., In Vitâ Apoll., l. vi., c. 11. (p. 34)

[158] Schol., In Vitâ Sophocl.; Suidas, In Σοφοκλ.; Plutar., De Profect. Vitæ. (p. 34)

[159] Aristot., De Poët., c. 25. (p. 34)

[160] Aristoph., In Ran., v. 874 et 1075. (p. 35)

[161] Philostr., Vitâ Apoll., l. ii., c. 2; l. iv., c. 16; l. vi., c. 11; Vitâ Æschyl. apud, Robort., p. 11. (p. 35)

[162] Aristoph., In Ran.; Aristot., De Poët, c. 25. (p. 35)

[163] Plato, De Legib., l. ii. et iii. (p. 35)

[164] Hérodot., l. vi., 21; Corsin., Fast. attic., t. iii., p. 172; Aristot., De Poët., c. 9. (p. 36)

[165] Aristot., De Poët., c. 9. (p. 36)

[166] Susarion appeared 580 B.C., and Thespis some years after. The latter produced his tragedy of Alcestis in 536 B.C.; and the condemnation of Socrates occurred in 399 B.C. So that only 181 years elapsed between the initial presentation of comedy and the death of this philosopher. (p. 36)

[167] Aristot., De Poët., c. 3. (p. 36)

[168] Aristoph, In Pac., v. 740; Schol., ibid.; Epicharm., In Nupt. Heb. apud Athen., l. iii., p. 85. (p. 36)

[169] Plat., In Argum.; Aristoph., p. xi.; Schol., De Comœd.; ibid., p. xii. (p. 36)

[170] Thence arises the epithet of Eumolpique that I give to the verses which form the subject of this work. (p. 38)

[171] The proof that Rome was scarcely known in Greece, at the epoch of Alexander, is that the historian Theopompus, accused by all critics of too much prolixity, has said only a single word concerning this city, to announce that she had been taken by the Gauls (Pliny, l. iii., c. 5). Bayle observes with much sagacity, that however little Rome had been known at that time, she would not have failed to furnish the subject of a long digression for this historian, who would have delighted much in it. (Dict. crit., art. THEOPOMPUS, rem. E.) (p. 39)

[172] Diogen. Laërt., l. i., § 116. Pliny, l. v., c. 29. Suidas, In φερεχύδς. (p. 40)

[173] Degerando, Hist. des Systêm. de Phil., t. i., p. 128, à la note. (p. 40)

[174] Dionys. Halic., De Thucid. Judic. (p. 40)

[175] The real founder of the Atomic system such as has been adopted by Lucretius (De Rerum Natura, l. i.), was Moschus, Phœnician philosopher whose works threw light upon those of Leucippus (Posidonius cité par Strabon, l. xvi., Sext. Empiric., Adv. mathem., p. 367). This system well understood, does not differ from that of the monads, of which Leibnitz was the inventor. (p. 40)

[176] Fréret, Mytholog. ou Religion des Grecs. (p. 41)

[177] Voltaire, who has adopted this error, has founded it upon the signification of the word Epos, which he has connected with that of Discourse (Dictionn. philos. au mot EPOPÉE). But he is mistaken. The Greek word ἔπος is translated accurately by versus. Thence the verb επεῖν, to follow in the tracks, to turn, to go, in the same sense. (p. 41)

[178] The Greeks looked upon the Latin authors and artists as paupers enriched by their spoils; also they learned their language only when forced to do so. The most celebrated writers by whom Rome was glorified, were rarely cited by them. Longinus, who took an example of the sublime in Moses, did not seek a single one either in Horace or in Vergil; he did not even mention their names. It was the same with other critics. Plutarch spoke of Cicero as a statesman; he quoted many of his clever sayings, but he refrained from comparing him with Demosthenes as an orator. He excuses himself on account of having so little knowledge of the Latin tongue, he who had lived so long in Rome! Emperor Julian, who has written only in Greek, cites only Greek authors and not one Latin. (p. 42)

[179] Voyez l'ouvrage de Naudé, intitulé: Apologie des hommes accusés de magie. Le nombre de ces hommes est très-considérable. (p. 44)

[180] Allard, Bibl. du Dauphiné, à la fin. (p. 44)

[181] Duplessis-Mornai, Mystère d'iniquité., p. 279. (p. 44)

[182] This Ballad tongue, or rather Romance, was a mixture of corrupt Latin, Teutonic, and ancient Gallic. It was called thus, in order to distinguish it from the pure Latin and French. The principal dialects of the Romance tongue were the langue d'oc, spoken in the south of France, and the langue d'oïl, spoken in the north. It is from the langue d'oïl that the French descend. The langue d'oc, prevailing with the troubadours who cultivated it, disappeared with them in the fourteenth century and was lost in numberless obscure provincial dialects. Voyez Le Troubadour, poésies occitaniques, à la Dissert., vol. i. (p. 45)

[183] Fontenelle, Hist. du Théâtre Français. (p. 45)

[184] Voyez Sainte-Palaye, Mém. sur l'ancienne Cheval.; Millot, Hist. des Troubad. Disc. prélim., on ce que j'ai dit moi-même dans le Troubadour, comme ci-dessus. (p. 45)

[185] It is necessary to observe that vau or val, bau or bal, according to the dialect, signifies equally a dance, a ball, and a folly, a fool. The Phœnician, root על (whal)

expresses all that is elevated, exalted. The French words bal, vol, fol, are here derived. (p. 45)

[186] The sonnets are of Oscan origin. The word son signifies a song in the ancient langue d'oc. The word sonnet is applied to a little song, pleasing and of an affected form.
The madrigals are of Spanish origin as their name sufficiently proves. The word gala signifies in Spanish a kind of favour, an honour rendered, a gallantry, a present. Thus Madrid-gala arises from a gallantry in the Madrid fashion. The sylves, called sirves or sirventes by the troubadours, were kinds of serious poems, ordinarily satirical. These words come from the Latin sylva which, according to Quintilius, is said of a piece of verse recited ex-tempore (l. x., c. 3). (p. 45)

[187] Voyez Laborde, Essai sur la Musique, t. i., p. 112, et t. ii., p. 168. On trouve, de la page 149 à la page 232 de ce même volume, un catalogue de tous les anciens romanciers français. On peut voir, pour les Italiens, Crescembini, Della Volgar Poësia. (p. 46)

[188] See Laborde. It is believed that this Guilhaume, bishop of Paris, is the author of the hieroglyphic figures which adorn the portal of Notre-Dame, and that they have some connection with the hermetic science. (Biblioth. des Phil. Chim., t. iv. Saint-Foix, Essai sur Paris.) (p. 46)

[189] Perhaps one is astonished to see that I give the name of sirventes, or sylves, to that which is commonly called the poems of Dante; but in order to understand me, it is necessary to consider that these poems, composed of stanzas of three verses joined in couplets, are properly only long songs on a serious subject, which agrees with the sirvente. The poems of Bojardo, of Ariosto, of Tasso, are, as to form, only long ballads. They are poems because of the unity which, notwithstanding the innumerable episodes with which they are filled, constitutes the principal subject. (p. 46)

[190] Pasquier, Hist. et Recherch. des Antiq., l. vii., ch. 12. Henri-Etienne, Précellence du Lang. Franç., p. 12. D'Olivet, Prosod., art. i., § 2. Delisle-de-Salles, Hist. de la Trag., t. i., p. 154, à la note. (p. 48)

[191] D'Olivet, Prosod., art. V., § 1. (p. 48)

[192] Ibidem. (p. 48)

[193] William Jones, Asiatic Researches, vol. i. (p. 50)

[194] Ibid., vol. i., p. 425. (p. 50)

[195] William Jones, Asiatic Researches, vol. i., p. 430. (p. 50)

[196] Wilkin's Notes on the Hitopadesa, p. 249. Halled's Grammar, in the preface. The same, Code of the Gentoo-Laws. Asiat. Research., vol. i., p. 423. (p. 50)

[197] Asiat. Research., vol. i., p. 346. Also in same work, vol. i., p. 430. (p. 51)

[198] W. Jones has put into English a Natak entitled Sakuntala or The Fatal Ring, of which the French translation has been made by Brugnières. Paris, 1803, chez Treuttel et Würtz. (p. 51)

[199] See Asiat. Research., vol. iii., p. 42, 47, 86, 185, etc. (p. 51)

[200] Asiat. Research., vol. i., p. 279, 357 et 360. (p. 51)

[201] Institut. of Hindus-Laws. W. Jones, Works, t. iii., p. 51. Asiat. Research., vol. ii., p. 368. (p. 52)

[202] Hist. génér. de la Chine, t. i., p. 19. Mém. concern. les Chinois, t. i., p. 9, 104, 160. Chou-King. Ch. Yu-Kong, etc., Duhalde, t. i., p. 266. Mém. concern., etc., t. xiii., p. 190. (p. 52)

[203] The She-King, which contains the most ancient poetry of the Chinese, is only a collection of odes and songs, of sylves, upon different historical and moral subjects. (Mém. concer. les Chinois, t. i., p. 51, et t. ii., p. 80.) Besides, the Chinese had known rhyme for more than four thousand years. (Ibid., t. viii., p. 133-185.) (p. 52)

[204] Le P. Parennin says that the language of the Manchus has an enormous quantity of words which express, in the most concise and most picturesque manner, what ordinary languages can do only by aid of numerous epithets or periphrases. (Duhalde, in-fol., t. iv., p. 65.) (p. 52)

[205] Ci-dessus, p. 31. (p. 52)

[206] Voyez la traduction française des Rech. asiatiq., t. ii., p. 49, notes a et b. (p. 52)

[207] Voyez ce que dit de Zend, Anquetil Duperron, et l'exemple qu'il donne de cette ancienne langue. Zend-Avesta, t. i. (p. 52)

[208] D'Herbelot, Bibl. orient., p. 54. Asiat. Research., t. ii., p. 51. (p. 53)

[209] Anquetil Duperron, Zend-Avesta, t. i. (p. 53)

[210] Asiat. Research., t. ii., p. 51. (p. 53)

[211] L'abbé Massieu, Histor. de la Poésie franç., p. 82. (p. 53)

[212] In Arabic /(diwan). דיואן (p. 54)

[213] D'Herbelot, Bibl. orient., au mot DIVAN. Asiat. Research., t. ii., p. 13. (p. 54)

[214] It must be remarked that the word Diw, which is also Persian, was alike applied in Persia to the Divine Intelligence, before Zoroaster had changed the signification of it by the establishment of a new doctrine, which, replacing the Diws by the Iseds, deprived them of the dominion of Heaven, and represented them as demons of the earth. See Anquetil Duperron, Vendidad-Sadè, p. 133, Boun-Dehesh., p. 355. It is thus that Christianity has changed the sense of the Greek word Δαίμων (Demon), and rendered it synonymous with the devil; whereas it signified in its principle, divine spirit and genius. (p. 54)

[215] Asiat. Research., t. ii., p. 13. (p. 54)

[216] Voyez Anquetil Duperron, Zend-Avesta, t. iii., p. 527 et suiv. Voyez aussi un ouvrage allemand de Wahl, sur l'état de la Perse: Pragmatische-Geografische und Statische Schilderung . . . etc. Leipzig, 1795, t. i., p. 198 à 204. (p. 54)

[217] Voyez plusieurs de leurs chansons rapportées par Laborde, Essai sur la Musique, t. ii., p. 398. (p. 54)

[218] Laborde, ibid., t. i., p. 425. (p. 55)

[219] I will give, later on, a strophe from Voluspa, a Scandinavian ode of eumolpique style, very beautiful, and of which I will, perhaps, one day make an entire translation. (p. 55)

[220] It was said long ago that a great number of rhymed verses were found in the Bible, and Voltaire even has cited a ridiculous example in his Dictionnaire philosophique (art. RIME): but it seems to me that before concerning oneself so much as one still does, whether the Hebraic text of the Sepher is in prose or in verse, whether or not one finds there rhymed verses after the manner of the Arabs, or measured after the manner of the Greeks, it would be well to observe whether one understands this text. The language of Moses has been lost entirely for more than two thousand four hundred years, and unless it be restored with an

aptitude, force, and constancy which is nowadays unusual, I doubt whether it will be known exactly what the legislator of the Hebrews has said regarding the principles of the Universe, the origin of the earth, and the birth and vicissitudes of the beings who people it. These subjects are, however, worth the pains if one would reflect upon them; I cannot prevent myself from thinking that it would be more fitting to be occupied with the meaning of the words, than their arrangements by long and short syllables, by regular or alternate rhymes, which is of no importance whatever. (p. 55)

[221] Vossius, De Poematum cantu et viribus rhythmi; cité par J. J. Rousseau, Dictionnaire de Musique, art. RYTHME. (p. 56)

[222] Nearly all of the Italian words terminate with one of four vowels, a, e, i, o, without accent: it is very rare that the vowels are accentuated, as the vowel ù. When this occurs as in città, perchè, dì, farò, etc., then, only, is the final masculine. Now here is what one of their best rhythmic poets, named Tolomèo, gives as an hexameter verse:
Questa, per affeto, tenerissima lettera mando A te...
To make this line exact, one feels that the word mando, which terminates it, should be composed of two longs, that is to say, that it should be written mandò, which could not be without altering the sense entirely. Marchetti has translated into blank verse the Latin poem of Lucretius. I will quote the opening lines. Here is evident the softness to which I take exception and which prevents them from being really eumolpique, according to the sense that I have attached to this word.
Alma figlia di Giove, indite madre Del gran germe d'Enea, Venere bella, Degli uomini piacere e degli Dei: Tu, la sotto il volubili e lucenti Segni del cielo, il mar profundo, e tutta D'animai d'ogni specie orni la terra: . . . etc. (p. 68)

[223] One must not believe that the mute e with which many English words terminate represents the French feminine final, expressed by the same vowel. This mute e is in reality mute in English; ordinarily it is only used to give a more open sound to the vowel which precedes it, as in tale, scene, bone, pure, fire. Besides it is never taken into account, either in the measure or in the prosody of the lines. Thus these two lines of Dryden rhyme exactly:

"Now scarce the Trojan fleet with sails and oars Had left behind the fair Sicilian shores. . . . " Æneid, b. i., v. 50.
It is the same in these of Addison:

"Tune ev'ry string and ev'ry tongue, Be thou the Muse and subject of our song...."
St. Cecilia's Day, i., 10.
or these from Goldsmith:

"How often have I loiter'd o'er thy green, Where humble happiness endeared each scene." The Deserted Village, i., 7. (p. 68)

[224] There remains to us of this poetry the very precious fragments contained in the Edda and in Voluspa. The Edda, whose name signifies great-grandmother, is a collection, fairly ample, of Scandinavian traditions. Voluspa is a sort of Sibylline book, or cosmogonic oracle, as its name indicates. I am convinced that if the poets of the north, the Danes, Swedes, and Germans, had oftener drawn their subjects from these indigenous sources, they would have succeeded better than by going to Greece to seek them upon the summits of Parnassus. The mythology of Odin, descended from the Rhipæan mountains, suits them better than that of the Greeks, whose tongue furthermore is not conformable here. When one makes the moon and the wife (der Mond, das Weib) of masculine and neuter gender; when one makes the sun, the air, time, love (die Sonne, die Luft, die Zeit, die Liebe) of feminine gender, one ought wisely to renounce the allegories of Parnassus. It was on account of the sex given to the sun and the moon that the schism arose, of which I have spoken, in explaining the origin of the temple of Delphi.

The Scandinavian allegories, however, that I consider a débris of Thracian allegories, furnishing subjects of a very different character from those of the Greeks and Latins, might have varied the poetry of Europe and prevented the Arabesque fiction from holding there so much ascendancy. The Scandinavian verses, being without rhyme, hold moreover, to eumolpœia. The following is a strophe from Voluspa:

"Avant que le temps fût, Ymir avait été; Ni la mer, ni nes vents n'existaient pas encore; Il n'était de terre, il n'était point de ciel: Tout n'était qu'un abîme immense, sans verdure." "In the beginning, when naught was, there Was neither sand nor sea nor the cold waves, Nor was earth to be seen nor heaven above. There was a Yawning Chasm [chaos] but grass nowhere. . .
Ár vas alda pat-es ekki vas; vasa sandr né sær né svalar unnir, iærð fansk æva né upp-himinn; Gap vas Ginnunga, enn gras ekki, . . .

Voyez Mallet, Monuments celtiques, p. 135; et pour le texte, le poëme même de la Voluspa, in Edda islandorum, Mallet paraît avoir suivi un texte erroné. As to the Gallic poetry of the Scotch bards, that Macpherson has made known to us under the name of Ossian, much is needed that they may have a sufficient degree of authenticity for them to be cited as models, and placed parallel with those of Homer, as has been done without reflection. These poems, although resting for the greater part upon a true basis, are very far from being veritable as to form. The Scotch bards, like the Oscan troubadours, must be restored and often entirely remade, if they are to be read. Macpherson, in composing his Ossian, has followed certain ancient traditions, has put together certain scattered fragments;

but has taken great liberties with all the rest. He was, besides, a man endowed with creative genius and he might have been able to attain to epopœia if he had been better informed. His lack of knowledge has left a void in his work which demonstrates its falsity. There is no mythology, no allegory, no cult in Ossian. There are some historic or romanesque facts joined to long descriptions; it is a style more emphatic than figurative, more bizarre than original. Macpherson, in neglecting all kinds of mythological and religious ideas, in even mocking here and there the stone of power of the Scandinavians, has shown that he was ignorant of two important things: the one, that the allegorical or religious genius constitutes the essence of poetry; the other, that Scotland was at a very ancient period the hearth of this same genius whose interpreters were the druids, bards, and scalds. He should have known that, far from being p. 101 without religion, the Caledonians possessed in the heart of their mountains, the Gallic Parnassus, the sacred mountain of the Occidental isles; and that when the antique cult began to decline in Gaul, it was in Albion, reckoned among the holy isles by even the Indians, that the druids went to study. Voyez Les Commentaires de César, iv., 20; L'Introduction de l'histoire de Danemark, par Mallet; L'Histoire des Celtes, par Pelloutier; et enfin les Recherches asiatiques (Asiat. Research.), t. vi., p. 490 et 502.

In order to seize the occasion of applying eumolpique lines to a greater number of subjects, I am going to quote a sort of exposition of Ossian, the only one I believe, which is found in his poems; because Macpherson, for more originality, neglected nearly always to announce the subject of his songs. I will not give the text, because the English translation whence I obtained it does not give it. It concerns the battle of Lora. After a kind of exordium addressed to the son of the stranger, dweller of the silent cavern, Ossian said to him:

Le chant plait-il à ton oreille? Ecoute le récit du combat de Lora. Il est bien ancien, ce combat! Le tumulte Des armes, et les cris furieux des guerriers, Sont couverts par un long silence; Ils sont éteints depuis longtemps: Ainsi sur des rochers retentissants, la foudre Roule, gronde, éclate et n'est plus; Le soleil reparaît, et la cime brillante Des coteaux verdoyants, sourit à ses rayons.

Son of the secret cell! dost thou delight in songs? Hear the battle of Lora. The sound of its steel is long since past. So thunder on the darkened hill roars, and is no more. The sun returns with his silent beams, The glittering rocks, and green heads of the mountains smile.

This example serves to prove that eumolpique lines might easily adapt themselves to the dithyramb. (p. 69)

[225] The tragedy of the Cid, given by Pierre Corneille in 1626, upon which were based the grandeur and dominant character of the Théâtre Français, as well as the renown of the author, is taken from a Spanish ballad very celebrated in Spain. The Cid, who is the hero of it, lived towards the close of the eleventh century. He was a

type of the paladins and knights errant of the romanesque traditions. He enjoyed a wide reputation and attained a high degree of fortune. Voyez Monte-Mayor, Diana, l. ii.; et Voltaire, Essai sur les Mœurs, t. iii., stéréotype, p. 86.

In the course of the sixteenth century, the Spanish held a marked superiority over the other peoples: their tongue was spoken at Paris, Vienna, Milan, Turin. Their customs, their manners of thought and of writing, subjugated the minds of the Italians, and from Charles V. to the commencement of the reign of Philip III., Spain enjoyed an importance that the other peoples never had. Voyez Robertson, Introduction d l'Histoire de Charles-Quint.

It would be necessary to overstep considerably the ordinary limits of a footnote, if I should explain how it happens that Spain has lost this supremacy acquired by her, and why her tongue, the only one capable of rivalling and perhaps effacing the French, has yielded to it in all ways, and by which it was eclipsed. This explanation would demand for itself alone a very lengthy work. Among the writers who have sought for the cause of the decadence of the Spanish monarchy, some have believed to discover it in the increase of its wealth, others, in the too great extent of its colonies, and the greater part, in the spirit of its government and its superstitious cult. They have all thought that the tribunal of the Inquisition alone was capable of arresting the impulse of genius and of stifling the development of learning. In this they have taken effects for causes, and consequences for principles. They have not seen that the spirit of the government and the cult is always not the motive, but the result of the national spirit, and that the wealth and the colonies, indifferent in themselves, are only instruments that this spirit employs for good or evil, according to its character. I can only indicate the first cause which has prevented Spain from reaching the culminating point which France is very near to attaining. This cause is pride. Whilst Europe, enveloped in darkness, was, so to speak, in the fermentation of ignorance, Spain, conquered by the Arabs, received a germ of science which, developing with rapidity, produced a precocious fruit, brilliant, but like hot-house fruit lacking internal force and generative vigour. This premature production having raised Spain abruptly above the other European nations, inspired in her that pride, that excessive amour propre, which, making her treat with contempt all that did not belong to her, hindered her from making any change in her usual customs, carried her with complacency in her mistakes, and when other peoples came to bring forth fruits in their season, corrupted hers and stamped her with a stationary movement, which becoming necessarily retrogressive, must ruin her, and did ruin her. (p. 69)

[226] In comparing the first lines of Homer with those of Klopstock, it is seen that the Greek contains 29 letters, 18 of which are vowels; and the German 48 letters, 31 of which are consonants. It is difficult with such disparity in the elements to make the harmony the same. (p. 71)

[227] The final sigma is printed in the original book as the medial form here.—JBH (p. 77)

[228] The final sigma is printed in the original book as the medial form here.—JBH (p. 82)

[229] The epsilon in these words is rotated 180 degrees in the printed original.—JBH. (p. 83)

[230] Hiérocl., Comment. in Aur. Carmin. Proem. (p. 86)

[231] Fabric., Bibl. græc., p. 460; Dacier, Remarq. sur les Comm. d'Hiéroclès. (p. 86)

[232] Jamblic., De Vitâ Pythag., c. 30 et 33; Plutarch., De Gen. Socrat. (p. 86)

[233] Plutarch, De Repug. stoïc.; Diog. Laërt., l. viii., § 39; Polyb., l. ii.; Justin., l. xx., c. 4; Vossius, De Phil. sect., c. 6. (p. 86)

[234] Hiérocl., Aur. Carm., v. 71. (p. 86)

[235] Voyez Dacier, Rem. sur le Comment. d'Hiérocl. (p. 87)

[236] Bacon, Novum Organum, Aph., 65 et 71. (p. 89)

[237] Asiat. Res., t. iii., p. 371 à 374. (p. 89)

[238] Mém. concern. les Chin., t. ii., p. 26. (p. 89)

[239] Eulma Esclam. Note du Boun-Dehesh, p. 344. (p. 89)

[240] Porphyr., De Antr. Nymph., p. 126. (p. 89)

[241] Αὐτόν δ᾽ ἐκ ὁράω περὶ γὰρ νέφος ἐσήρικται. Voyez Dacier, dans ses Remarques sur les Comment. d'Hiérocl. (p. 89)

[242] Vitâ Pythagor.; Phot., Cod., 259; Macrob., Somn. Scip., l. i., c. 6, l. ii., c 12; August., De Civit. Dei, l. iv., c. 9 et 11; Euseb., Præp. Evang., l. iii., c. 9; Lactant., De Fals. Relig., l. i., c. 6 et 7; Plot., Ennead., iii., l. ii. (p. 90)

[243] Plutar., De Isid. et Osirid., p. 377. (p. 90)

[244] Hiérocl., Aur. Carm., v. i. (p. 91)

[245] The Greek word κόσμος expresses a thing put in order, arranged according to a fixed and regular principle. Its primitive root is in the Phœnician אוש (aôsh) a principle Being, the fire. The Latin word mundus renders the Greek sense very imperfectly. It signifies exactly, that which is made neat and clean by means of water. Its nearest root is unda, and its remotest root is found in the Phœnician אוד (aôd), an emanation, a vapour, a source. One can see, according to this etymology, that the Greeks drew the idea of order and beauty from fire, and the Latins from water. (p. 91)

[246] Diogen. Laërt., l. viii., 125; Plutar., De Decret. philos., ii., c. 6; Sext. Empir., Adv. Math., x., § 249; Stob., Eccl. phys., p. 468. (p. 91)

[247] Plutar., In Numa. (p. 91)

[248] Jambl., Vitâ Pythag., c. 28, 32 et 35. (p. 91)

[249] Ἑν, δύο. The symbol of Fo-Hi, so celebrated among the Chinese, is the same and is expressed by a whole line —— 1, and a broken line — — 2. I shall make myself better understood upon this subject, in speaking as I intend to do upon music and upon what the ancients understood by the language of Numbers. (p. 91)

[250] Vitâ Pythag.; Phot., Bibl. Codex, 259. (p. 91)

[251] Vie de Pythag. par Dacier. (p. 92)

[252] Hiérocl., Aurea Carmin., v. 1. (p. 92)

[253] Ci-devant, p. 81. (p. 92)

[254] Timée de Locres, ch. 3; Edit. de Batteux, § 8; Diod. Sicul., l. ii., p. 83; Herod., l. ii., c. 4; Hyde, De vet. Pers. Relig., c. 19; Plato, In Tim., In Phæd., In Legib., etc. (p. 92)

[255] Bailly, Hist. de l'Astr. anc., l. iii., § 10. (p. 92)

[256] Pythagoras, at an early age, was taken to Tyre by Mnesarchus, his father, in order to study there the doctrine of the Phœnicians; later he visited Egypt, Arabia, and Babylon, in which last city he remained twelve years. It was while there that he had frequent conferences concerning the principle of things with a very learned magian whom Porphyry names Zabratos; Plutarch, Zaratas; and Theodoret, Zaradas. (Porphyr., Vitâ Pythag.) Plutarch is inclined to believe that this magian is the same as Zardusht, or Zoroaster, and the chronology is not here entirely contrary. (Plutar., De Procreat. anim.; Hyde, De Relig. vet. Pers., c. 24, o. 309 et c. 31, p. 379.) (p. 92)

[257] Asiat. Research., t. vi., p. 174. (p. 92)

[258] Holwell's, Histor. Interest. Events, ch. iv., § 5. (p. 92)

[259] Beausobre, Hist. du Manich., t. i., p. 164. (p. 92)

[260] Macrob., Somn. Scip., l. i., c. ii. (p. 92)

[261] Böhme, Les Six Points, ch. 2. (p. 93)

[262] The word קבל signifies, in Hebrew, Arabic, and Chaldean, that which is anterior, that which one receives from the ancients by tradition. (p. 93)

[263] Aurea Carm., v. 48. (p. 93)

[264] Synes, Hymn., iii., v. 174; Hymn., iv., v. 68. (p. 93)

[265] Beausobre, list. du Manich., t. i., p. 572. (p. 93)

[266] The word Eon, in Greek Αἰών, is derived from the Egyptian or Phœnician אי (aï), a principle of will, a central point of development, and יון (ion), the generative faculty. This last word has signified, in a restricted sense, a dove, and has been the symbol of Venus. It is the famous Yoni of the Indians and even the Yn of the Chinese: that is to say, the plastic nature of the Universe. From there, the name of Ionia, given to Greece. (p. 94)

[267] Herm. Trismég., c. 11. (p. 94)

[268] Gods, Heroes, and Demons signify in the Greek words θεός, Ἥρωες, Δαίμων, whence they are derived, the Principle-Beings attained to perfection; the ruling Principle-Beings; Terrestrial Existences. The word θεός is formed from the word אוש (aôs), a Principle-Being, preceded by the hemantique letter ת (θ, th), which is the sign of perfection. The word Ἥρωες is composed of the same word אוש (aôc), preceded by the word ררה (herr), expressing all that rules. The word Δαίμων comes from the ancient word Δῆμ, land, united with the word ὤν, existence. (p. 95)

[269] Κάθαρσις καὶ τελειότης. (p. 95)

[270] Lil. Greg. Gyral., Pythag. Symb. Interpret., p. 92. (p. 95)

[271] Apud Phot. Cod., 249. (p. 95)

[272] Dict. Crit., art. PYTHAGORAS, rem. Q. (p. 96)

[273] Not long since, a man rather well organized mentally, but very slightly enlightened by the true science, brought out a book entitled Ruverabhoni, in which, heaping up all the ancient and modern sophisms pronounced against the social organization founded upon the establishment of the family, he aspired to change the instinct of nature, in this respect, and to found true happiness upon the débris of all the ties of blood, of all the affections of the soul, and of all the duties of consanguinity. (p. 96)

[274] As I give the same meaning as did Moses and not that of the Septuagint copied by the Vulgate, I transcribe here the original text, so that those who understand Hebrew may see that I have not deviated from it.
לך וְתנ רְיהלא הזהי-רשא המדאח לע רימי ווב דאי וְעמל רמא-תאו רְיבא-תא דככ
Exodus, ch. 20, v. 12. (p. 96)

[275] This country of Adam, in Hebrew האדמה (ha-adamah), adaméenne. This word, which has been vulgarly translated by the Earth, signifies it only by metaphor. Its proper sense, which is very difficult to grasp, depends always on that which is attached to the name of Adam, whence it is derived. Jhôah, in Hebrew יהוה, pronounced very improperly Jehovah, on account of a defective punctuation of the Masoretes, is the proper name of GOD. This name was formed by Moses in a manner as ingenious as sublime, by means of the contraction of the three tenses of the verb הוה (hôeh), to be. It signifies exactly will be-being-been; that which is, was, and shall be. One renders it well enough by Eternal. It is Eternity, or the Time-without-Limit of Zoroaster. This name is quite generally followed, as it is here, with the words אלהיך (Ælohî-cha), thy Gods, in order to express that the Unity contained in Jhôah, comprehends the infinity of the gods, and takes the place of it with the people of Israel. (p. 97)

[276] Mémoires concern, les Chinois, t. iv., p. 7. (p. 97)

[277] Nemesis, in Greek Νέμεσις, is derived from the Phœnician words נאמ (nam or næm), expressing every judgment, every order, every decree announced by word of mouth; and אשיש (æshish), all that serves for principle, as foundation. This last word has root אש (as, os, or æs). (p. 98)

[278] Hiao-King, ou Livre de la Piété filiale. (p. 99)

[279] Kong-Tzée, dans le Hiao-King qui contient sa doctrine. (p. 99)

[280] Hiérocl., Comment. Aurea. carmin., v. 5. (p. 99)

[281] Hiéroclès, ibid., v. 7. (p. 99)

[282] Porphyr., in Vitâ Pythag., p. 37. (p. 99)

[283] Dacier, Vie de Pythag. (p. 99)

[284] Diog. Laërt., l. v., § 21. (p. 99)

[285] Hiérocl., Aurea. carm., v. 8. (p. 99)

[286] Evang. de S. Math., ch. 22. (p. 99)

[287] Zend-Avesta, 30e hâ, p. 164; ibid., 34e hâ, p. 174; ibid., 72e hâ, p. 258. (p. 99)

[288] Herm. Trismeg., In Pœmand. (p. 101)

[289] Senac., De Sen., vi., 2. (p. 101)

[290] Aul. Gell., l. vi., c. 2. (p. 101)

[291] Plutar., De repugn. Stoïc. de Fato. (p. 102)

[292] Chalcidius, in Tim., not. 295, p. 387. (p. 102)

[293] Hist. du Manich., t. ii., l. v., ch. 6, p. 250. (p. 102)

[294] Dict. crit., MANICHEENS, rem. D. (p. 102)

[295] Cicéron, Tuscul., l. i.; Clem. Alex., Strom., l. v., p. 501. (p. 102)

[296] Justin., Cohort ad Gent., p. 6; Cyrill., Contr. Julien; Fabric., Bibl. græc., t. i., p. 472. (p. 102)

[297] Plutar., De Procr. anim. (p. 102)

[298] Plat., Epist., 2 et 7, t. iii., p. 312, 313, 341, etc. (p. 103)

[299] Voyez l'excellent ouvrage de Beausobre à ce sujet, L'Histoire du Manichéisme. (p. 103)

[300] When Zoroaster spoke of this Cause, he gave it the name of Time without Limit, following the translation of Anquetil Duperron. This Cause does not still appear

absolute in the doctrine of this theosophist; because in a passage of the Zend-Avesta, where in contemplation of the Supreme Being, producer of Ormuzd, he calls this Being, the Being absorbed in excellence, and says that Fire, acting from the beginning, is the principle of union between this Being and Ormuzd (36e hâ du Vendidad Sadé, p. 180, 19e fargard, p. 415), One finds in another book, called Sharistha, that when this Supreme Being organized the matter of the Universe, he projected his Will in the form of a resplendent light (Apud Hyde, c. 22, p. 298). (p. 103)

[301] In Tim., not. 295. (p. 104)

[302] Voyez Photius, Cod., 251. Plotin, Porphyre, Jamblique, Proclus et Symplicius ont été du même sentiment qu' Hiéroclès, ainsi que le dit le savant Fabricius, Bibl. græc., t. i., p. 472. (p. 104)

[303] Iliad, L. ult., v. 663. (p. 104)

[304] Cicér., de Natur. Deor., l. i., c. 15. (p. 104)

[305] Axiômes de Pythagore conservés par Stobée, Serm. 6. (p. 105)

[306] Hiérocl., Aur. carm., v. 10 et 11. (p. 106)

[307] Strab., l. xvi., p. 512; Sext. Empir., Adv. Mathem., p. 367. (p. 106)

[308] Atom, in Greek ἄτομος, is formed from the word τόμος, a part, to which is joined the a privative. (p. 106)

[309] Huet, Cens. Phil. Cartesian., c. 8, p. 213. If one carefully examines the systems of Descartes, Leibnitz, and Newton, one will see that, after all, they are reduced either to atoms, or to inherent forces which move them. (p. 106)

[310] Cicér., de Fato, c. 77. (p. 106)

[311] August., Epist., 56. (p. 106)

[312] August., Epist., 56. (p. 106)

[313] Cicér., de Nat. Deor., l. i., c. 19; Quæst. Acad., l. iv., c. 13; de Fato, c. 9. (p. 106)

[314] Diog. Laërt., l. x., §123; Cicér., de Nat. Deor., l. i., c. 30. (p. 107)

[315] Senec., Epist., 88; Sext. Empir., Adv. Math., l. vii., c. 2; Arist., Métaphys., l. iii., c. 4. (p. 107)

[316] Arist., Physic., l. vi., c. 9; voyez Bayle, Dict. crit., art. ZENON, rem. F. (p. 107)

[317] Cicér., de Natur. Deor., l. i., c 15. (p. 107)

[318] Semel jussit, semper paret, Seneca has said. "The laws which God has prescribed for Himself," he adds, "He will never revoke, because they have been dictated by His own perfections; and that the same plan, the same design having pleased Him once, pleases Him eternally" (Senec., Præf. ad Quæst. nat.). (p. 107)

[319] Cicer., De Fato, cap. 17. (p. 107)

[320] Cicer., ibid., c. 9. (p. 107)

[321] Aul. Gell., l. vi., c. 2. (p. 107)

[322] Cicer., De Nat. Deor., l. i., c. 9; Plutar., De repug. Stoïc.; Diogenian. Apud.; Euseb., Præp. Evang., l. vi., c. 8. (p. 108)

[323] Herodot., Euterp., §171; Julian Firm., De Error, prof., p. 45. (p. 108)

[324] Meurs., Græc. Feriat., l. i.; Plutar., In Alcibiad.; Porphyr., De Abst., l. § 36; Euseb., Præp. Evang., l. i., c. 1; Schol. Apoll., l. i., v. 917; Pausan., Corinth, p. 73. (p. 108)

[325] Porphyr., Vitâ Pythag., p. 10. (p. 108)

[326] The doctrine of Krishna is found especially recorded in the Bhaghavad Gita, one of the Pouranas most esteemed by the Brahmans; in the Zend-Avesta and in the Boun-Dehesh, that of Zoroaster. The Chinese have the Tchun-Tsieou of Kong-Tse, historic monument raised to the glory of Providence; in the Pœmander and Æsculapius, the ideas of Thoth. The book of Synesius upon Providence contains the dogmas of the Mysteries. Finally one can consult in the course of the Edda, the sublime discourse of Odin, entitled Havamâl. The basis of all these works is the same. (p. 108)

[327] This, as I observed in my Second Examination, should be understood only by the vulgar. The savant and the initiate easily restored to Unity this infinity of gods, and understood or sought the origin of evil, without the knowledge of which, divine Unity is inexplicable. (p. 109)

³²⁸ Talès, cité par Platon, De Republ., l. x.; Aristot., Metaph., l. iii.; Cicer., Acad. Quæst., iv., c. 37. (p. 109)

³²⁹ Anaximandre, cité par Aristot., Phys., l. i.; Sext. Empir., Pyrr., iii. (p. 109)

³³⁰ Anaximène, cité par Arist., Metaph., l. i., c. 3; Plutar., De Placit. Phil., i., 3. (p. 109)

³³¹ Héraclite, cité par Platon, Theætet.; Arist., Metaph., l. i., c. 6; Sext. Empir., Adv. Math., l. vii. (p. 109)

³³² De Gérando, Hist. des Syst. de Phil., t. iii., p. 283; Arist., Metaph., l. i., c. 6; Diog. Laërt., l. ix., c. 19. (p. 109)

³³³ Cicer., De Nat. Deor., l. i., c. 9. (p. 109)

³³⁴ Boët, De Consol., l. i., prosa 4. (p. 109)

³³⁵ Plutar., Adv. Stoïc., p. 1075. (p. 109)

³³⁶ Cicer., De Fato, c. 10; Lucret., l. ii., v. 216, 251, 284. (p. 109)

³³⁷ Cicer., De Fato, c. 9 et 17; Diogenian., Apud.; Euseb., Præp. Evan., l. vi., c. 8. (p. 109)

³³⁸ Cicer., De Natur. Deor., l. iii., c. 38 et 39. (p. 109)

³³⁹ Aul. Gell., l. vi., c. 1. (p. 109)

³⁴⁰ Plutar., Adv. Stoïc. (p. 110)

³⁴¹ The name given to the sect of the Pharisees signifies, in general, that which is enlightened, illumined, glorified, illustrious. It is derived from the root אור (aor), the light, governed by the article פה (phe), which expresses the emphasis; thence פאר (phær), an aureola, a tiara, and פרתמים (pharethmim), men illustrious, sublime. The name given to the sect of the Sadducees is derived from the word שד (shad) which, expressing all diffusion, all propagation, is applied to productive nature in general, and in particular to a mammal, its symbol among the Egyptians; it signifies properly the Physicists, or the Naturalists. (p. 110)

³⁴² The original name of the Book of Moses is ספר (sepher); the name of the Bible, that we attribute to it, is derived from the Greek Βίβλος, adopted by the so-called translators of the Septuagint. (p. 110)

[343] Joseph., Antiq., l. xii., c. 22; l. xiii., c. 9 et 23; l. xvii., c. 3; Budd, Introd. ad Phil. Hebr.; Basnage, Histoire des Juifs, t. i. (p. 110)

[344] This is founded upon a great number of passages, of which it will suffice to cite the following. One finds in Amos, ch. iii., v. 6: "Shall there be evil in a city which the Lord hath not done?" And in Ezekiel, ch. xxi., v. 3: "And say to the land of Israel, Thus saith the Lord God: Behold, I come against thee, and I will draw forth my sword out of its sheath, and will cut off in thee the just, and the wicked . . . against all flesh, from the south even to the north. . . . That all flesh may know that I the Lord have drawn my sword." (p. 110)

[345] Vitâ Pythag.; Photius, Bibl. Cod., 259. (p. 112)

[346] Kircher, Œdip., t. i., p. 411; Edda Island Fabl.; Macrob., Saturn., l. i., c. 20. (p. 112)

[347] Plotin, Ennead., iii., l. 2; Euseb., Præp. Evan., l. iii., c. 9; Macrob., Somn. Schip., l. ii., c. 12; Marc. Aurell., l. iv., c. 34. (p. 112)

[348] Pan, in Greek πᾶν, signifies the All, and Phanes is derived from the Phœnician word אנש (ânesh), man, preceded by the emphatic article פ (ph). It must be observed that these two names spring from the same root אן (ân), which, figuratively, expresses the sphere of activity, and literally, the limitation of the being, its body, its capacity. Hence אני (âni), me, and אניה (aniha), a vessel. (p. 112)

[349] Mém. concern. les Chinois, t. ii., p. 174 et suiv.; Edda Island; Beau-sobre, Hist. du Manich., t. ii., p. 784; Bœhme, De la triple Vie de l'Homme, c. ix., § 35 et suiv. (p. 112)

[350] Πάντι εν Κόσμῳ τριὰς·ἧς Μονὰς ἄρχει.
        Zoroast. Oracul. (p. 112)

[351] Hiérocl., Aurea Carmin., v. 14. (p. 113)

[352] Hermès, In Pœmandr. (p. 115)

[353] Evang. St. Math., ch. 18. (p. 117)

[354] Vendidad Sadé, p. 89. (p. 117)

[355] 34e hâ, p. 174. (p. 117)

[356] 3e fargard., p. 284. (p. 117)

[357] Jeshts Sadès, p. 151. (p. 117)

[358] Hafiz, cité par les auteurs Des Recherches asiatiques, t. iv., p. 167. (p. 118)

[359] L' Arya, cité comme ci-dessus:
"L'homme de bien, paisable au moment qu'il expire, Tourne sur ses bourreaux un œil religieux, Et bénit jusqu'au bras qui cause son martyre: Tel l'arbre de Sandal que frappe un furieux, Couvre de ses parfums le fer qui le dechire." (p. 118)

[360] Edda Island; Hâvamâl. (p. 118)

[361] Diogen. Laërt., In Prœm., p. 5. (p. 118)

[362] Pœmander et Asclepius. (p. 118)

[363] This is the vast collection of Brahmanic morals. One finds there many of the lines repeated word for word in the Sepher of Moses. (p. 118)

[364] Senec., De Sen., l. vi., c. 2. (p. 119)

[365] Hiérocl., Aur. carmin., v. 18. (p. 120)

[366] Jamblic., De Vitâ Pythag.; Porphyr., ibid., et de Abstin.; Vitâ Pythag. apud; Phot., Cod., 259; Diog. Laërt., In Pythag., l. viii.; Hierocl., Comment. in Aur. Carm.; ibid., De Provident.; Philost., In Vitâ Apollon; Plutar., De Placit. philos.; ibid., De Procreat. anim.; Apul., In Florid.; Macrob., In Saturn. et Somn. Scip.; Fabric., Bibl. græc. in Pythag.; Clem. Alex., Strom., passim., etc. (p. 120)

[367] Hiérocl., Aur. Carm., v. 14; Phot., Cod., 242 et 214. (p. 120)

[368] Diog. Laërt., In Pythag.; ibid., In Emped. (p. 121)

[369] Hiérocl., Pont. apud Diog. Laërt., l. viii., § 4. (p. 121)

[370] Maximus Tyrius has made a dissertation upon the origin of Evil, in which he asserts that the prophetic oracles, having been consulted on this subject, responded by these two lines from Homer:
"We accuse the gods of our evils, while we ourselves By our own errors, are responsible for them." (p. 121)

[371] Hiérocl., Aur. Carm., v. 18. (p. 121)

[372] Plutar., De Repugn. Stoïc. (p. 121)

[373] In Gorgi. et Phileb. (p. 122)

[374] Hiérocl., Aur. Carmin., v., 18. (p. 122)

[375] Hiérocl., Aur. Carmin., v. 18, 49 et 62. (p. 122)

[376] In Phédon; In Hipp., ii.; In Theæt.; De Rep., l. iv., etc. (p. 122)

[377] Hyde, De Relig. Vet. Pers., p. 298. (p. 122)

[378] Evan. S. Math., ch. xvii., v. 19. (p. 122)

[379] Vie de Kong-Tzée (Confucius), p. 324. (p. 122)

[380] Meng-Tzée, cité par Duhalde, t. ii., p. 334. (p. 122)

[381] Krishna, Bhagavad-Gita, lect. ii. (p. 122)

[382] XL Questions sur l'Ame (Viertzig Fragen von der Seilen Orstand, Essentz, Wesen, Natur and Eigenschafft, etc. Amsterdam, 1682). Quest. 1. (p. 122)

[383] Ibid. (p. 122)

[384] IX Textes, text. 1 et 2. (p. 123)

[385] XL Questions, quest. 6. (p. 123)

[386] Clem. Alex., Strom., l. iv., p. 506; Beausobre, Hist. du Manich., t. ii., p. 28. (p. 124)

[387] This is the signification of the Greek word πιλόσοφος. (p. 124)

[388] Dans le Tchong-Yong, ou le Principe central, immuable, appelé Le Livre de la grande Science. (p. 124)

[389] Evan. S. Math., ch. vii., v. 6. (p. 125)

[390] Bhagavad-Gita, lect. 8 et 13. (p. 125)

[391] Evang. S. Luc., ch. xiv., v. 26. (p. 125)

[392] 50e hâ Zend-Avesta, p. 217; 45e hâ, ibid., p. 197. (p. 125)

[393] Nombres, ch. xxxi.; Deutéronome, ch. iii., xx., etc. (p. 125)

[394] Exode, ch. xxxiv., v. 6. (p. 125)

[395] Koran, i., ch. 4, 22, 23, 24, 25, 50, etc. (p. 125)

[396] Voyez la fin du dernier Examen. (p. 125)

[397] S. Math., ch. v., v. 44. (p. 125)

[398] Ibid., c. xii., v. 20, etc. (p. 125)

[399] Ibid., ch. x., v. 34. (p. 125)

[400] S. Luc, ch. xii., v. 52, 53. (p. 126)

[401] Bacon, Novum Organum. (p. 127)

[402] Novum Organ., Aphor., 38 et seq. (p. 128)

[403] Voyez La Vie de Kong-Tzée et le Ta-Hio, cité dans les Mém. concern. les Chinois, t. i., p. 432. (p. 128)

[404] Mém. concern. les Chin., t. iv., p. 286. (p. 128)

[405] Novum Organum in Præf. et Aph., 1. (p. 128)

[406] Ibid., Aph., 11. (p. 128)

[407] Ibid., Aph., 13. (p. 128)

[408] Ibid., Aph., 14 et 15. (p. 128)

[409] Ibid., Aph., 38 et seq. (p. 128)

[410] Novum Organum in Præf. et Aph., 73. (p. 128)

[411] Ibid., Aph., 63. (p. 129)

[412] Ibid., Aph., 65. (p. 130)

[413] Hermes, In Asclepio; Porphyr., De Antr. Nymph., p. 106; Origen, Contr. Cels., l. vi., p. 298; Hyd., De Vet. Pers. Relig., p. 16; Jamblic., De Myster-Egypt., c. 37. (p. 132)

[414] Hist. des Voyag., t. lii., p. 72; Divd., l. iv., c. 79; Plutar., In Vitâ Num. (p. 132)

[415] Boulanger, Antiq. dévoil., l. iii., ch. 5, § 3. (p. 132)

[416] Mém. de l'Acad. des Insc., t. i., p. 67; Tit.-Liv., Decad., i, l. ix.; Aul. Gell., l. vi., c. 9. (p. 132)

[417] Duhald., t. ii., p. 578; t. iii., p. 336, 342; Const. d'Orville, t. i., p. 3. (p. 132)

[418] Philostr., In Vitâ Apoll., l. iii., c. 13. (p. 133)

[419] Dans mon 21e Examen, où j'ai cité particulièrement Diogène Laërce, l. viii., § 4. (p. 133)

[420] Syncell., p. 35. (p. 133)

[421] Senec., Quæst. Nat., l. iii., c. 30; Synes., De Provid., l. ii., sub fin. (p. 133)

[422] Plato, In Tim.; Ovid, Metam., l. xv., fab. v.; Senec., Epist., 35; Macrob., In Somn. Scip., l. ii., c. 2; Hist. des Voyages, t. xii., p. 529; Dupuis, Orig. des Cultes, l. v., in 12, p. 474; Bailly, Hist. de l'Astr. Anc., l. ix., § 15. (p. 133)

[423] Ciceron, De Divin., l. ii., c. 97. (p. 134)

[424] Cicer., De Natur. Deor., l. ii., c. 20; ibid., De Divin., l. ii., c. 97. (p. 134)

[425] Plato, In Tim. (p. 134)

[426] Souryâ-Siddhanta. (p. 134)

[427] Asiat. Research., t. ii., p. 378. (p. 134)

[428] Biot., Astr. Phys., ch. xiv., p. 291. (p. 134)

[429] Vitâ Pythag.; Phot., Bibl. Cod., 259; Plato, In Tim.; Macrob., In Somn. Scip.; Virg., Æneid, l. vi., v. 724; Sevius, Comm., ibid.; Cicer., De Nat. Deor., l. i., c. 5, 11, 14, et 15; Diog. Laërt., In Zon.; Batteux, Causes premières, t. ii., p. 116; Beausob., Hist. du Manich., t. ii., l. vi., c. 6, § 14. (p. 134)

[430] Stanley, De Phil. Chald., p. 1123. (p. 134)

[431] Kircher, Ædip., t. i., p. 172, et t. ii., p. 200. (p. 134)

[432] Maimon., More Nevoch., i., part., c. 70. (p. 134)

[433] Salmas, Ann. Climat., Præf., p. 32. (p. 136)

[434] Homer, Odyss., K. V. 494; Diodor. Sic., l. v., C. 6; Plin., l. vii., C. 56; Plutar., De Oracul. Defect., p. 434. (p. 136)

[435] Hierocl., In Aurea Carm., v. 31. (p. 137)

[436] Alcibiad., i. et ii.; Lachès, etc. (p. 137)

[437] In Alcibiad., i. (p. 137)

[438] Voyez Burette, Mém. de l'Acad. des Belles-Lett., t. v.; Laborde, Essai sur la Musique, t. i., introd., p. 20.
Our painters have hardly treated Greek painting better; and perhaps if the Pythian Apollo and the Chaste Venus had not again astonished Europe, but had disappeared as did the masterpieces of Polygnotus and of Zeuxis, the modern sculptors would have said that the ancients failed as much in pattern as in colouring. (p. 138)

[439] Wood, Essai sur le Génie orig. d'Homère, p. 220. (p. 138)

[440] Bryant, cité par Desalles, Hist. d'Homère, p. 18. (p. 138)

[441] Wolf et Klotz, cités par le même. Ibid., p. 36 et 117. (p. 138)

[442] Paw, Recherches sur les Grecs, t. ii., p. 355. (p. 138)

[443] C'est un certain Grégoire, cité par Leo Allazi, dans son Livre de Patriâ Homeri. Voltaire, Dict. philos., art. EPOPÉE. (p. 138)

[444] The name of Pagan is an injurious and ignoble term derived from the Latin Paganus, which signifies a rustic, a peasant. When Christianity had entirely triumphed over Greek and Roman polytheism, and when by the order of the Emperor Theodosius, the last temple dedicated to the gods of the nations had been destroyed in the cities, it was found that the people in the country still persisted a considerable time in the ancient cult, which caused them and all their

imitators to be called derisively Pagans. This appellation, which could suit the Greeks and Romans in the fifth century who refused to submit to the dominating religion in the Empire, is false and ridiculous when one extends it to other times, and to other peoples. It cannot be said without at once offending chronology and common sense, that the Romans or Greeks of the time of Cæsar, of Alexander, or of Pericles; the Persians, Arabs, Egyptians, Indians, the Chinese, ancient or modern, were Pagans; that is to say, peasants disobedient to the laws of Theodosius. These are polytheists, monotheists, mythologists, whatever one wishes, idolators perhaps, but not Pagans. (p. 138)

[445] Novum Organ., aph. 48. (p. 139)

[446] De Dign. et Increm. Science, l. iii., c. 4. (p. 139)

[447] Ut suprà. (p. 140)

[448] Bacon, de le Vie et de la Mort; Sueton., in Tiber., § 66. (p. 141)

[449] Hierocles, Aur. Carm., v. 33. (p. 142)

[450] Bacon assures, following the ancients, that the envious eye is dangerous and that it has been observed that after great triumphs, illustrious personages having been the object of an envious eye have found themselves ill-disposed for some days following (Sylva Sylvarum, § 944). (p. 143)

[451] Aul. Gell., l. iv., c. 11. (p. 143)

[452] Athen., l. vii., c. 16; Jambl., Vitâ Pythag., c. 30. (p. 143)

[453] Jambl., ibid., c. 24. (p. 143)

[454] Diog. Laërt., l. viii., §9; Clem. Alex., Pæd., l. ii., p. 170. (p. 143)

[455] Jambl., ibid., c. 21; Porphyre, Vitâ Pythag., p. 37; Athen., l. x., p. 418; Aul. Gell., l. iv., c. 11. (p. 143)

[456] Hiérocl., Aur. Carm., v. 32. (p. 144)

[457] Proverbes du Brahme Barthrovhari. (p. 144)

[458] Chou-King, ch. Yu-Mo. (p. 144)

[459] On trouve ce passages dans le Tchong-Yong, ou Livre du Juste-Milieu; ouvrage très célèbre parmi les Chinois. (p. 145)

[460] Porphyr., Vitâ Pythag., p. 27. (p. 146)

[461] Institutes of Manu, ch. 1, v. 5. (p. 146)

[462] Xénophon, Mém., l. iv., p. 796; Plat., in Alcib., i.; ibid., in Charm.; Pausan., l. x.; Plin., l. vii., c. 32. (p. 147)

[463] In Alcibiad., i. (p. 147)

[464] Cicér., Acad. Quæst., l. iv., c. 24; Sext. Empir., Hypotyp., l. i., c. 4 et 12. (p. 147)

[465] Diog. Laërt., l. iv., §10; Cicer., Acad. Quæst., l. iv., c. 18. (p. 147)

[466] Desland, Hist. Critiq. de la Philosoph., t. ii., p. 258. (p. 147)

[467] Euseb., Præp. Evan., l. xiv., c. 4. (p. 147)

[468] The Greek word is derived from the verb καλυπρεῖν, to cover with a veil. (p. 148)

[469] Bayle, Dict. crit., art. ARCÉSILAS. (p. 148)

[470] Sextus Empiricus, who was not a man to advance anything thoughtlessly, alleges that Arcesilaus was only a skeptic in semblance and that the doubts which he proposed to his listeners had no other aim than that of seeing if they had enough genius to understand the dogmas of Plato. When he found a disciple who evinced the necessary force of mind, he initiated him into the true doctrine of the Academy (Pyrrh. hypotyp., l. i., c. 33). (p. 148)

[471] Sext. Empir., Pyrrh. hypotyp., l. i., c. 4, 12, 15; l. ii., c. 4, etc. (p. 148)

[472] Ὄιν περ φύλλων γενεή, τοίη δὲ καὶ ανδρῶν. Iliad, l. vi., v. 146. (p. 148)

[473] The Brahmans call the illusion which results from this veil maya. According to them, there is only the Supreme Being who really and absolutely exists; all the rest is maya, that is to say, phenomenal, even the trinity formed by Brahma, Vishnu, and Rudra. (p. 149)

[474] De Gérando, Hist. comp. des Systèmes de philos., t. iii., p. 360. (p. 149)

[475] De Gérando, Hist. comp. des Systèmes de philos., t. iii., p. 361. (p. 149)

[476] Zeno raving been thrown by a storm into the port of Piræus at Athens, all his life regarded this accident as a blessing from Providence, which had enabled him to devote himself to philosophy and to obey the voice of an oracle which had ordered him to assume "the colour of the dead"; that is, to devote himself to the study of the ancients and to sustain their doctrine. (p. 149)

[477] Plutarch, in Catone majore. (p. 149)

[478] Plutarch, ibid.; Cicér., de Rep., l. ii.; Apud Nonium voce Calumnia. Lactant. l. v., c. 14. (p. 150)

[479] Kritik der Reinen Vernunft (Critique de la Raison pure), s. 6. (p. 152)

[480] Du mot grec κριτικός, celui qui est apt à juger. (p. 152)

[481] L'Histoire comparée des Systèmes de Philos., par De Gérando, et des Mélanges de Phil., par Ancillon de Berlin. These two writers, whatever one may say, have analysed very well the logical part of Kantism, and have penetrated, especially the former, into the rational part, as far as it was possible, for men who write upon the system of a philosopher without adopting the principles and making themselves his followers. (p. 153)

[482] Krit. der Reinen Vernunft; çà et là, en plusieurs endroits. (p. 153)

[483] This is taken from the Vedanta, a metaphysical treatise attributed to Vyasa and commented upon by Sankarâchârya. (p. 153)

[484] Justin, Cohort. ad Gent., p. 6; Cyrill., Contr. Julian. (p. 153)

[485] Plutar., de Procr. anim.; Chalcid., in Tim., n. 293. (p. 154)

[486] Plato, in Tim.; ibid., in Theet.; ibid., de Rep., l. iv. Conférez avec Proclus, Comment. in Tim., l. i.; Marc-Aurel., l. iv., l. ix., et l. x.; et Beausobre, Hist. du Manich., t. ii., p. 175, etc. (p. 154)

[487] The idea of making the quaternary spring from the unity, and the decade from the quaternary is expressed literally in the following lines of Pythagoras, preserved by Proclus:
. . . Πρόεισιν ὁ θεῖος ἀριθμὸς Μονάδος ἐκ κευθμῶνος ἀκηράτκ, ἔς τ᾽ ἂν ἵκηται Τετράδ᾽ ἑωὶ ζαδέην, ἣ δὴ τέκε μητέρα πάντων, Πανδοχέα, ὠρέσβειραν, ὅρον ωερὶ πᾶσι τιθεῖσαν, Ἄτροπον, ἀκαμάτην, δεκάδα κλείκσι μιν ἁγνήν·

The Monad, of Number is the sacred source; From it Number emanates and holds the virtues With which shines the Tetrad, Universal Mother, Which produces all things and conceals in its depths The immortal Decade, honoured in all places. (p. 154)

⁴⁸⁸ The nearest root of this word is find, whence is derived finden, to find; its remote root is hand, the seat of touch, whence comes finger, that which feels; its primitive root is אד or יד (âd or id), the hand in Phœnician. This last root, becoming nasal at the final and aspirate at the initial, has produced hand; fang, a capture, and find, a discovery. The syllable emp, which precedes the root find, expresses the movement which lifts up from below; lich designates that which disqualifies by identity, and keit, that which substantiates. (p. 155)

⁴⁸⁹ The root of this word is stand, a fixed thing, a state; its remote root is stat, that which is permanent. Its primitive root is שדד (shdad), firmness, force, constancy. The initial syllable ver expresses the movement which carries far away, which transports from the place where one is, to that where one is not. (p. 155)

⁴⁹⁰ The nearest root of this word, as well as its remote root, has disappeared from the modern German, where one finds only its derivatives. Its primitive root is in the Latin word opt, whence comes opto, I choose; and optime, best. This root is attached to the Phœnician עיף (whôph), anything which is raised above another thing. It becomes nasal in the German word and has changed the ph to ft. From it is derived the Saxon, English, Belgian, and Danish word up, which expresses the movement of everything which tends above. Also from it, the German word luft, air, and the English word aloft, that which is elevated. The preposition ver has taken the final n, placing it before unft, as it carries it constantly in its analogue fern, that which is distant. Likewise one says fernglass, a telescope with which one sees at a distance. (p. 155)

⁴⁹¹ De Gérando, Hist. des Systèmes de Philos., t. ii., p. 193. (p. 155)

⁴⁹² Brit. der Rein. Vernunft, s. 24. (p. 156)

⁴⁹³ In the Oriental languages רו (rou) indicates the visual ray, and רד (rad), all movement which is determined upon a straight line. This root, accompanied by a guttural inflection, is called recht, in German, and right in English and Saxon. The Latins made of it rectum, that which is straight. In French rature and rateau. The Teutons, taking right in a figurative sense, have drawn from this same root, rath, a council, and richter, a judge. (p. 156)

494 In Tim., cité par Beausobre, Hist. du Manich., t. ii., p. 174. (p. 157)

495 The word intelligence, in Latin intelligentia, is formed of two words, inter eligere or elicere, to choose, to attract to self interiorly, and by sympathy. The etymology of the word expresses exactly the use of the faculty. (p. 157)

496 Kritik der Reinen Vernunft, s. 662, 731; De Gérando, Hist. des Systèm., t. ii., p. 230. (p. 157)

497 Krit. der Reinen Vernunft, s. 306, 518, 527, etc. (p. 157)

498 Ibid., s. 135, 137, 399, etc. (p. 157)

499 Kritik der praktischen Vernunft (Critique de la Raison pratique), s. 5, 22, 219, 233, etc. (p. 158)

500 Characteristics, London, 1737. (p. 158)

501 A System of Moral Philosophy, t. i., eh. 4. (p. 158)

502 Enquiry into the Human Mind, on the Principle of Common Sense. (p. 158)

503 An Appeal to Common Sense, etc., Edinburgh, 1765. (p. 158)

504 In Greek τὸ ἡγεμονικόν, that which dominates and rules, that which is intelligible. (p. 160)

505 In Greek τὸ φυσικόν, that which pertains to generative nature, that which is physical, and sentient. (p. 160)

506 In Greek τὸ λογικόν, that which pertains to reasonable nature, that which is logical, the thing which proves that another thing is. Voyez Platon, in Tim., et conférez avec Beausobre, Hist. du Manich., t. ii., p. 174. (p. 160)

507 Plutar., de Facie in Orb. lun., p. 943. (p. 161)

508 The first kind of virtue is called ἀνθωπίνη, human, and the second ἡρωικὴ καὶ δία, heroic and divine. Attention should be given to these epithets which are related to the three principal faculties of man. Aristot., ad Nicom., l. vii., c. 1; Plato, in Theætet.; Gallien, in Cognit et Curai. morb. anim., l. i., c. 3, et 6; Theod. Marcil, in Aur. Carmin. (p. 161)

509 In Somn. Scip., c. 8. (p. 161)

[510] Aristot., de Cælo et Mundo, l. i.; Philo, de Mund. opific. (p. 161)

[511] Pausan., in Corinth., p. 72; Tzetz., in Schol. (p. 161)

[512] Suidas, in Εποπ; Harpocr., ibid. (p. 161)

[513] Clem. Alex., l. v., p. 582. (p. 162)

[514] Psellus, Ad Oracul. Zoroastr. (p. 162)

[515] Meurs. Eleus., c. 12; Dion. Chrysost., Orat. xii. (p. 162)

[516] Sophocl. apud Plutar., De Audiend. Poet. Schol.; Aristoph., De Pace. (p. 162)

[517] Porphyr., Vitâ Pythag., p. 5. (p. 163)

[518] γνῶσις, savant. (p. 163)

[519] Epiph., l. i.; Plucquet, Dictionn. des Hérésies, t. ii., p. 72. (p. 163)

[520] Diod. Sicul., l. i.; Herodot., l. ii. (p. 163)

[521] Aristot., Polit., l. ii.; Strab., l. viii. (p. 163)

[522] Voyez DANIEL, et conférez avec Court de Gébelin, Monde primitif, t. viii., p. 9. (p. 163)

[523] Zend-Avesta, 14e hâ, p. 127. (p. 163)

[524] Pomp. Mela, iii., c. 2; César, l. vi., c. 14; Pelloutier, Hist. des Celtes, l. iv., ch. 1, § 27 et 30. (p. 163)

[525] The first Shastra is entitled Djatimala. I am ignorant of the title of the other, that I cite from Henry Lord: Discovery of the Banian Religion, in Church, Collect., vol. vi. (p. 164)

[526] Asiat. Research., tom. vi., p. 254. (p. 164)

[527] Mémoir. concern. les Chin., t. ii., p. 174 et suiv. (p. 165)

[528] Vie de Kong-Tzée, p. 237 et suiv. (p. 166)

[529] Porphyr., Vitâ Pythag. (p. 169)

[530] Plato, ut suprà. (p. 169)

[531] Synes., De Provident., c. 5. (p. 169)

[532] Beausobre, Hist. du Manich., t. ii., p. 33. (p. 169)

[533] Tatian, Orat. contr. Cræc., p. 152. (p. 171)

[534] Diogen. Laërt., l. x., § 123; Cicero, De Nat. Deor., l. i., c. 30. (p. 172)

[535] Cicer., ibid., c. 8 et seq. (p. 172)

[536] Cicer., ut suprà. (p. 173)

[537] Diogen. Laërt., l. x., § 123. (p. 173)

[538] Dict. critiq., art. EPICURE, rem. T (p. 175)

[539] Mém. concern. les Chin., t. i., p. 102 et 138. (p. 175)

[540] Asiat. Research., vol. vi., p. 215. Voyez les Pouranas intitulés, Bhagavad-Vedam et Bhagavad-Gita, et conférez avec les Recherches asiatiq., t. v., p. 350 et suiv., et avec l'ouvrage de Holwell (Interest. Hist. Events), ch. 4, § 5, etc. (p. 175)

[541] Cicer., cité par S. August., Contr. Pelag., l. iv.; Pindar, Olymp., ii., v. 122. (p. 175)

[542] Meurs., Eleus., c. 11; Dion. Chrysost., Orat. 12. (p. 175)

[543] Boun-Dehesh, p. 347. (p. 175)

[544] Vendidad-Sadé, 30e M. (p. 176)

[545] Homil. Clement., xix., § 4, p. 744. (p. 176)

[546] Ibid., cité par Beausobre, Hist. du Manich., t. i., p. 38. (p. 176)

[547] It is necessary before all, to restore the language of Moses, lost, as I have said, for more than twenty-four centuries; it must be restored with the aid of Greek and Latin which chain it to the illusory versions; it is necessary to go back to its original source and find its true roots: this enormous work that I have undertaken, I have accomplished. (p. 176)

[548] Fortun. apud August., Disput., ii.; August., Contr. Faust., l. xxi., c. ult. (p. 176)

[549] Origène, cité par Beausobre, Hist. du Manich., t. ii., v., ch. 6. (p. 176)

[550] Beausobre, ibid., t. ii., p. 346. (p. 177)

[551] Hierocl., Aur. Carmin., v. 49 et 50. (p. 177)

[552] Plat., In II. Alcibiad.
"Accordez-moi, grands Dieux, ce qui m'est nécessaire, Soit que je pense ou non à vous le demander; Et si de mes désirs l'objet m'était contraire, Daignez, grands Dieux, daignez ne pas me l'accorder." (p. 177)

[553] Vendidad-Sadé, 68e hâ, p. 242. (p. 178)

[554] Zend-Avesta, Jeshts-Sadés, p. 113. (p. 178)

[555] Hiérocl., Aur. Carm., v. 48 et 49, et ibid., v. 46. (p. 179)

[556] Plat., In Georgiâ, In Phæd.; Ibid., De Rep., l. vii.; August., De Civit. Dei, l. iii., c. 1 et l. x., c. 29. (p. 179)

[557] Acad. des Inscript., t. xxxi., p. 319. (p. 179)

[558] Procl., In Tim., l. v., p. 330; Cicer., Somn. Scip., c. 2, 3, 4, et 6; Hierocl., In Aur. Carm., v. 70. (p. 180)

[559] Veda, cité par W. Jones, Asiat. Resear., t. iv., p. 173. (p. 180)

[560] Premier Pourâna, intitulé Matsya. (p. 180)

[561] Boushznda-Ramayan. (p. 180)

[562] Institut. of Menou, ch. 1, v. 1. (p. 180)

[563] Shanda-Pourdna. (p. 180)

[564] Ekhamesha. (p. 181)

[565] Aurore naissante (Morgens röte im Aufgang: durch Jacob Böhmen zu Amsterdam, 1682), ch. 14, § 41. (p. 182)

[566] Brahma, Vishnu, and Rudra. (p. 182)

[567] Jupiter, Neptune, and Pluto. (p. 182)

[568] In the Tao-te-King of Lao-Tse, a work which has held a high reputation among the numerous followers of this theosophist, one finds that the absolute, universal Being which he declares can neither be named, nor defined, is triple. "The first," he said, "has engendered the second; the two have produced the third; and the three have made all things. That which the mind perceives and the eye cannot see is named Y, the absolute Unity, the central point; that which the heart understands and the ear cannot hear is named Hi, the universal Existence; that which the soul feels and the hand cannot touch is named Ouei, the individual Existence. Seek not to penetrate the depths of this Trinity; its incomprehensibility comes from its Unity." "This Unity," adds Lao-Tse, in another passage, "is named Tao, the Truth; Tao is Life; Tao is to itself both rule and model. It is so lofty that it cannot be attained; so profound that it cannot be fathomed; so great that it contains the Universe; when one looks on high one sees no beginning; when one follows it in its productions, one finds in it no end." (p. 182)

[569] One of the principal dogmas of Fo-Hi is the existence of one God in three persons, whose image is man. All his doctrine is limited to leading, by meditation and repression of the passions, the human ternary to its perfection. This ternary is composed, according to him, of Ki, Tsing, and Chen, that is to say, of the material, animistic, and spiritual principle. It is necessary that, being joined together, this ternary should make but One. Then its duration will have no limit and its faculties will be indestructible. Voyez Duhalde, t. iii., in fol., p. 50. (p. 183)

[570] This is noticeable particularly in Bayle. (p. 184)

[571] Herod., In Clio, § 131; Strab., l. xv.; Boehm., Mores Gentium. (p. 184)

[572] Pelloutier, Hist. des Celtes, t. v., c. 3. (p. 184)

[573] Tacit., De Morib. Germ., c. 9; Lactant., Præm., p. 5. (p. 184)

[574] August., De Civit. Dei, l. iv., c. 31; Clem. Alex., l. i., p. 304; Strom. (p. 184)

[575] Plutar., In Vitâ Numa; ibid., In Mar.; Pelloutier, Hist. des Celt., l. iv., c. i.; Lucan., Phars., l. iii., v. 412; Clem. Alex., Cohort. ad Gent., p. 57. (p. 184)

[576] Porphyr., Sent., no. 10, p. 221; Stanl., In Pythag., p. 775. (p. 185)

[577] Stanley, De Phil. chald., p. 1123; Beausob., Hist. du Manich., t. ii., l. ix., c. 1, § 10. (p. 185)

[578] Τρισμέγιστος, thrice greatest. (p. 185)

[579] It is said that this famous table of Emerald was found in the valley of Hebron, in a sepulchre where it was between the hands of the cadaver of Thoth himself. Krigsmann, who assures us that this table must have read in Phœnician and not in Greek, quotes it a little differently from what one reads in the ordinary versions. Voyez Tabula Smaragdina, citée par Fabric., Bibl. Græc., p. 68. (p. 185)

[580] Homère, cité par Maxime de Tyr.; Pline, l. ii., c. 7; BIBLE, psalm. 73 et 93; Job, c. 23; Habacuc, c. 1; Malach., c. 3; Balzac, Socrate chrétien, p. 237. (p. 188)

[581] Plucquet, Dict. des Hérés., art. PRÉDESTINATIENS. (p. 188)

[582] Noris., Hist. pelag., l. ii., c. 15. (p. 189)

[583] Origen, Comment. in Psalm., p. 38 et 39. (p. 189)

[584] S. Léon., Epist. Decret., ii.; Niceph., l. xvii., c. 27. (p. 189)

[585] Conc. Rom., Gelas., t. iii. (p. 189)

[586] Dict. des Hérés., art. PÉLAGIENS. (p. 190)

[587] Plucquet, comme ci-dessus, t. ii., p. 454. (p. 190)

[588] Pelag., apud S. August., De Nat. et Grat., l. iii., c. 9. (p. 190)

[589] Pelag., apud August., De Grat. Christ., c. 4. (p. 190)

[590] Comment. in Aur. Carm., v. 62. (p. 191)

[591] S. August., De Grat. Christ., cité par Plucquet, Dict. des Hérés., art. PÉLAGIENS. (p. 191)

[592] Calvin, Institut., l. ii., c. 1 et 2. (p. 191)

[593] Ibid., t. ii. (p. 192)

[594] Maimbourg, Hist. du Calvinisme, l. i., p. 73. (p. 192)

[595] Plato, In Alcibiad., ii. (p. 193)

[596] Ibid. (p. 194)

[597] Ut suprà, v. 10 et 11. (p. 194)

[598] Ut suprà, v. 22. et 24. (p. 195)

[599] Ut suprà, v. 54 et 55. (p. 195)

[600] Burnet, Archæolog., l. i., c. 14. (p. 195)

[601] De la Triple Vie de l'Homme, ch. vi., § 53. (p. 195)

[602] Ibid., ch. v., § 56. (p. 195)

[603] Prod., In Tim., l. v., p. 330; Plethon, Schol. ad. Oracl. magic. Zoroast. (p. 195)

[604] Aur. Carm., v. 62-77. (p. 196)

[605] Lactant., De Irâ Dei, c. 13, p. 548. (p. 196)

[606] Dict. crit., art. MANICHÉENS, rem. D. (p. 197)

[607] Dict. crit. art. MARCIONITES, rem. E et G. (p. 197)

[608] Ibid., art. PAULICIENS, rem. E. (p. 198)

[609] Bayle, Dict. crit., art. PAULICIENS, rem. E. (p. 198)

[610] De Irâ Dei, c. 13, p. 548. (p. 198)

[611] Basilius, t. i., In Homil. quod Deus non sit auctor mali, p. 369; Bayle. Dict. crit., art. MARCIONITES, rem. E et G. (p. 198)

[612] Traité de Morale. (p. 198)

[613] Réponse à deux object. de M. Bayle, par Delaplacette, in-12, 1707. (p. 198)

[614] Essai de Théodicée, part iii., No. 405 et suiv. (p. 199)

[615] Essai de Théodicée, part. iii., No. 405 et suiv. (p. 199)

[616] Ci-dessus, 25e Examen. (p. 200)

[617] Cité par De Gérando, Hist. des Systèmes, t. ii., p. 100. (p. 204)

[618] Hist. des Animaux, in-4, p. 37. (p. 204)

[619] System des transcendental Idalimus, p. 441; Zeitschrift für die speculative Physick. (p. 204)

[620] Buffon, Théorie de la Terre; Linné, De Telluris habitab. Increment; Burnet, Archæolog., etc. (p. 204)

[621] Nouv. Dict. d'Hist. nat., art. QUADRUPÈDE. (p. 204)

[622] Ovid., Metamorph., l. xv. (p. 204)

[623] Nouv. Dict. d'Hist. nat., art. QUADRUPÈDE. (p. 204)

[624] Nouv. Dict. d'Hist nat., art. ANIMAL. (p. 205)

[625] Nouv. Dict., art. NATURE. (p. 205)

[626] Lettre à Hermann. (p. 205)

[627] Charles Bonnet, Contempt. de la Nat., p. 16; Lecat., Traité du Mouvement musculaire, p. 54, art. iii.; Robinet, De la Nature, t. iv., p. 17, etc. (p. 205)

[628] Nouv. Dict., art. QUADRUPÉDE. (p. 205)

[629] Cicer., De Finib., l. v., c. 5; Aul. Gell., l. xx., c. 5; Clem. Alex., Strom., l. v.; Hiérocl., Aur. Carm., v. 68; Lil. Gregor. Gyrald., Pythag. Symbol. Interpret.; Dacier, Vie de Pythag.; Barthelemi, Voyage du Jeune Anarch., t. vi., ch. 75, etc. (p. 207)

[630] Jambl., Vitâ Pythag., C. 29, 34, et 35. (p. 207)

[631] Porphyr. apud Euseb., Præp. Evang., l. iii., c. 7; ibid., De Abstinent., l. iv., p. 308; Jambl., De Myst. Egypt., c. 37. (p. 207)

[632] Clem. Alex., Stromat., l. v., p. 556. (p. 207)

[633] Hierocl., Aur. Carm., v. 70. (p. 209)

[634] Prod., In Tim., l. v., p. 330 (p. 209)

[635] Apud Plutar., De Audiend. Pœtis. (p. 209)

[636] Pind., Olymp., iii.; Apud, Plutar., Consol. ad Apoll. (p. 209)

[637] Plat., In Phædon (p. 209)

www.ingramcontent.com/pod-product-compliance
Lightning Source LLC
Chambersburg PA
CBHW051544010526
44118CB00022B/2569